MYSTERIOUS
SOMERSET AND BRISTOL

Daniel Codd has spent years delving into the supernatural history of the East Midlands, a fascination borne out of a belief that truth is far stranger than fiction and that even the most outlandish of folkloric stories probably has a basis in fact. His research into the paranormal has seen him spending a less-than-healthy amount of time poring through archive documents, and he is endlessly fascinated by the stories of curiosities and strange phenomena that people tell him. He gains great satisfaction from people's interest in the subject matter, and from seeking out locations that are supposedly haunted or which have other legends attached to them. He is constantly asked if he has ever seen a ghost himself (to which the answer is sadly not). Much of his spare time is taken up with searching for missing car keys and/or spectacles. His motto is: 'Those who have never attempted anything can honestly say they've never failed at anything' and he sometimes wishes he could live by this rule himself. He has previously written *Mysterious Lincolnshire* (2007), *Mysterious Northamptonshire* (2009), *Mysterious Cambridgeshire* (2010) and is currently working on a novel inspired by some of the strange tales he has learned.

MYSTERIOUS
SOMERSET AND BRISTOL

DANIEL CODD

First published in Great Britain in 2011 by The Derby Books Publishing Company Limited, 3 The Parker Centre, Derby, DE21 4SZ.

ISBN 978-1-85983-947-8

Printed and bound by Melita Press, Malta.

CONTENTS

	Acknowledgements	6
	Foreword	7
Chapter 1	Enigmatic Events from County History	10
Chapter 2	In the Realm of Miracles	29
Chapter 3	Supernatural Evil	52
Chapter 4	Curses, Portents and Superstitious Belief	73
Chapter 5	Ghost Stories of Somerset	85
Chapter 6	Modern Ghostly Encounters	114
Chapter 7	Animal Enigmas	137
Chapter 8	Creatures of Myth and Legend	155
Chapter 9	Inexplicable Incidents, Bizarre Behaviour & Peculiar Places	174
	Index of Place Names	192

ACKNOWLEDGEMENTS

Directors of the Ship and Castle, Congresbury; Carla Pilkington of High Ham Parish Council for providing information on Low Ham Church (for information the village, see www.highhamparishcouncil.co.uk); Karen Cook for arranging to let me see the spear at Low Ham; David Catton (The Camelot, South Cadbury, for his fascinating information); staff at the Garrick's Head, Bath; Susan Kerton (Higher Farm, Chilton Cantelo) for allowing me to see Theophilus Brome's skull; staff at Gough's Cave, Cheddar Gorge; Denise Dumbleton and staff at Glastonbury Abbey; staff at Somerset Rural Life Museum, Glastonbury; Carole Moore (Wellington Museum); John Wood (House Manager, Dunster Castle and Gardens); wardens of St Mary's Church, Wellington; also St Mary's at Crewkerne; June Hope, Parish Councillor at Corfe, Ken Brown, and all at www.corfevillagesomerset.org.uk; Guy Arnold (The Monkton Inn, West Monkton); John Trebilcock (The White Horse Inn, Stogumber); Stephen Minnitt, Taunton Castle Museum; John Sharman (The Ring O'Bells, Ascott); Victoria Langford; Ann Meddings at the Theatre Royal, Bath; Hilde Bucknell, Church Warden, St Michaels and All Angels at Haselbury; Lizzie Myers at Huntstile Organic Farm; administrators at St Peter and St Paul's Church, Wincanton, for relating the story of St Eligius, and providing information on Nathaniel Ireson; curate et al of St Andrew's Church, Congresbury, for showing me St Cungar's tree; Director of the Castle Hotel, Taunton; John Richards, Chairman, Watchet Chamber of Trade; Women's Institute at Carhampton; owners of Temple Farm, Chedzoy; staff at Roman Baths, Bath; curators of St Michael's Church, Bawdrip; Gemma Halliwell of Woodlands Castle, Taunton; Stephen Clews, Roman Baths and Pump Room Manager (Heritage Services, Bath and NE Somerset Council: for more information see the National Trust website); Fiona Shearer of the Halfway House, Dunwear (many thanks!); Nick Goff, Museum Curator at North Somerset Museum, Burlington Street, Weston-super-Mare; Karen Langford, Martin Williams and Mary Dempster, all for their anecdotes on Somerset folklore.

All images are copyright D. Codd, except: pages 102, 111 and 120 (with kind permission, from the collection of Philip S. Evans, for further information see www.oldphotos.com); page 63 (with the kind permission of Gayle Pennington, Wookey Hole Caves, for further information please see www.wookey.co.uk); pages 88 and 112 (reproduced from an original copy of *An Exploration Of Exmoor*, J.L.W. Page, 1890, in possession of the present author); page 51 (Wendy Clacker and the George Muller Charitable Trust); pages 60, 122 and 161 (with the consent of the Mary Evans Picture Library, London).

FOREWORD

'To the traveller', F.J. Snell writes in *Memorials Of Old Somerset* (1906), 'Somerset…is not all flat, yet the typical scene is ever the turf-clad moor, with its long "rhines" and invariable willows. That is the Somerset on which one looks down from the central peak of the Glastonbury Tor, with Mendip in the far dim vista. The broad pleasance of Taunton Dene, worthily named the garden of England, and the happy hunting grounds of Exmoor and Quantock, are also integral parts of the county; and east and south, round Yeovil and round Chard, are many lovely nooks, not to mention the superb beauty of the Avon. Still, the region of the peat and the gorges of Cheddar stand out distinct and individual. They are the heart and midriff of the land; in an imaginative sense, they make Somerset at once a fief of the sea.' This is still true today; it is no understatement to say that Somerset boasts some of the most breathtakingly beautiful views in the whole of England.

The past is very much in evidence in Somerset, by which not only do I mean the near past, as personified in such places as Wells Cathedral and Glastonbury Abbey, but also the distant past. From the massive ancient hill fort at South Cadbury to the mysterious stone circles at Stanton Drew, there are evidences of our distant, even pre-historic, ancestry that conjure up a curiously eerie realisation of just how far we, as a nation and as a species, have come. Perhaps the best example of this is Cheddar Gorge and Caves, which can truly be classed as one of the most awe-inspiring natural wonders in the United Kingdom. I will never forget my first visit to this place, outside of the peak season, when the

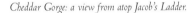

Cheddar Gorge: a view from atop Jacob's Ladder.

drive through the rabbit warren that is the village of Cheddar gave no indication as to the impressiveness of the gorge; it is akin to driving though a rent torn in the land by an earthquake, and the limestone cliffs close in and tower above the observer as they snake through the pass. It is easy to see why they say that the Devil was responsible for such a geological curiosity. In actual fact, this chasm was carved through the Mendip Hills by Ice Age meltwater. Upon my first visit here more years ago than I care to remember, I found myself unconsciously slowing down my car to around 5mph, such is the amazement that this place creates, particularly when it is deserted and populated only by the rare breed of British Primitive goats that trot across the road between the sides of the chasm with impunity and little fear of cars. In 1903 the oldest complete skeleton of a prehistoric man was found some 90ft from the entrance to Gough's Cave, embedded in cave earth beneath a stalagmite, when Richard Gough excavated and opened up to the public what had previously been known as Sand Hole. Cheddar Man, as the remains became famously called, appeared to have died a violent death in his early 20s around the year 7150 BC, and for many years now there have been suggestions that the Cheddar tribes practised cannibalism. There seems little doubt about this now: as early as 1954, a survey of the Mendips observed of other remains found hereabouts that, 'It has been suggested that some of the limb bones may have been split for marrow.' Some of these remains have been estimated to be around 13,000 years old, dating to the Upper Paleolithic era. Electric lighting was installed in Gough's Cave as long ago as 1899, and the tourist industry has now long caught up with Cheddar Gorge; perhaps this is no bad thing. But, for me, the most mesmerizing thought is the suggestion that if you could remove the tarmac from the roads, and the buildings, and the town of Cheddar, and somehow transport Cheddar Man through time, he would easily recognise this place that he called home over 9,000 years ago. It is also interesting to note the automatic association between the caves in this county and the sinister and unexplained; in August 2010 a resident of Banwell told me of the caves there, 'Banwell Bone Caves are pretty interesting, too. There are loads of prehistoric bones. They were found when the caves were opened up and are thought to have been washed in when the area was flooded or part of the sea. There are a few Paganist sacrifice tables too, but I don't know much about them or how they ended up at the caves…'

And so this compilation covers all regions of modern Somerset: from Exmoor, the Brendon Hills and the Quantocks, through Taunton and Yeovil, the Somerset Levels, Glastonbury, the Mendips and Wells, to the newly-created North Somerset and Bath and North East Somerset unitary authorities (these latter formerly part of Avon). Since the geographic area of Somerset is so large and diverse, it also made sense to go that bit further and include, in some small way, references to southern Bristol, given its proximity to Somerset and the observation that they were once classed as one region. This we learn from a charter granted to the city on 8 August 1373 by King Edward III, dictating that, '…the town of Bristol be forever separated from the counties of Gloucester and Somerset, and that it be a county of itself, called the County of Bristol.' A gazetteer describes Bristol thus, 'Til Bristol was made an independent county, it was usually reckoned to belong to Somersetshire, occupying the southern extremity of Gloucestershire, and the northern of Somersetshire. It is now usually mentioned in connection with the latter of these two counties.' This was written in 1813. In truth, Bristol is probably worthy of a book in its own right, but I also feel that the inclusion of elements of Bristol folklore allows the reader to observe the juxtaposition between the city and the countryside, or between the urban and the rural, in terms of the types of stories contained within this book.

It has to be said that, in many ways, in Somerset's corners and away from the sizeable towns, and certainly Bristol, it is easy to forget the modern world about you, and bathe in the aura of the many mysterious places that this county hides. Exmoor and its coastline, the Tarr Steps, Glastonbury Tor, South Cadbury hill fort, Burrow Mump, Athelney, and Sedgemoor all encapsulate, in the correct conditions, not only what is mythical and mysterious about Somerset, but also about Great Britain as a nation. In some places, the modern world appears to have not quite caught up with Somerset. This is not a criticism, but maybe a blessing. Even the landscape is curious – perfectly flat here, miles of hills there, heathland of gorse, heather and bracken, or else moorland or woodland, with cliffs, mounds, caves and prehistoric stones deposited everywhere. Sometimes the roads – some of which are perilously, terrifyingly thin – dip all of a sudden and take the driver, it seems, into the bowels of the earth, where before one never knew that they were even on a slope. Some of these roads are so pitch black at night that even high beams make no difference in penetrating the gloom, and it almost becomes a relief to see any sign of civilisation. Following rainfall, these very roads seem to run with water after the fact, the water forming little rivers at the sides of the roads almost everywhere. In many places, Somerset's hills and heights are crowned by monuments or follies, which are visible from miles around. Little wonder that Somerset is fertile ground for stories of the Devil, fairies, ghosts, miracles, strange beasts and mythology. In fact, in many instances such is the atmosphere of parts of Somerset that these stories seem not only possible, but also likely. On a bright spring day Somerset is enchanting; conversely, when storm clouds gather overhead and the streets are deserted it can become a gloomy, eerie and even sinister place.

Mysterious Somerset And Bristol has taken many years to compile fully, but it should be observed that this is not a history book; I apologise in advance for any unwitting historical inaccuracies that the sharp-eyed may pick out, and can only assure the reader that all sources drawn upon were considered reliable. Having spent much time in Somerset I can but only repeat what I was told many years ago, that 'to spend three days in Somerset is to fall in love with it' and I can vouch on every level that this is an absolute truism. Somerset is, in every sense, perhaps the most mysterious county in Britain.

The view from Glastonbury Tor.

CHAPTER I:

ENIGMATIC EVENTS FROM COUNTY HISTORY

INTRODUCTION

As befits any sizeable region, there have been many historical riddles throughout the ages in Somerset. John L.W. Page's *An Exploration Of Exmoor* (1890) makes numerous observations concerning this part of Somerset's origins, observations that illustrate that there are some aspects of our history that we will never be clear about, despite shaky indicators: 'The district now called Somersetshire was in ancient times inhabited by the Belgae, a brave Gaulish people, but of Celtic origin, who migrated hither out of Gaul [France] A.M. 3650, 313 years before the birth of Christ, and repelled the Britons – the aboriginal inhabitants of the country, whose carneds [prehistoric sites] still crown some of our highest mountains.' Page suggests that Somerset 'generally became English' only in AD 926, when the advancement of Anglo-Saxon rulers finally succeeded in expelling the remnants of these Belgic-Britons and began to fix boundary lines: 'No doubt many Wealhas, as the Saxon scornfully called the poor Briton, haunted the wild hill country for centuries after.'

The northern coastline suffered greatly from invasions by the Lidwiccas – pirate armies from Brittany intent on plunder – in the 10th century, with Watchet and Porlock suffering greatly. In AD 918 we are told that the Lidwiccas were repulsed back into the sea by the English, who were commanded by Aelle, 'Lord of the Castle of Brystowe in dais of yore.' The pirate army was forced to settle on Flat Holm, an island in the Bristol Channel, where many of them starved to death. In 988 and 997 more pirates entered the Bristol Channel and landed at Watchet, where they 'wrought much evil by burning and man-slaying.' From this era, Page observes, there were numerous sites considered by the local peasantry to have been locations where violent and bloody confrontations occurred. Some thought (in Page's time) that a titanic battle had been enacted in AD 878, between Danish pirates under the warlord Hubba and the English under Alfred, at the site of Cannington Park fort, where a heroic handful of remaining combatants successfully defended the fort and killed Hubba. Hubba was considered by many to have been buried under the tumulus that can be found on North Moor, north of Shurton. In a field called Knap Dane in Nettlecombe parish there were many stories of a vast deposit of skeletons being uncovered – supposedly casualties of the invasion of AD 918 – while at nearby Williton there were a number of fields, collectively called Battlegore, where tradition said 'much armour and many weapons' were found at one time. A tumulus on private land between the A39 and the West Wood junction still bears the peculiar name of Bleary Pate; 100 years ago it bore the even stranger name of Bloody Pate – the reason for which had been lost to the ages even by Page's time.

Tumuli and carneds like this literally scatter the county of Somerset. And place names such as Robber's Bridge, crossing Weir Water west of Porlock in Exmoor National Park, remind us that there was also a long tradition of outlawry in these parts. This region is, of course, legendary as the setting for R.D. Blackmore's classic romance *Lorna Doone*, and many locales here are linked to Lorna's story: among them the church at Oare, where Lorna was hit by a gunshot on her wedding day, and Cloven Rocks near Simonsbath, where her assailant, Carver Doone, was engulfed by the 'black bog' during the final confrontation with John Ridd. The notorious Doone clan are likely to have had a basis in reality and to have infested Exmoor in the 17th century, and Blackmore's preface to his novel declares that 'any son of Exmoor, chancing on this volume, cannot fail to bring to mind the nurse-tales of his childhood – the savage deeds of the outlaw Doones in the depth of Bagworthy Forest, the beauty of the hapless maid [Lorna herself] in the midst of them, the plain John Ridd's Herculean power…' In 1890 John L.W. Page wrote of the church window through which Carver Doone fired at Lorna, 'People who do not know that the chancel is a comparatively recent addition, will wonder how he could possibly have hit her. It need scarcely be said that the story that her bloodstains still mark the altar is as mythical as it is romantic. The grave of the "gert Jan Ridd" will be sought for in vain, but a witness to his Samson-like strength may be seen in Mr Snow's grounds hard by. Here is a mighty ash, whose lower limbs, bending curiously earthwards, are said to have been forced into that position by the mighty muscles of Lorna's lover.' Time ran out for the Doones, according to Charles Harper's *The Somerset Coast*, when they were fired at by the wife of Yenworthy Farm, Culbone, using a long duck gun that was, in 1909 at least, still preserved within the farm. At Exford the remnants of the raiding party killed an infant in a farmhouse burglary and for this the clan were massacred by a band of local men, who also destroyed their stone huts on the Weir Water. Separating fact from fiction is difficult with the legend, but apparently the Doone line lingered – until the last of the clan, an old man and his granddaughter who sang carols at Christmastide, were found together frozen to death by the roadside between Simonsbath and Challacombe, Devon, around 1800.

Such is the mythology of the Doones in Exmoor. It is with crime in mind that there have been many whispers of dark deeds throughout the centuries. In 1744, during repairs to the Bishop's Palace, Bristol (which stood behind the cathedral on Canon's Marsh until it was largely destroyed during the Bristol uprising of 1831), an underground dungeon was accidentally discovered, together with a claustrophobic underground tunnel leading to an 'apartment in the house'. In this cell were found a great many human bones, and 'instruments of iron, supposed to have been used for torture.' In May 1828 labourers digging a garden in Shepton Mallet unearthed three skeletons, and it was observed at the time that an adjacent premises had once been an inn of poor reputation at which several persons had supposedly disappeared some time back. Legends of wicked innkeepers murdering their drunken clients are fairly common in folklore worldwide, but on this occasion it seems to have been the case. It goes without saying that there have been many notable crimes throughout the ages in Somerset and Bristol, but it is quite often the ones that go unsolved that capture the imagination. The man fished out of the River Avon at Twerton, Bath, in 1790 was never even identified, let alone served justice. He had been battered to death at an unknown time and his pockets loaded with stones so as to sink his body beneath the water, according to the *Sherborne And Yeovil Mercury* of 15 March that year. Today, the horror and sadness of some of the unsolved crimes over the last 50 years is still felt very deeply, the open wound in the community felt all the more keenly because of the lack of closure and the agonising knowledge that the culprit evaded all efforts to catch them. The landscape of the region has also claimed many who were simply never seen again. This is especially evident near the coastline: the ocean floors beneath the choppy waters north of Somerset must be littered with the submerged hulks of many a vessel that sailed into oblivion when departing Bristol; Evans' *A Chronological Outline Of The History Of Bristol* (1824) certainly indicates that this is the case. This chapter, however, is not so much concerned with these tragedies and criminal riddles as it is with the legends and myths from

Somerset's dim and distant past: King Alfred at Athelney, King Bladud at Bath, legendary deposits of treasure and, just possibly, the echoes of King Arthur himself at Glastonbury and South Cadbury. In a county so rich in history and folklore, the following legends might possibly have more than just a glimmer of truth to them.

KING BLADUD OF BATH

The legend of the origin of the city of Bath is a very well-known one. Bladud was the princely son of King Lud-Hudibras who, when a young man, was banished by his father after contracting leprosy. Bladud's mother, the queen, presented her son with a ring in order that, should he ever return to the capital if cured, he would be recognisable. Wandering into exile, the prince swapped his clothes with that of a shepherd and eventually entered into the service of a swineherd who resided near what is now Keynsham. Unfortunately for Bladud, the pigs caught leprosy also, and so to hide this from the swineherd Bladud drove them along the banks of the River Avon, which he crossed at what became Swineford. Staying on the other side of the Avon, Bladud was interrupted during his prayers to the sun one morning by the spectacle of his herd rushing in madness up the valley, where all the pigs threw themselves into the warm, oozy bog that at that time covered the site. For some time the porcine herd submerged themselves in the 'boiling fountains' before hunger got the better of them and a much-relieved Bladud was able to tempt them out of the swamp with bags of acorns. This routine continued until, eventually, he realised that the pigs performed this ritualistic act to benefit from the warm mud when the weather was cold. Furthermore, the bog seemed to be doing the pigs some good, so Bladud penned each animal in separately to lessen the chance of the disease returning and then submerged his own person in the mud; much to his astonishment, his own condition began to improve and within time he was well enough to return to his father's court, where he was recognised by the ring he had kept rather than by his much-improved appearance. Needless to say, the legendary spa resort of Bath grew from these humble origins.

In time Bladud became king in his own right, and there are other tales of his life as ruler, including the end of his reign during a disastrous attempt to fly in New Troy (modern-day London). This story began *c*.1136 with the renowned scholar and churchman Geoffrey of Monmouth, and was alluded to as a historical 'fact' in his *History Of The Kings Of Britain*. Bladud died *c*.850 BC and was succeeded as king by his son Leir – Shakespeare's King Lear.

That Bath has existed since shortly after the Roman invasion of summer AD 43 – it began life as Aquae Sulis – is not in doubt, and it is highly likely

This gilt bronze head, found in 1727 in Stall Street, belongs to the goddess Sulis-Minerva and may date to the first century.

King Bladud's image looks out over King's Bath from his alcove.

that the site was well known long before the Romans occupied it from the Celtic Britons, who appear to have previously venerated their goddess Sulis at a shrine there. And what of Bladud himself? Geoffrey of Monmouth makes no mention of leprosy and pigs, merely telling us that 'Bladud built the town of Kaerbadum, that we now call Bath, and it was he who constructed the hot baths there that are so suited to the needs of mortal men.' He dedicated the baths to the goddess Minerva and had fires lit that never went out. It seems the story of the leprosy episode was a later elaboration of Geoffrey's original anecdote, itself either an invention or built on little more than an oral tradition. The funny thing is that, as myths go, it is fairly plausible, and one can only wonder – despite the huge improbability of it all – whether there is just the tiniest grain of truth in any of it. Former generations certainly believed so, hence the somewhat-unsettling image of Bladud himself dated *c*.1699 that can be seen in an alcove looking over the King's Bath. John Wood's huge tome, *A Description Of Bath* (1765), devotes much text to the serious consideration that Bladud was a real person, although he describes the statue as resembling 'a dressed puppet, seated in a ducking stool.' Curious as this carving is, one before it that adorned Bath's North Gate was apparently so vulgar that the town clerk penned a satire declaring that Bladud's ghost haunted Bath and was disgusted and shamed by his own depiction. The original statue was replaced by the one we see now, coloured and 'painted to the life.' An interesting aside is Wood's observation that the front of the North Gate was 'from the remotest ages adorned with a statue of King Bladud.' Whatever the truth of the king's legend, much of the original Roman Baths (together with their Georgian embellishments) can now still be seen as their builders intended, including the magnificent centrepiece that is the Great Bath – 111ft long and 68ft wide.

As a point of interest, King Bladud is not the only legendary figure from Britain's mythological past to have connections with Bath: King Coel (the 'Old King Cole' of nursery rhyme and supposedly the grandfather of Constantine the Great) granted the city a charter. If there is any truth in this it must have happened in the third century. And some say that Bristol was founded in 380 BC by Brennus, a mythical first king of the Britons. Certainly, as early as AD 560 the monk Gildas recorded Bristol as being a fortified and eminent British city when the Romans abandoned the island in AD 409.

HERE 'STANDETH CAMALLATE'

On 5 February 2010 I visited the village of South Cadbury, between Yeovil and Castle Cary. Beyond the crossroads and the inn called The Camelot can be found the signs directing the walker towards 'Castle Lane – leading to Camelot Fort.'

This simple sign belies the significance of this place in both historical and mythological terms. From the Castle Lane, the immense hill that towers beside the southern road out of the little village bears scant resemblance to a castle; small patches of woodland obscure much of it from the road, and it looks rather like a gigantic hill, very similar to another that can be seen away to the east.

Yet this landmark of limestone, towering some 500ft above sea level, is historically reckoned to have been the basis for – if not the actual location of – Camelot, the legendary seat and court of the semi-mythical Romano-British King Arthur himself.

The 'castle' at South Cadbury was clearly strategically placed to defend this area of south-western Britain, and as early as 1542 the Tudor traveller John Leland wrote that the remains of the fort here had long been supposed locally to have been the base from which Arthur led his troops into the heroic, legendary battle of Mons Badonis against the Barbarians AD *c*.500 – a disputed location in its own right: the battle might have taken place in Dorset, northern Wiltshire or somewhere near Bath. Nennius, the Welsh monk whose *Historia Brittonum* (AD *c*.830) affords us the first glimpses of the 'historical' Arthur, recorded, 'Nine hundred and forty fell by his hand alone, no-one but the Lord affording him assistance.' The Battle of Badon Hill is almost certainly an actual historical event, as an even earlier historian and cleric, Gildas, implied in AD *c*.540 that the clash was recent history. The snag here – for which historians and mythologists have never forgiven Gildas – is that he does not mention Arthur, although he does mention a shadowy Romano-British general of high rank called Ambrosius Aurelianus, whose 'degenerate progeny' still existed in Gildas' day. Many feel that this man, whose parents had been slain in the political turmoil sweeping the nation following the Roman withdrawal, and who was reputedly exceptionally brave, was the real template for the person later called Arthur.

But to get tied up in the murky history of Arthur is perhaps missing the point. On a gloomy Friday morning I set off along the stony track that takes one upwards in a meandering fashion as though alighting a mere hill; before long, however, it becomes apparent that one is walking upwards through a gully, or channel if you like, with the hill beginning to soar on either side of you as though you were walking up and into the entrance to something. Trees gather in close on either side and the sun filters through them, lending this passage a curious green and shadow effect, until you finally alight onto the top of this landmark and a great panoramic of the surrounding Somerset countryside is displayed before one's eyes. It becomes apparent very quickly that this is no ordinary hill: it is a natural landmark fortified into a man-made structure, and its eastern side displays obvious – and substantial – evidence of defensive earthworks being fashioned to fortify this great plateau. These surround it and at one time must have enclosed and protected the community that resided here. At any rate, someone clearly lived here at one time...but who?

Excavations at the site have revealed much. For a long time it was accepted that the fortification was of Roman origin, these being the peoples to whom the famous 18th century antiquarian Stukeley ascribed it. Excavations in the 1960s, however, suggested it was much, much older, with evidence being unearthed that the site was occupied as early as the Late Bronze Age and throughout the Iron Age. There are indications that in the AD first century there were one or more violent skirmishes here, and perhaps Cadbury hill fort was partly destroyed by fire. But the suggestion is that the site was occupied around the middle 400s to the late sixth century. This is the exact era that Arthur – or the warrior chieftain whom Arthur is based upon, about whom we know so little – flourished in the years following the Roman withdrawal from Britain. The site was reoccupied during the late Saxon era, when it would appear to have been refortified and used as a mint for making coins sometime *c*.1009. By Leland's time it had once more been abandoned for centuries, but he made some interesting observations. Although in the Norman era the site was Cadanbyric, in 1542 Leland very definitely identifies it with Camelot: 'At the very south ende of the chirche of South Cadbyri standeth Camallate, sumtyme a famose toun or castelle...The people can telle nothing there but that they have hard

Is this really the entrance to 'Camelot'?

say that Arture much resortid to Camallate.' He noted that it was still possible to see the remnants of foundations and walls once constructed of the 'dusky blew [blue] stone' that the villagers had pillaged throughout the years. These were likely to be the remains of the Norman encampment, but Leland noted that much older gold, silver and copper Roman-era coins had been turned over during ploughing, and that a remarkable silver horseshoe had lately been found. He also identified the nearby village we now call Queen Camel as Quene Camalet, and observed that people said Pomparles Bridge, between Glastonbury and Street, was the spot where 'Arture cast in his swerd.' So this spot was identified as the exact spot where Excalibur was submerged by the water of the River Brue! Generations later, William Stukeley recorded that a ditched area within the higher reaches of the hill fort was known as King Arthur's Palace, and might have been a praetorium, or commander's area. There was also a never-failing spring in the fourth ditch called King Arthur's Well, which can still be sought out today.

In the *Annales Cambriae* (AD *c.*960) it is written that the historical Arthur died, along with one Medraut, during a titanic clash between the Britons and Saxons at somewhere called Camlann around AD 539. Camlann has been tentatively placed at Queen Camel, or Annis Hill, West Camel, both near South Cadbury, although such associations are only educated guesswork. It is claimed that farm workers at some point unearthed a mass grave containing many skeletons to the west of Cadbury Castle.

The shadowy figure of Arthur was already a legend by the Middle Ages, and the Welsh churchman and scholar Geoffrey of Monmouth's *History Of The Kings Of Britain* introduced many now-famous elements of the Arthurian myth. His expansive work drew upon as much local lore as historical fact, and it references one regional ruler named Cado (or Cador, Cadorius), a member of the Dumnonian (south-west) royal family allied to Arthur. Geoffrey's *History* (*c.*1136) alludes to Arthur's queen, Guinevere, being raised by Cado and possibly his being related to Arthur himself. It may, in fact, have been Cado whose kingdom occupied South Cadbury hill fort and not Arthur's

The confusion notwithstanding, some historians will affirm that speculation as to the location of Camelot is academic, since technically Camelot never existed: it was an element woven into the Arthurian myth in the Middle Ages. But if we accept that Arthur was based on a real figure, then it follows that this shadowy Romano-British leader must have lived, courted, dined, hidden and made war plans from some kind of fortified base. The elevated position of Cadbury Castle, and its antiquity, would appear to make it at least a plausible location for the site of the historical Camelot. Although later researchers disregarded Camallate as a name and called this structure South Cadbury hillfort, if this is not Camelot then surely nowhere is. It is certainly not difficult to get caught up in the romance of the idea, and to imagine Arthur (or the warrior chieftain his legend is based on) charging out of the hill fort along the very entrance in which I stood and away into the forestry to fight the battles that founded his mythology. When one's imagination is stretched, the whole suggestion of this place actually being the template for Camelot suddenly becomes very plausible, even likely. And what a world of thought is suggested.

'MIND THEE KE-AKS MAN!'

There are many sites in Somerset that harbour traditional links to the Danish invasions, as we have already seen. *The Reader's Digest Folklore, Myths And Legends Of Britain* (1973) tells us that Bleadon, a village south of the glacial Bleadon Hill, was formerly called Bleed Down on account of a clash between red-headed Danish pirates and locals here in the Dark Ages, which was also the reason behind a supposed mistrust of red-headed people that lingered for centuries. It was also widely believed in former times that 'brent' was a derivation of 'burnt', it being supposed that the area of East Brent 'suffered much from the flames during the invasions of the Danes', according to *Somerset Notes And Queries* (1856). Nearby can be found the curious, conical Brent Knoll rising almost 1,000ft above sea level. This hill is estimated to have been used as a fortified base since the Roman era, and by the West Saxons as an alarm post; tradition has it that Alfred is also said to have defended himself here, at one period, against the Danes. The nearby hamlet of Battleborough retained its name on account of some violent encounter lost in the mists of history.

One of the most famous stories connected to King Alfred is also one of the most famous British legends of all. Around Easter AD 878 Alfred was forced to seek refuge from the Norse invaders in the Somerset marshes at Athelney, then a complete island on the north side of Stan Moor and near to East Lyng. Here, Alfred concealed himself in the rough hut of one Denwulf, where he devoted his time as a fugitive to secret prayer and devotion. Alfred had taken the guise of an ignorant peasant, and one day offended his protector's wife by neglecting the bread that was burning at the hearth. She ran in hastily and removed the loaves, furiously scalding Alfred (of whose true identity she was ignorant) with the words, 'You man! You will not turn the bread you see burning, but you will be glad to eat it when done!' A Somerset rhyme was sung thereafter of this episode:

Ca'sn thee mind the ke-aks, man, an' doossen zee 'em burn?
I'm boun thee's eat 'em vast enough, az zoon az 'tiz the turn.

This simple legend has captured the public's imagination for centuries, in no small part due to its reflection of the king's sorry situation and state of mind prior to his emergence from hiding and ultimate triumph over the hitherto all-conquering Danish invaders in May 878. The nearby pub at Burrowbridge is called the King Alfred Inn, and on Athelney Hill can be observed King Alfred's Monument, a pillar, erected by John Slade in 1801, bearing an inscription and protected by railings, although this is inaccessible to the public. According to folklorist C.H. Poole, the story of the burning loaves was circulating at the time of events, and although *Somerset Notes And Queries* disputes whether Alfred hid himself in the guise of a peasant — contesting that he built a fortress in Athelney and retained his position as a warrior while awaiting his followers throughout the country to flock to his cause — it is highly likely that one of Britain's most famous legends contains more than a grain of truth. According to *An Encyclopaedia Of Superstitions* (1949), a curious reminder of these times was ever after practised: 'Since time immemorial it has been a Christmas Eve custom in Somerset and Devon to burn the "Ashen Faggot" in local inns and taverns, as in King Alfred's time.'

THE BURIAL PLACE OF KING ARTHUR

Within the grounds of Glastonbury Abbey, near to the ruined structure of the Lady Chapel, can be found a sign — easy to miss — planted in the grass that bears the simple inscription: 'Site of the ancient graveyard where in 1191 the monks dug to find the tombs of Arthur and Guinevere.'

Many of the elements of the Arthurian legend with which we are now familiar began with Geoffrey of Monmouth's *History Of The Kings Of Britain*, among them the prophecies of Merlin, an amalgamation of a character largely based on 'Merddin, the bard of Ambrosius' who was said to have set forth from the coast in a ship of glass and headed westward with nine 'Cylveirrd Bards' and 13 British curiosities. Apart from being glimpsed from the Irish coast, the ship of glass was not to be seen again. Geoffrey is also considered the first to mention Caliburn — Arthur's legendary sword, Excalibur — as being wielded by the king during a battle at Bath and as having been forged in the Isle of Avalon. Geoffrey's work is largely romance, an interweaving and exaggeration of incidents drawn from written historical sources and folklore. Nonetheless, Geoffrey tells us that Arthur was mortally wounded at Camlann, where thousands were slain on the battlefield (including the treacherous usurper, Mordred, presumably the historical Medraut). Arthur was reverently cast off towards the Isle of Avalon in a boat so that his wounds might be healed, leaving his cousin Constantine to rule in his stead; however, he was not heard from again — although Geoffrey appears to imply that the king will return at some future point, for Merlin prophesied that God did not wish the Britons to rule any longer and the king would lie within the Isle of Avalon until the moment came for him to be resurrected to lead the Britons to greatness. As for Guinevere, she fled York upon her betrayal of Arthur to live the life of a nun in the church of Julius the Martyr at the City of the Legions, which is thought to be Caerleon, Wales.

In the romantic mediaeval era this prose had enormous appeal, and for many centuries Geoffrey's work was acknowledged as historical fact without question, with the idea of a resurrected king very popular among a people subjugated and colonised for centuries by the Scandinavians and, lately, the Normans.

Although Geoffrey of Monmouth does not tie the Isle of Avalon to a location, implying that it is a place of paradise, the Celtic Isle of the Blessed, where the heroic justly go to when they leave the mortal coil, the conical hill of Glastonbury Tor would at one time have been a striking landmark rising like an

Glastonbury Tor was at one time surrounded by fenland, before drainage.

island out of the swamps and marshes of the Somerset Levels, and many consider that this might be the historical location of such a place. The story was phenomenally popular, and in 1113 a violent fracas between Cornishmen and visiting French canons from Laon was sparked by the latter scoffing at suggestions Arthur still lived, waiting to be resurrected. For mythologists, this event has huge significance, as it evidences the sincere belief among western Britons that Arthur would return to lead them – long before Geoffrey of Monmouth records it in 1136.

In 1191 there was the staggering revelation that monks at Glastonbury had actually discovered the whereabouts of the legendary king in their churchyard. King Henry II suggested to the clergy of Canterbury that perhaps Arthur's gravesite was at Glastonbury because of its ancient holy associations and the topographical possibility that Glastonbury Tor may have been Avalon; this was how he understood it from the writings of an ancient historical poet of the Britons. Henry II died before the monks made their astonishing discovery, but one Giraldus Cambrensis (*c.*1146–*c.*1223) wrote afterwards that 'in our times' Arthur's remains were found buried deep in the earth, concealed in a hollow oak between two stone pyramids in the abbey cemetery. A lead cross was found affixed to a stone slab, bearing an inscription in Latin: *Hic jacet sepultus inclitus rex Arthurus cum Wenneveria uxore sua secunda in insula Avallonia*, roughly translated as, 'Here lies buried the famous King Arthur with Guinevere his second wife in the island of Avalon.' Giraldus had seen this personally. The king's bones were observed to be of enormous size, the shinbone surpassing the kneecap of the tallest man present, with the skeleton displaying 10 severe wounds, of which all had healed – except the last, a gaping head wound that appeared to have killed him. At the feet of

Arthur lay the remains of Guinevere, a lock of whose golden hair was lifted out of the sepulchre by a monk…only to crumble into dust. The site of the grave had, according to Giraldus, been further deciphered by ancient scriptures at Glastonbury, cryptic markings on the two stone pyramids and visionary revelations.

Henry II may have feared that Arthur might become a figurehead for a rebellion in Wales, since the legends that he would return to lead the Britons to glory were clearly prevalent in western Britain.

The timing and the state of the body strongly suggest an attempt to draw a line under the mythology. It is stated that historically Glastonia was called 'Insula Avalonia' and that Aval was the ancient British word for apples (of which the region abounded; others had previously even referred to Avalon as 'The Isle of Apples', or 'The Fortunate Isle') and there seems to have been an attempt to tie up all the loose ends of the story. Geraldus added that the Welsh formerly called Glastonbury Tor 'the island of glass', and that from this the invading Saxons labelled the place Glastingebury. He also wrote that 'Morganis, a noble matron and ruler' of those parts, who was allied by blood to Arthur, was the one responsible for bearing the mortally wounded king away to 'the island now called Glastonia.'

Glastonbury's abbot at the time of the discovery would have been Henri de Soilli. Whatever the truth behind the discovery, it is an event that was corroborated, to a certain extent, by another historian of the time, Ralph de Coggeshall. At Glastonbury Abbey itself, near the remnants of the High Altar, can be found the site of Arthur and Guinevere's reburial. A sign here informs us that on 19 April 1278 the remains of the pair were taken from the south side of the Lady Chapel and placed in a black marble tomb where they remained until the dissolution of the abbey in 1539. There is a suggestion, however, that the two skulls were kept separate and ordered to be retained in the Treasury by King Edward I and Queen Eleanor, who performed the ritualistic reburial. At any rate, by the time of the Dissolution, the lead cross apparently still existed, for the Tudor traveller John Leland observed its Latin engravings and actually held it, although I cannot find any suggestion that he observed the skulls, and they were probably appropriated to London.

This is, unfortunately, where this story ends. As we shall see, in September 1539 the abbey fell victim to Henry VIII's infamous and systematic suppression of the monasteries, known as the Dissolution. Abbot Richard Whyting was hanged on Glastonbury Tor, and Glastonbury's treasures were looted and pillaged, an act of plunder legally sanctioned by the signing of a document. Many of England's true treasures vanished forever during this time, and the popular supposition is that King Arthur is once again truly lost to history. *The Gentleman's Magazine* in 1834 speculated that several antiquities from Glastonbury Abbey were transferred to Naworth Castle, Cumberland, then owned by Lord Howard, who history recalled as a believer in the truth of Arthur's mythology; but, for all intents and purposes, the bones of the heroic king and queen, if that is what they were, are lost.

These days the site of the tomb is marked by a rectangular stone outline in the grass and 28 stone slabs that stand before it, which were presumably used for prayer and veneration at the tomb. During one visit I took the opportunity to ask a resident of Glastonbury if they knew what became of the king and queen, to which the reply was, 'Do you think they kept them here when they knew the king's soldiers were coming?' And like everywhere else in Somerset, Glastonbury has its ghosts; an administrator at the abbey told me, 'There have been stories of sightings of a dark warrior, which may have connections with the King Arthur legend…'

Could this really be where King Arthur and his queen's remains were unearthed at Glastonbury?

This is a very condensed version of the Arthurian legend. There are many different dimensions to this story, much of it borne out of the myth taking on a life of its own. The legend of the Holy Grail being buried in the vicinity of Chalice Well (formerly, it would appear, Chalk Well) off Wellhouse Lane on Chalice Hill at the foot of the Tor, and of Arthur's knights embarking on a quest for it, is a relatively modern addition to the Glastonbury myth.

KING ARTHUR: AWAITING RESURRECTION

Particularly interesting, however, are the allusions that Arthur still rests somewhere, ready to defend Britain at a time of national crisis, since this appears to be a story that King Henry II failed utterly to stem. As late as 1469 Thomas Malory's *Morte d'Arthur* further embellished the legend, adding for the benefit of his readership, 'Yet some men yet say in many parts of England that king Arthur is not dead, but had by the will of Our Lord Jesu in another place. And men say that he shall come again, and he shall win the Holy Cross…' The Welsh chronicler Elis Gruffud *c.*1552 states that there was a general belief that Arthur slept within a hill near to Glastonbury and that, according to tradition, in the middle of the 13th century he actually emerged and interacted with numerous people. This reflects the ancient, well-known legend that Arthur resides in this fashion beneath Cadbury Castle, and that on Midsummer Eve iron or golden gates open to display the interior of the hill fort for the briefest of moments and Arthur himself can be glimpsed in supernatural slumber awaiting the day of reckoning. Others say that the spectral figure of Arthur leads a retinue of ghostly knights out of the hillside on the nights of the full moon to allow their horses to drink at King Arthur's Well. Edric Holme's *Wanderings In Wessex* (1922) tells us that 'Every intelligent native for miles around' knew that the hill was hollow and that 'twelve knights, led by their prince' rode round the hill on silver-shod horses and through the trees towards Glastonbury, from whence the distant note of a silver trumpet could be discerned. He adds, tantalisingly, that, 'Some say that of late the Prince and his followers did come forth…'

The story is a well-known one today. The owner of The Camelot Inn, South Cadbury, told me in March 2010:

'We have been here at the Camelot for over two and a half years and have picked up several pieces of anecdotal evidence as to King Arthur, mainly that on Midsummer Day (or Night) a white horse with a knight (perhaps King Arthur) has been seen by many at night riding down Folly Lane. This appears to be witnessed more when Midsummer Night falls on a Tuesday, which is why years ago this pub used to closed on a Tuesday! Even I have heard horses hooves at night while taking the dogs out for a walk, and in full knowledge that no one in their right mind would ride out after midnight around here!'

THE RIVAL CHURCH TOWERS

South-east of Langport there is a very simple, but well-known, story concerning the respective church towers of St Mary's at Huish Episcopi and – to the south – St Martin's at Kingsbury Episcopi. The three-tiered west tower of St Martin's was built by a master architect in the early 1500s, while that at Huish was allegedly built by his new apprentice around the same time. They were meant to be built to compliment each other, but when construction had finished the church at Huish Episcopi – designed by the apprentice – was judged the better, and, at this, the master architect either committed suicide by leaping from the top of Huish church, or murdered his apprentice by thrusting him from the 100ft tower.

I wonder if this story has something to do with a 'fact' that I was told about these churches: that they were, indeed, both built *c*.1500, but that while Huish church tower is exactly 100ft high, Kingsbury church tower is only 99ft high.

BURIED TREASURES

South of Williton can be found the village of Monksilver, where the south aisle window of All Saints Church depicts a hammer, nails, horseshoe, pincers and buttress. The story behind these delineations is that the village blacksmith sent away for a 100-weight of iron from Bristol and, in due course, received a heavy sack that, when opened, turned out not to contain his iron but the same weight in pure gold. He used part of his mysterious windfall to add the south isle to the church, the implements of his trade allegedly being depicted in the windows.

If the stories are to be believed, chances are that wherever you live you are not too far from a huge, undiscovered horde of buried treasure. Many of the legends concern curses, ghosts or fairy guardians and are suitable for other chapters, but some suggest hoards of such fantastical riches that they must be myth…or must they not? For example, west of Luccombe, at the Chisland Lane junction, can be found the remains of a wayside chapel built on the edge of moorland – a site suggestive of its being positioned to keep the unearthly inhabitants of the demon-haunted moors away from the villages near Porlock. In 1903 an excavator at these meagre ruins was told that it was common knowledge that a chest of gold lay buried near Chapel Cross.

A golden coffin is said to be buried on Murtry Hill, Buckland Dinham, near the Orchardleigh Stones, and there was an apparent attempt at excavation here around 1872 in which three holes were dug, although whether this was on account of the legend or an attempt at understanding the stones is not clear. The stones themselves are largely hidden from view of the thin road that climbs the hill – a steep windy affair that passes a solitary farmstead and ultimately leads nowhere. Such is the random position of the stones – a small one leaning against an upright larger one – that I suppose it is only natural that they were considered to be a 'marker' for something; after all, there is no suggestion that they formed a communal gathering point as at Stanton Drew. There is another tradition of a golden coffin buried near Shepton Mallet, a rumour perhaps linked to the discovery around 1840 of urns containing ashes and bone fragments at the Beacon Hill tumuli, south of Oakhill.

The village of Priddy is literally surrounded by ancient long barrows and tumuli, and at Priddy Nine Barrows on North Hill the Somerset Archaeological and Natural History Society noted in 1971 the legend that one of the barrows hid the site of a golden coffin. The ancient fort at Small Down Knoll, Chesterblade, north-east of Evercreech, concealed another golden coffin. What is instantly clear is that all the sites of fabled riches are beneath or near some prehistoric antiquity, and the traveller John L.W. Page observed another such landmark on Winsford Hill, Winsford: the standing stone at the crossroads, engraved in Latin with 'Son of Curatacus' (a British chieftain), supposedly marked the deposit of a hoard of treasure. This object – formerly the Longstone, now called the Caratacus Stone – bore the wear and tear of the elements, indicating that it had stood at this site for many centuries, and in 1890 it had been recently vandalised.

The barrows on the western side of the B3170, south of Corfe and at the Fyfett junction, bear the extremely curious name of Robin Hood's Butts but, as William Phelps's *History of Antiquities of Somersetshire* (1839) says, 'but how they acquired this appellation there is no record.' Suffice to say that one had been

The Caratacus Stone, high on blustery Winsford Hill.

opened in 1818, according to the Somerset antiquarian William Phelps, whereupon nothing was discovered but some flints in the centre. There was no evidence of internment, and the meagreness of the discovery within is maybe what generated the following legend. The biggest barrow covered a deposit of gold, but it was impossible to dig it out as the harder one worked, the less progress was made. This was largely on account of supernatural elements filling in the excavations and other such mischief being wrought overnight. Perhaps this is the misfortune that befell the treasure-seeker in 1818! F.W. Mathews's *Tales Of The Blackdown Borderland* (1923) also observed that in his time there was a tradition that the mounds hid the remains of hundreds of slaughtered Cromwellian soldiers, and that after dark the country people gave Robin Hood's Butts a wide berth in the belief that they were haunted. A Victorian gazetteer also remarked of these mounds, now found with trees growing from them, '…the vulgar maintain [they] marked the distance to which Robin Hood and Little John were accustomed to throw their quoits.'

Robin Hood in Somerset? Some of these sites were clearly thought to be not just hiding places, but also magical, with stories of their 'guardian stones' being possessed of the ability to move and turn over.

Finally, an amazing story was told by Revd Joseph Collins of Bridgwater to the *British Archaeological Association Journal* in 1857 concerning Ruborough Camp, an Iron Age hill fort at Wind Down, north of Broomfield in the Quantocks. The enclosure of the camp was called Money Field by locals, on account of gold found there and the belief that 'underneath the surface [was] an iron castle full of gold and silver, guarded by gnomes and spirits.' In the 1840s an aged labourer told Collins that there was more treasure under their feet at the site than 'was contained in the palaces of all the kings in the world.' The entrance to this subterranean castle was an iron door that could only be found on nights with a full moon.

Collins was informed that two generations earlier one Doctor Farrer, a parishioner who was not only well-read, but also (it was implied) a necromancer, located the iron door by use of a 'shoot of hazel' that acted like a divining rod. A servant began to dig at the spot, but when his spade made a 'clank' against something solid, a terrifying thing happened: groans, shrieks and screams came from just beneath the earth, and grasping hands grabbed the servant's legs as terrifying spirits materialized all around him in the pit he had dug. Placing a Bible as protection on the man's head, Dr Farrer managed to wrestle him out to the surface, and afterwards, according to the labourer, 'The pit was at once closed up, and the door, I believe, is changed, as no one else has been able to find it since.' Other labourers told Collins that they had, in their own lifetimes, tried digging on the night of the full moon at Ruborough Camp but been put to flight by mournful sounds they heard – sounds which Revd Collins put down to the wind whistling among the pine trees. Nonetheless, in the Revd Collins's time the legend was fed by stories of treasure – a gold bar, a turquoise ring set in gold, pieces of armour – actually having been found in the last 100 years.

ODD INTERNMENTS AND EXHUMATIONS

In 1834 an interesting discovery was made in a field called Sparborough, 950 yards north east of Willett Tower, in the Brendon Hills. A circle of 3ft-high standing stones was discovered, 6ft in diameter, within which was found a large chevron-decorated urn full of human ashes and burnt bone fragments. Such accidental exhumations as this, while containing no supernatural mystery, are still extremely fascinating: it is a direct, accidental connection with a prehistoric ritual, which – had it not been disturbed – possibly would have remained hidden and unknown for evermore, and there are other examples of odd deposits of human remains being unearthed in Somerset.

In 1782 there was a strange find on Cadbury Hill, a small hill with an Iron Age fortification on its summit that overlooks Yatton in North Somerset. Here were found '13 human bodies, some of them fresh and of unusual size', and a stone coffin about 2.5ft below the surface of the earth, according to a periodical called *The Church Of England Magazine* (1868). Perhaps it is no surprise that a solitary phantom Roman legionary is said to haunt this place.

During excavations at the remains of a third-century masonry house in Abbey Gate Street, Bath, the severed head of a young woman was found hidden in the flue of a large domestic oven. This act of barbarity was likely to have taken place in the fifth century, but now, of course, we can only guess at the ritualistic or criminal circumstances that brought about this grisly discovery. At Wells Cathedral a heart in a copper casket was accidentally discovered and supposed to belong to a mediaeval bishop. The curiosity was preserved in clear liquor and discovered in the hollow of a stone coffin in the crypt. Surely the strangest find of all was that unearthed in 1908 by archaeologist F.B. Bond in the clay outside the walls of Glastonbury Abbey church on the southern side of the nave: the skeleton of a battle-injured man with a second human skull ritualistically buried between his legs. The remains were thought to belong to one Radulphus Cancellarius, a Norman. Radulphus had received a devastating injury to his forearm in a fight with a Saxon earl; it was the earl's head that lay between Radulphus' legs, having been slain by the Norman. The discovery is outlined in Bond's *Gate Of Remembrance*, which details the remarkable psychic experiments that often dictated the excavations at Glastonbury.

While noting deliberate exhumations we also learn of a gruesome incident in Bristol in 1735. Captain James Newth went on trial for the murder of his wife on 10 September, but he poisoned himself before he could be convicted and was buried at a crossroads near the city. *The Gentleman's Magazine* reported that the mob felt thwarted by this and so subjected the corpse to a posthumous lynching: they dug him up and 'dragged his guts about the highway, poked his eyes out, and broke almost all his bones.'

A strange burial was recorded as having taken place on 4 August 1700. A woman with the surname Pugsley had died aged 80 and her will dictated bizarre conditions. She was to be wrapped in her wedding dress and laid out on a bier, which was then to be taken to a field called Nine Trees in Bristol. The funeral cortege was to make its way from St Nicholas' Church accompanied by a fiddler, with the way led by two maidens who were to scatter herbs before the bier. As the procession passed into Nine Trees, the church bells were to chime. She was not to be buried in a coffin. These wishes were adhered to, and the spectacle was played out before 10,000 Bristolians, earning itself a permanent place in the folklore of the town. This was also on no small account because of Dame Pugsley's life. As a young woman and recently married, her husband (who had held a command under Prince Rupert during the Civil War) was slain by a lucky shot fired from Montpelier during the siege of Bristol in 1645. His corpse had fallen in a ditch and was buried beneath the turf stained with his blood – in the very field where Dame Pugsley herself now desired to be buried. For the next 55 years of her life she habitually dressed in mourning clothes.

An 1824 survey of Bristol tells us that the site of her burial was known as 'Mother Pugsley's Well-Field in the S. E. portion of which stood Prior's Hill Fort.' Quite naturally, Dame Pugsley's 'troubled spirit' was held to haunt the site.

THE MISTLETOE BOUGH

Many tales concern that strange world where history, rumour and wishful thinking converge, and the tales are 'mysterious' by virtue of the fact that the legend cannot be absolutely proved one way or the other. One example of this is the song entitled *The Mistletoe Bough* by T.H. Bayly, which tells the story of a lovelorn young woman, 'Lord Lovell's bride', who dances before her proud father and erstwhile husband at a Christmas wedding ceremony, before taking herself off to play hide-and-seek. She subsequently vanishes off the face of the earth, to the dismay of her mystified family and friends, until years later, '...an old chest that had once laid hid; Was found in the castle – they raised the lid; A skeleton form lay mouldering there; In the bridal wreath of that lady fair.' This is supposed to have been based on a factual event and many old houses across the country lay claim to being the actual location where this incident happened. In Somerset the 19th-century rectory near St Michael's Church, Bawdrip, has been suggested as one site for the basis of the story, although its lack of antiquity would suggest that this is a mistake. The parish church has a memorial to the daughter of one Edward Lovell whose death was premature.

Lovell was rector at St Michael's for 14 years and died in 1675; a mere six years later his daughter Eleanor herself died. Her death was recorded on an inscribed tablet behind the altar, and although Bawdrip's claim to be the actual location of the event was, in the words of Sedgemoor historian Desmond Hawkins in 1954, 'not very convincing' the legend has endured. Although the mmemorial declares that Eleanor died on 14 June 1681 and her poor husband 'mourned her snatched away well nigh on her wedding day by a sudden and untimely fate', it would seem that a curious connection of coincidences is all that links Bawdrip to the legend of *The Mistletoe Bough* – were it not for the suggestion that the rectory was only inhabited by the incumbent vicar since 1860, and prior to this their traditional residence was a dilapidated farmstead elsewhere in Bawdrip and not the 19th-century building observed to be the rectory today...

Could this stone tablet be the basis for the legend of The Mistletoe Bough?

THE LEGEND OF JACK THE TREACLE EATER

The eastern boundary marker on the Barwick Park Estate near Yeovil is a folly: a peculiar structure consisting of an archway of rubbled stone about 5m high, crowned by a conical rocket-shaped tower with a bolted wooden doorway in its side. On the pinnacle is a winged figure made of lead. It possibly dates to *c.*1775 and is one of four follies that apparently function as boundary markers: the Fish Tower to the north, the Rose Tower to the west, the Needle to the south and the eastern marker, which is known as Jack the Treacle Eater.

All of these buildings are shrouded in mystery as to their actual purpose, but Jack the Treacle Eater is the strangest-looking of the lot. The structure's name is the subject of much guesswork, with some saying that it was named after a local runner who lived on treacle and took messages to London for the Messiter family. The winged figure on its apex is 'Swift Jack' himself and children are told that this figure comes to life at midnight, making his way to the small lake at Barwick House to drink treacle. The Messiter family obtained the estate in the early 1800s, however, by which time the follies appear to have been built for some decades. Another story is that the archway and its conical tower date to the Middle Ages and in the 1200s the husband (or son) of the milkmaid who served Barwick House committed a murder and was successfully hidden in the tower for seven months, with his wife regularly leaving a milk churn full of food by the archway to support him. He was supposedly very fond of treacle.

The first legend seems to be too late, the second is far too early, although the name of this curiosity is so specific that it is possible that there is some misremembered truth in one, or both, of the stories behind it.

PRINCESS CARABOO

There are many characters from Somerset and Bristol who have earned a special place in folk-memory due to the historical circumstances of their life. When King John of England claimed the throne (despite many insisting that the seat belonged to his nephew, Arthur, the Duke of Bretagne) among the prisoners he claimed following a decisive battle at Mirebeau, France, was the Duke's sister, Princess Eleanor. This lady was known as the Beauty of Bretagne, but unfortunately for her John and his successor, Henry III, had her confined for the next 40 years in the castle at Bristol. Following Arthur's disappearance and supposed murder, this lady — also known as the Pearl of Brittany — became heiress presumptive to the English throne, but her confinement effectively removed her from the pages of history. It is the thought of this poor, beautiful young woman hidden away and growing old while the world moved on that has led to a belief that the sad ruins of the castle in Castle Park must be haunted by Eleanor's ghost.

There are rather more intriguing enigmas elsewhere, however. It was in Nether Stowey that the poet Samuel Taylor Coleridge chose to hide himself away, and in 1797 he experienced a wondrous dream: a vision of the legendary world of Xanadu. This resulted in the composition of his poem *Kubla Khan*, but at 54 lines it was only a mere fragment of the glorious vision that Coleridge had experienced. The reason for the shortness of the poem was this: Coleridge had awoken in an ecstatic rapture (highly likely to have been opium-induced) and immediately put pen to paper. He had gotten as far as 'For he on honey dew has fed/And drunk the milk of Paradise' when a knocking at the door announced the arrival of 'a person on business from Porlock', who somehow managed to detain Coleridge for over an hour. By the time the poet had got rid of this insurance salesman, his vision of Xanadu had left him forever, and although he had a dim and misty memory of the place, ultimately the poem was left unfinished, and for some 20 years he did not consider it worth publishing.

'A person from Porlock' became a byword for an unwanted visitor, but the mystery here is whether the awful intruder actually ever existed, or was just an invention of Coleridge's who was woven into his explanation of why he was unable to complete *Kubla Khan*. But surely one of the most curious of historical figures was Mary Baker, better known as Princess Caraboo.

Briefly, the general version of the story is that on 3 April 1817 a young woman appeared as if out of nowhere in the village of Almondsbury, Gloucestershire, at the door of a cottage. She was attractive, dressed exotically, and appeared disorientated. The language she spoke was completely unheard of, and when she was taken before a magistrate named Worrall, he — instead of committing her as a vagrant — took her to his home in Knole Park, where he and his wife managed to learn that her name was Caraboo and that she was fascinated by Chinese imagery and symbols. She slept on the floor of a nearby inn, and it appeared she had come from Indo-China — this was gleaned by her identifying a picture of a pineapple with the terminology 'ananas'. Her writing was also unknown and consisted of symbols that resembled combs, birdcages and pans. Worrall could make neither head nor tail of her, so committed her to gaol in Bristol for vagrancy. During her incarceration a 'gentleman from the East Indies' called Manuel Eyenesso announced that Caraboo was, in fact, speaking Javanese and he translated her story: she had been strolling in her garden in Java when she was kidnapped by pirates. After a long journey imprisoned on a sailing vessel she managed to fling herself into the sea — which happened to be the Bristol Channel — and make her way ashore. And she was royalty, too — a princess in her native land.

Worrall took the 'princess' back into his home, which subsequently played host to all sorts of dignitaries who scratched their heads in puzzlement or proclaimed the whole thing a nonsense. Eventually the truth came out: a woman in Devonshire recognised Caraboo's portrait in the *Bristol Journal* and the girl was identified as a cobbler's daughter from Witheridge called Mary Baker (née Willocks), who had travelled England as a domestic servant. Thereby came a full and very detailed confession, and the Worrall family quickly paid for Mary to travel to Philadelphia, perhaps out of embarrassment at the uproar the affair was creating across England by this time.

Mary did eventually return to Bristol in 1821, apparently trying to carve a career out of her notoriety, but she was reduced to selling leeches to Bristol Infirmary Hospital and died on Christmas Eve 1864. She was buried in a pauper's grave in the Hebron Road cemetery in the city. Charles Fort, the Albany-born compiler of all things out-of-place, observed in *Lo!* (1931) that the whole episode of Princess Caraboo remained – in his opinion – a strange enigma. Eyenesso's translation of Caraboo's story must in itself have been an fabrication, since her language was not Javanese, but (it was later decided) a mixture of invention and gypsy. It was either that or she really did speak Javanese, which was unthinkable. Fort cited a number of contemporary reports as conflicting heavily in their detail, even to Mary Willocks' identity, making the whole story as 'officially' explained implausible and utterly meaningless; it was even clear that there were falsifications in her alleged 'confession'. Fort even hinted his belief that there had been some almighty cover-up to get the woman out of the country as soon as possible. Even now, none of it seems to make much sense, and the meaning behind the imposture – if such it was – was never fully explained. The last word must go to Charles Fort: 'All I can make of the story is that the girl mysteriously appeared.'

Montacute House, near Yeovil. These days, there are many romantic legends of subterranean passages in Somerset; I was told of one that ran from here to Ham Hill fort. The manager here told me, 'Detailed architectural and structural inspections have been carried out and have never shown any indication of the existence of a tunnel. The tunnel tradition seems to be one that refers to many mansions.' However, this does not deter such popular myths.

CHAPTER 2:

IN THE REALM OF MIRACLES

INTRODUCTION

Surely one of the most thought-provoking things I have heard repeated on many occasions is the sincere belief that as a boy Jesus Christ was brought to the British Isles and resided for a time in Somerset. It is commonly believed that as a boy of around 12, Jesus came to the West Country with Joseph of Arimathea (whom some say was a relative, possibly his uncle) to learn the trade of a tin merchant, and his course took him to Glastonbury. Glastonbury at this time in its history is considered to have been a comparatively high society, inhabiting the waterlogged landscape and existing in advanced (for the time) mud and wattle settlements that may have originated in Neolithic times. Needless to say, this circumstance is supposed to have led to the situation of Glastonbury Abbey here, a story perhaps helped by the fact that the abbey's actual origins are shrouded in the mists of the historical Dark Ages. William Blake's hymn *Jerusalem* is based on the belief that Christ came to England:

And did those feet in ancient time
Walk upon Englands mountains green;
And was the holy Lamb of God,
On England's pleasant pastures seen...

Somerset folklorist Ruth Tongue painted a picture of this popular belief, writing in her definitive *Somerset Folklore* (1965), 'Our Lord when a boy came voyaging with a sailor uncle to Britain. Their trading ship put in at Watchet, and from there He walked across the Quantocks to Bridgwater where He boarded a punt and crossed the lakes and marshes to the foot of Mendip', where primitive lead mines operated, en route to Glastonbury. This is a story that resurrects itself from time to time, with some academics considering it at least feasible, and there is a time period for which very little is known of Jesus except that he was away from home, possibly far abroad. The Virgin herself might even have accompanied the travellers, and some believed that while in Glastonbury Jesus helped to construct a primitive wattle hut, which would later become a site of pilgrimage for the disciples he was survived by. They supposedly completed and edified the hut in AD 64, a rude and misshapen affair, but nonetheless it was the first Christian church in Britain and later the site of the abbey.

There is also a famous phrase in the Mendip Hills: 'As sure as Our Lord visited Priddy', and it seems that in the past this was often quoted as a truism during Sunday sermons in the area. There is no doubt that this is a fascinating prospect, however unlikely; ultimately it is an issue of belief. Many people have quoted this tale in some form to me and believe it a truism, and we shall have to leave this story at that.

This belief goes hand in hand with another of Somerset's, if not Britain's, most famous legends. The story of Joseph of Arimathea's associations with Glastonbury is so well known it almost need not be told, but no chapter on the heritage of the county would be complete without a condensed version of a tale that, in the words of folklorist C.H. Poole, 'will retain its hold on the hearts of men until the Second Advent.'

It is commonly said that in AD c.63 Joseph of Arimathea came to Britain accompanied by 11 monks via the ancient Phoenician trading route, carrying with him two phials containing the blood and sweat of Jesus himself, procured when Joseph had washed Jesus's body after the Crucifixion. (Incidentally, it was widely believed at one time that the Avon Gorge was created AD 33 on the day of the Crucifixion by a worldwide earthquake.) Joseph landed at Burnham-on-Sea and declared the region would be known as 'Paradise'. The small group navigated their way 17 miles (possibly along the now-disappeared Siger River) to Glastonbury through the marshland and, at a site that was ever after known as Wearyall Hill, an exhausted Joseph thrust his staff in the ground. The staff, brought with him from Palestine, took root and spontaneously (so it is said) began to blossom and bud, forever after being known as the Holy Thorn. Joseph had travelled to Britain to seek out the ancient wattle church in the Glastonbury marshes, and it is said that from these meagre beginnings Glastonbury Abbey was born. Joseph was believed to have been buried in a linen shirt at Glastonbury along with the two phials.

Christianity had certainly arrived in Britain by the early AD 200s, although there is no mention in the earliest scriptures of Joseph of Arimathea being its ambassador. We learn from William of Malmesbury of the likelihood that 'No other hands than those of the Disciples of Christ erected the church of Glastonbury.' He does not mention Joseph of Arimathea by name, however.

There are no real details of Joseph of Arimathea's death, a circumstance that no doubt fuelled the belief in this story. *Memorials Of Somerset* explains that in 1345 a man named Blome obtained permission from King Edward III to undertake excavations at Glastonbury, and in 1367 thereby unearthed what were said to be Joseph's remains. In a curious parallel to the unearthing of King Arthur's remains, what was thought to be Joseph's tomb was reverently placed in the ancient Lady Chapel, where it became the focus of pilgrimage. In 1502–03 at least three miracles were observed to occur at the shrine, including the remarkable restoration of life to a child who had earlier been considered dead at Wells. The other miraculous occurrences were the curing of a Wells vicar's lameness, and a would-be suicide who saw his wounds heal at Banwell. The tomb appeared to survive the destruction of the Dissolution – it was seen in the chapel at the end of the great church by a Mr Ray in 1662 – but this is, apparently, the last we hear of it and it is possible that the whole discovery was fraudulent.

Of the hawthorn shrub on Wearyall Hill, it had grown immense in size and had sprouted a double trunk. In the reign of Queen Elizabeth I a Puritan zealot had taken an axe to the trunk and hewn off half of this remarkable thorn bush; however, he was prevented from chopping off the second trunk when he wounded himself with his own axe and blinded himself with flying woodchips. Another assault was made on the tree by a soldier during the reign of Charles I. Richard Baxter's *The Certainty Of The World Of Spirits* (1691) tells us that by Baxter's time there was a long-standing belief that the thorn 'flowereth just on Christmass-Day' and he collected several accounts affirming this curiosity. In one instance, an 'ancient man' had found on Christmas Day that the shrub 'blossoms as though it was the midst of May' – whereas the day before the thorn had appeared as though dead. What is most interesting is correspondence dated 1659 to Baxter from a Wells man named John Chetwind, who explained, '...the old thorn in the times of the war was rooted up, and is utterly gone.' Poole noted in 1870 that the supposed site of this relic was marked by a flat slab bearing the inscription 'I,A,,A.P.P.DXXXI'.

All vestiges of the Holy Thorn were not lost, however, for it had been budded and grafted many times over. Some had apparently made a living off it, marketing its thorns as holy relics, and John Chetwind

Some believe this carving at Crewkerne to be Joseph's likeness.

observed that one graft from it at a Mr Gallop's house did shoot forth and bud at around Christmas time, but not on the exact day. This, it should be remembered, was not the original thorn, but one grown from it. *The Gentleman's Magazine* recorded in 1753 that an offshoot of the original Holy Thorn had been seen by many curious spectators to blossom on 5 January – which, owing to a change in the calendar, would have been the old-style Christmas Day.

The current Glastonbury Thorn at the abbey is a distant relative of the original.

There are said to have been other related horticultural oddities: a walnut tree that stood near St Joseph's Chapel (Lady Chapel) that only budded on the feast day of St Barnabas, and a legend that an oak was planted to the north east of the Tor upon Joseph's arrival in the Glastonbury marshes. This mighty landmark was for centuries called the Oak of Avalon, until *c.*1906 when it seems to have been cut down. Other trees from the same grove displayed some 2,000 season rings.

Near St Patrick's Chapel can be found a proud thorn bush, a sign before it declaring, 'Glastonbury Thorn'. The original grew on Wearyall Hill. I have been told that this bush – which is supported by three poles, as befits such a venerable antiquity – is a descendent of the great, great original, and near Yeovil I was told a peculiar story. It seems there are some that cling to the hope that that selfsame original still exists on Wearyall Hill and that it is only its children we are allowed to see, for, according to one of the owners of Higher Chiltern Farm, 'if people knew it was still there, it'd be attacked and all sorts.' The crucial point to remember here is that to believe any of this we first have to have faith that it was Joseph who came to Somerset and planted it in the first place – without one, there cannot be the other. There is also a tradition that Joseph established a hermit's cell at Crewkerne. Perhaps the final comment on all of this should be that given in *Memorials Of Somerset*: 'There *is* a thorn growing there, planted in 1951 and believed to be a descendent of the long-gone original. Coincidentally, the *Mail* reported in December 2010 it had been vandalised.'

St John's Church in Pilton contains an atmospheric banner depicting the arrival of the boy Jesus at a waterlogged Glastonbury in a boat with his uncle. He sits on the stern, a halo adorning his head as he surveys the unfamiliar land. As we shall see, there is almost too much lore and heritage surrounding the iconic ruins of Glastonbury to take in. The theme of devotion and faith is rich in Somerset, perhaps richer than anywhere else in Britain. And this chapter is concerned with the marvellous and mystical attached to such faith: Somerset is very much a land of miracles, and the feet of saints have truly walked among the common people in this county.

LOST IN TIME: LEGENDS OF SAINTS FROM THE DARK AGES

To the west of Crewkerne, on the southern side of the A30, can be found the hill called St Rayn Hill. *Somerset Notes And Queries* noted simply in 1856 that here 'there was formerly a chapel, dedicated to St Ranus, which contained his bones.' The hill was also known as Strayn Hill, and little is known of Ranus, Rayn or Reigne himself. He was thought to have been buried beside St White, an equally obscure saint whose name accounted for many a place name hereabouts. These two are indicative of the hazy memory of hermits, martyrs and holy men from the Dark Ages of English history, and are fascinating by virtue of the fact that in some cases literally nothing is known of their lives or deeds, although their memory survived through place names; sometimes, the lack of detail allowed folklore and storytelling to fill in the gaps.

Legend has it that the first real abbot of Glastonbury was the famous Saint Patrick around AD 450. According to tradition, he returned to Britain from captivity in Ireland and made his way to Glastonbury. Upon his death in about AD 493 it was widely believed that he was buried there. L.S. Lewis, the Glastonbury historian, wrote, 'It is extremely probable that after the great fire in 1184, when the remains of Saint Patrick were placed in a pyramid to the south of the altar of St Mary's Chapel, some were placed in the altar of Saint Patrick's Chapel. There is a very big recess in the south side of the altar.' Saint Patrick's Chapel at Glastonbury appears to be of Norman origin, although his associations with Glastonbury are disputed and some think that the earliest chronicler of this legend, William of Malmesbury, confused Patrick with another saint: Petrock of Padstow in Cornwall. The confusion is touched upon by Malmesbury, who affirms that a certain brother had a vision, at a time when the saint's associations with Glastonbury were being questioned, in which a mysterious personage confirmed that proof of Patrick's burial at the abbey could be found 'inscribed in golden letters' somewhere. Writing in 1120, Malmesbury stated, 'He lies on the right side of the altar in the old church. Indeed, the care of posterity has enshrined his body in silver. Hence the Irish have an ancient usage of frequenting the place to kiss the relics of their patron.' Another renowned Irish saint, Brigid, may also have been buried at Glastonbury, according to William of Malmesbury. Even if she was not, certainly left a number of keepsakes at the abbey: her necklace, script and instruments for embroidery, which were on display in Malmesbury's time and 'are efficacious in curing diverse diseases.'

The 13th-century Church of St Dubricius in Porlock reflects the belief that the Welsh saint of that name spent time on the Exmoor coast, and there are traditions of him building a chapel at Dunkery Hill. Here, the bells were supposed to be so loud that they drove all the forest demons away from the hill, allowing travellers to pass safely. The obscurity of Dubricius has given rise to many fantastic stories, notably that he died c.612 aged around 150 years old, and that he officiated at the wedding of Arthur and Guinevere as the Archbishop of Wales.

The Patron Saint of Wales, David, also visited Glastonbury around AD 530 to consecrate the Chapel of Our Lady and donate an altar containing a large sapphire. The night before the ceremony David experienced a vision of Jesus Christ, in which Jesus declared that he had dedicated the church a long time ago and that David should desist. This Saint David did, after Christ touched his hands and produced the

A depiction of Patrick in the saint's chapel at Glastonbury.

stigmata on David's palms. Many saw and the touched the wounds, which miraculously healed themselves during Mass the following day upon David speaking in Latin, 'Per Ipsum, et cum Ipso, et in Ipso.' Henry VIII's agents appropriated the sapphire altar during the Dissolution and there is a rumour that the jewel is the same one that now adorns the royal crown.

It is well known that Keynsham, south-east of Bristol, is supposed to have been named after Keyna, daughter of Braghan, Prince of Wales. She lived here as an anchoress (female hermit) and is famously credited with ridding the area of serpents. Saint Keyna the Virgin left her native soil, possibly in an attempt to throw off suitors, in the later 5th century and directed her journey beyond the River Severn to the woodland outside the settlement of Keynsham. The local prince facilitated her residence here after she — by the power of prayer — turned all the snakes and vipers in the area to stone. A contributor to *The Gentleman's Magazine* in 1811 wrote of this, 'And to this day all the stones in that country resemble the windings of serpents, through all the fields and villages.' The Tudor antiquarian Camden wrote '…there be stones figured like serpents wound into circles found in the quarries of stone about Cainsham.' It is very possible that these were fossilised ammonites, an enormous example of which, discovered at Shepton Mallet, can be found at the Somerset Rural Life Museum. This story about Keyna has been around since at least the 1300s. Eventually, she was sought out by the Welsh saint Cadoc, who desired her to return to her native land with him; she initially refused, as the inhabitants of Keynsham regarded her highly, but eventually departed Somersetshire for good after being admonished by an angel.

The Bishopric of Somersetshire is supposed to have been established by the crusading Saints Fagan and Deruvian in AD 167 at Congresbury, and it continued for over 600 years. Congresbury earned its name from Cungar, a religious hermit who hid himself away in what was at the time a solitary place, during the reign of King Ina. Around 711 Cungar founded a Collegiate church for 12 canons in the honour of the Holy Trinity. Cungar is traditionally said to have been the son of the Emperor of Constantinople, who was directed by an angel to leave his home and make a pilgrimage in the footsteps of Joseph of Arimathea, and Cungar lived a life of great denial at Congresbury. Here, he fasted, prayed and supposedly immersed himself in freezing water, even in wintertime. He eventually deserted this place for South Wales in the face of Saxon advances, it being said (more realistically) that he was actually the son of Geraint, Prince of Devon. Hill's *The Place Names Of Somerset* certainly indicates that a huge question mark hangs over this legend as told, and that a 'cynegar' may have been a term for a hermit, rather than a specific person. But upon visiting the church I was told that some 15 years ago excavation work in the car park had to be abandoned when wooden foundations of what seemed to be an Anglo-Saxon church were discovered, indicating an even earlier association with a religious community here than the Norman-era church suggests. These ruins had to be preserved, and apparently are now beneath the tarmac of the car park. There is a feeling among churchgoers here that Congresbury might have been the centre of religious life in Somerset, at least rivalling — and possibly outshining — Glastonbury for a while.

There are almost too many figures such as this from Somerset's history to keep track of. Saint Carantoc, a Welshman, allegedly tamed a serpentine dragon at Carhampton on the orders of King Arthur in the sixth century, as a condition of recovering his prized stone altar that had been found by Arthur and Catho (another regional ruler) on the banks of the River Avill. Carantoc had some time previously pushed this alter out into the Severn estuary, intending to let it guide him to a place where God desired him to set up a chapel and monastery, but he had lost track of it until he encountered Arthur near Carhampton. At Doulting we learn that another saint, Aldhelm, breathed his last here and, knowing he was to die, directed his attendants to carry him to the little wooden church, where, 'commending his soul to God, he tranquilly breathed his last.' This was about 25 May 709 and the mediaeval church here was dedicated to Aldhelm in his veneration. St Aldhelm's Well by the River Sheppey can still be found. Robert Hope's *Legendary Lore Of The Holy Wells Of England* (1893) describes its contents as 'wonder-working water.' The obscure seventh-century Welsh saint Collen, or Colan, settled in a hermit's cell under the shelf of a rock at the foot of

St Cungar's tree in Congresbury churchyard – grown from the saint's staff.

Glastonbury Tor and may – if folklore is to be believed – have met Gwynn ap Nudd, King of the Fairies and Lord of Annwfn (or possibly demons impersonating him), who held his elfin court from a golden chair within that very hillock. Equally remarkable stories are told of Saint Eligius (or Eloi) in Wincanton. This French missionary, who died around AD 660, miraculously removed the leg of an old, unruly carthorse brought to him by a carter, re-shod it and then replaced the animal's entire leg, following an accident that had damaged its hoof. S. George, the Wincanton historian, tells us that an oolitic stone found in the church c.1735 depicts this legend: 'On the left side is a mitred bishop standing with a horse's leg in his hands with the foot resting on an anvil. At the foot of the bishop kneels a man evidently entreating the bishop to do something for him. On the right hand is a horse or ass minus one leg...' Sadly, this carving is incomplete, as administrators of the parish church explained to me: 'The carving is sharp and crisp, but the figures have all had their heads crudely knocked off – almost certainly by Protestant extremists, "iconoclasts" or "idol-breakers", at the time of the Reformation. So here is a tiny piece of the pre-Reformation decoration of the church.'

Saint Aethelwyn, brother of the Anglo-Saxon king Cenwealh (died AD c.674), may have lived as a hermit in the barren marshes of Athelney Island over two centuries before King Alfred sought refuge there. In 878 the king himself is said to have experienced a vision of Saint Cuthbert, who spoke to him in a dream and assured the fugitive ruler that in the end he would triumph. Upon his victory Alfred had a monastery erected at the spot. In 1693 the story was borne out to a certain extent when a gold amulet was discovered in Newton Park, bearing on one side an image of Saint Cuthbert and the inscription 'Aelford Mec Heit Gevorcan' – 'Alfred had me made.'

Depiction of the miracle at Wincanton.

SAINT DUNSTAN AND GLASTONBURY

Dunstan, whose likeness scribing an ancient text graces the visitor centre at Glastonbury Abbey, is perhaps the abbey's best-known abbot. Dunstan is described in F.J. Snell's *Memorials Of Old Somerset* (1906) as 'at once the greatest man of his time in England and the greatest of the early English abbots of Glastonbury.' He was born AD *c.*909 (his date of birth is the subject of some dispute, though) into a well-connected aristocratic Wessex family in Baltonsborough (Ballsbury), south-east of Glastonbury. As a boy he was placed by his father, Heorstan, under the tutorage of a colony of Irish monks who had settled near the (then) semi-ruined and Danish-ravaged monastery at Glastonbury. While serving in the Chapel of St Mary his intelligence, articulacy and skill with art caught the attention of the royal court, with Dunstan also becoming friendly with Elfleda, a niece of King Athelstan, who had chosen the life of an anchoress in a small abode near the western side of the monastery. It is during Saint Elfleda's residency here that a miracle supposedly occurred: upon being forewarned that her uncle, the king, would shortly be arriving, and finding herself in want of provisions, she prayed that mead be provided for the king's retinue. Following Mass, at lunch, when greedy companions of the king emptied the drinking vessel, providence miraculously filled it to the top so that it did not run dry and all were sustained throughout the meal. When told of the marvel, Athelstan said, 'We have sinned too much in vexing this servant of God with our excessive superfluity.' Dunstan spent much time with Elfleda, regarding the old woman as highly as his own mother. As she lay upon her deathbed Dunstan beheld a dove of the purest brilliant white flying towards her window from the abbey, and when he went to her bedside he was amazed to see that, although the curtains were drawn around her bed, Elfleda appeared to be conversing with someone invisible, and the nurse told Dunstan that a bright light had appeared behind the curtains shortly before he entered. When all was quiet, Dunstan poked his head through the curtains and asked Elfleda who she was conversing with; she replied, 'Surely with who you saw flying this way, whilst you were standing outside the church.' The following morning she received the last sacraments and died.

He was also close to Athelstan's successor King Edmund, to whom he owed his elevation to the position of Abbot of Glastonbury in AD 942, and his life can almost be chronicled by the monumental achievements he undertook: his implementation of strict Benedictine rules at Glastonbury and his ousting of the secular priests and slack monks; his ascension to the posts of Bishop of Worcester and, then, Bishop of London; his elevation to the position of Archbishop of Canterbury in October 960; his organisation of the spectacular coronation of King Edgar at Bath in 973. He is even held to have given the foolish 15-year-old King Eadwig the back of his hand when he caught the young monarch cavorting with a mistress (and her mother) on a sofa, the king having slipped away from his own coronation at Kingston Upon Thames in January 956.

Under Dunstan, Glastonbury became a favourite place of pilgrimage for the contemporary kings of England, and here were buried his patron, King Edmund I, along with King Edgar and King Edmund Ironside. Dunstan was canonised in the century after his death, and there are many stories of miracles associated with his time at Glastonbury, as put forward by his great hagiographer, Osbern, in his *Life Of Dunstan* (*c.*1070).

The ancient chronicler Matthew of Westminster suggests that Dunstan's future greatness was evidenced at the time of his birth. His mother was an exceptionally devout woman called Cynethryth who, while pregnant, was believed to have re-lit the candles of all those present in St Mary's Chapel when a mysterious wind extinguished all of the flames except the one flickering on her own candle. This was on the day of the purification of the Blessed Virgin, otherwise called Candlemas, on 2 February, and it evidenced that the as-yet unborn Dunstan was destined to be the 'minister of eternal light to the Church of England.'

We are also told that while undergoing his scholarship with the solitary group of Irish educators who frequented Glastonbury, Dunstan envisioned the restoration of the abbey and also recovered from a near-fatal bout of marsh fever. His preservation was occasioned by the appearance of an angel at his bedside one night. But perhaps the two most famous legendary events associated with Dunstan occurred in adulthood, although before he obtained the abbacy of Glastonbury. As early as the following century it was already being written that he had won an encounter with the Devil in the little hermit's cell he had built near St Mary's: 'In this crude abode, five feet long and two and a half feet deep, he lived a hermit's life, studying, praying, and working at his various trades, with no relaxation save his beloved harp.' He also practised chemistry and ironmongery. Here, as Dunstan was forging a chalice, the Devil appeared at a window to tempt him, but he seized the creature with red-hot tongs by the nose and held him, bellowing furiously, a great part of the night. While many consider this a symbolic legend, some said that the Devil had taken the form of a beautiful woman to tempt him; when this is considered, it is possible that the legend is based on something of the sort happening to Dunstan during his lifetime, although the popular image is of his snaring a diabolical-looking creature by the face with the tongs. Some say that the incident occurred after his investiture as Archbishop of Canterbury, on the site of the Archiepiscopal Palace at Mayfield, East Sussex, which in 1868 was described as 'in part an ivied ruin; here are preserved St Dunstan's forge, and anvil, and tongs.'

The other famous story concerning Dunstan occurred *c.*942, during a hunting expedition in the Mendip Hills in which King Edmund, with whom Dunstan was currently estranged, nearly died. Axbridge being then a royal borough, the king was chasing a stag which, in its desperation, threw itself into the 'immense precipiece and horrid gulph, called by the inhabitants Cheddarclyffe.' The hounds also crashed over the edge, and as Edmund attempted to wrestle his unmanagable horse on the lip of the gorge he commended his soul to God. He spoke to the Lord, 'I do not recollect that I of late have injured anyone except Dunstan; and this fault I will amend by reconciling myself to him if time is allowed me.' The horse calmed down, scrambled away from the edge, the king was saved, and in recognition of this Dunstan was granted the abbacy of Glastonbury by a humbled Edmund.

Upon the death of King Eadred on 23 November 955, Dunstan — then still at Glastonbury — is said to have been appraised of the monarch's death at Frome by angels singing in the air, 'King Eadred has gone to his rest in peace.' This marked the turning point in his life in a direction away from Glastonbury.

St Dunstan defeats the Devil using tongs.

Dunstan – the man whose supporters insisted talked 'face to face with God' – died at Canterbury on 19 May 988, shortly before reaching his 80th year. Quite what became of his relics is unclear, as both Canterbury and Glastonbury were claiming to house his skeleton in the 1500s. Glastonbury claimed that around 1016 the then abbot, Beohtred, and four of his monks had cautiously approached Canterbury, which had been ravaged and deserted after Danish attacks, and stealthily returned Dunstan's remains to Somerset; this would have been some 28 years after his death. But in 1508 Archbishop Warham found Dunstan's tomb at Canterbury to be undisturbed, and the arguing continued until the whole affair was swallowed up in the confusion of the Dissolution of the Monasteries, when many relics were appropriated by the state, only to vanish forever.

Numerous other miracles concern Dunstan's ascension through the ranks of the church to the ultimate position of Archbishop of Canterbury; while Bishop of Worcestor he was purportedly led to the See of London c.958 by a vision of the Apostles. His most famous miracles, however, remain associated with his Someset upbringing. As the old folk-rhyme tells it:

> St Dunstan, as the story goes;
> Once pulled the Devil by the nose;
> With red-hot tongs, which made him roar;
> That he was heard three miles or more...

The church at Baltonsborough was built in the 15th century and dedicated to Dunstan in his honour, and today an accomplished ironwork weathervane made by a 19th-century blacksmith adorns the tower: quite naturally, since Dunstan is the patron saint of blacksmiths.

'ENGLAND'S ONE MIRACLE WORKER AND PROPHET'

Apart from Dunstan, Somerset's other famous native holy man is Wulfric, a mediaeval hermit popularly referred to as 'England's one miracle worker and prophet.'

Wulfric was born around 1080, although there is dispute as to where: Poole tells us he was born at Letona, a place about eight miles from Bristol, and perhaps Litton is meant, although many believe that he hailed from Compton Martin. Born into a middle-class family, he entered into holy orders at a young age; however, upon being ordained, and still being young and foolish, he spent much of his time hunting and hawking. At some point, however, he experienced a 'Road to Damascus'-type shift and began taking his holy vows seriously. The trigger for this seems to have been a relatively ordinary event: he was chastised by an unknown person dressed in the garb of a beggar, whom he encountered while out hunting and whom he refused alms to.

The significance of this in Wulfric's mind is unclear. Perhaps he believed that he had encountered Christ himself and had failed a test. But he immediately embarked upon a life of penance, acting first as chaplain to William Fitzwalter, lord of his home town, and then migrating to Haselbury Plucknett, where he took up residence in a vacant hermit's cell on the cold northern side of the chancel of St Michael's Church around 1125. The priest at St Michael's was, at the time, one Brichtric, married to Godida.

His transformation was remarkable. He lived a life of such denial and austerity that he wasted away to a near-skeleton, forcing himself to go without sleep, and when he did sleep, leaning his head painfully at an angle against a stone wall. His diet was oaten bread and gruel brought by Haselbury village boys from Montacute Priory, and his shirt rough and itchy; later he took to wearing a heavy coat of iron chain mail. In the depths of winter he would force himself to recite the whole psalter while up to his neck in freezing water in a stone bath and, like other anchorites, may have succumbed to bouts of illness in his solitude. Draughty wind blew through his little cell, and he might have endured perpetual darkness were it not for the monks illuminating the nearby church to provide him light. It is repeated that he fought internal battles against maddening temptation proffered him by Satan, and that when his piety won through he was scourged by that selfsame 'enemy of souls'.

Devotion such as this often caught the public imagination and many made pilgrimages to Wulfric, where he provided wise words of piety and counsel – although, seemingly, he did not meet his pilgrims face-to-face, but ordered his messages to be taken to them in a vestibule. As his fame spread, so did the stories; Wulfric was even reputed to have sent an emissary to a nearby stream to recover a half-drowned man whom he had known by divine means was being thrust under the water by the Devil. The man had in fact sold his soul, but changed his mind, and had been trying to get to Wulfric when the Devil got him at the Broad River and tried to teach him a lesson. Wulfric's counsellor, armed with a cross and holy water, saw the Devil off and brought the penitent man before Wulfric's feet. The saint dismissed him in peace.

The miracles attributed to Wulfric during his time at Haselbury Plucknett are many. He hailed Stephen of Blois as king when the future monarch rode past his cell with the words, 'It is no error – it is you, Stephen, that I mean. For the Lord hath delivered the realm into your hand. Protect the church and defend the poor.' Stephen became king in 1135, but the advice of Wulfric was ignored, for Stephen's reign was rent by 19 years of civil war and anarchy – a time when 'Christ and all his saints slept.' Wulfric also prophesied that the religious house of the Order of Canons, established by Walter, Lord of Haselbury, would not prosper.

Water blessed by Wulfric healed many, as did the rings from the chain mail coat that he bore on his shoulders until, in later life, its weight hindered his genuflection. At this point he bade his old patron, the knight Sir William, who had presented him with it, to try to cut the chain mail with a pair of sewing scissors. The scissors cut through the iron like a knife through butter. Christ-like, Wulfric turned water into wine and stolen bread into stone (and back again) to teach a thieving young boy a lesson. He also remonstrated with a mouse that had been nibbling his cape, at which the repentant animal scurried to his feet and expired before the holy man.

In 1154 Wulfric told his counsellor that he had been visited by God and that his death drew near, and the counsellor must prepare for Wulfric's death the following Saturday – 20 February. Upon his death there was fighting about the church as the Norman Cluniac monks from Montacute came to collect his remains and clashed violently with a crowd of villagers from Haselbury and Crewkerne assembled by Osberne, the parish priest who had succeeded his father, Brichtric. Osberne later removed Wulfric's remains from his cell to ensure their security, transferring them inside the church, where his tomb in the North Chapel was visited by pilgrims for generations.

Wulfric is widely regarded as a saint, although he does not appear to have been formally canonised. I was told by the Church Warden here that, 'There is regrettably no physical evidence of where his body was finally buried. Nor is there any depiction of Wulfric here in Haselbury. A window in St Michael's Church at Compton Martin – in the Mendips where Wulfric served as a priest before he came to Haselbury – has an artist's impression of him. We only have a modern panel commemorating his 29-year stay here.' But, tantalisingly, in 1878 Poole tells us, 'From time immemorial, a side aisle, now used as a baptistery, has borne the name of St Wulfric.'

The parish priest had apparently moved the remains yet again some years after Wulfric's death, reburying them at the western end of the putative Saxon church, the exact location being known only to himself and God. Wulfric's cell could itself still be observed as late as 1633, and presumably the man himself still lies buried hereabouts.

MIRACLES AT THE TOMBS OF THE BISHOPS

Most of Wells Cathedral, including the famous ornately-sculptured mediaeval West Front, dates from the late 12th and early 13th centuries, although its three towers were not built until the late 14th and 15th centuries. The cathedral stands on the site of an earlier church established around the year 705 by King Ina, on a site that may have itself once housed a Roman mausoleum. The present structure originated around 1176 and the mediaeval close that surrounds it is more or less intact, consisting of the residences of cathedral dignitaries. It is the seat of the Bishops of Bath and Wells, who lived at the adjacent moated Bishop's Palace.

Folklorist C.H. Poole noted that 'passing from the pillars to the tombs of this cathedral church' many miracles were wrought at the sepulchre of Bishop William of Bitton II, who was elected to that post in 1267 and who died on 4 December 1274. People afflicted with painful toothache made pilgrimages here, and – apparently – left with their teeth much healed.

Many extraordinary cures are also reputed to have been wrought at the tomb of one of Bitton's successors, William de Marchia, elected bishop in 1293 and who died around June 1302. He was buried between the door of the cloisters and the altar of Saint Martin, and for some considerable time after his death there was a petition for him to be canonized on account of these miraculous occurrences – as there had been during the tenure of Bishop Bitton 30 years earlier.

THE MIRACULOUS CHAINS

In the 17th century at Wellington Court House, the seat of the Popham family, a pair of ancient iron shackles hung on the wall, which legend said were evidence of a miracle. One of the early Pophams had been taken captive by the Turkish and his good lady back in Wellington despaired of ever seeing him again. She prayed continually until one day her husband was found in the mansion – miraculously transported by an invisible power, so they said in Somerset, where this story was accepted without a doubt. The shackles that manacled him were removed and hung in the hall as evidence. This legend is recorded in Aubrey's *Brief Lives*, and although the Popham line in south-west England went back to the time of King John, it is unclear which ancestor the legend was supposed to revolve around. The mansion itself was destroyed during the Civil War after being garrisoned by the Parliamentary army.

DELIVERANCE

Very often, miraculous escapes from death by common people were laid at the door of God's providence and the power of prayer. In Market House Lane, Minehead, can be found an ancient almshouse that, when established in 1630, consisted of 11 apartments and bore a brass plate over the door with a singular inscription:

Robert Quirke built this house Anno 1630, and doth give it to the use of the poore of this parish forever. And for better maintenance I do give my two inner cellers, at the inner end of the key; and cursed be that man that shall convert it to any other use than to the use of the poore, 1630.

This dire inscription can still be seen, and is part-explained by the second engraving: 'God's providence is my inheritance.'

A ship is engraved in the plaque, and the story is that, since Quirke was a mariner, he created the almshouse after being spared by the Almighty while at sea during some near catastrophe. Typical of the examples of God's providence experienced by mariners is the remarkable escape of the crew of a small vessel that set sail from Bristol for New England on 22 September 1681. Fierce winds changed their course to the West Indies and, when on the point of starvation and exposure, the Lord intervened, according to the 17th-century observer of the remarkable, Richard Baxter. He wrote:, 'When their victuals fail'd them, the merciful God, whose is the sea, for he made it, sent them a supply, by causing dolphins every now and then to come so near the vessel as to be catch'd; yet it was observable that they could never catch any but in an extream necessity; nor any more than would serve their present necessity.' By collecting rainwater, eating dolphins and roping themselves to the ship and being dragged in the water to keep cool, they managed to land at Barbados.

The Minehead plaque also carries a curse.

We learn of other escapes from near-death that were probably put down to providence. At the church of St Decuman's, Watchet, there is a curious legend of a close shave with a living burial. One of the ladies of the Wyndham line — some say that it was Lady Florence Wyndham, who died in 1596 — had a remarkable escape in her early years. In c.1557, and heavily pregnant, she was presumed to have died following an illness and so was laid out in the vault of St Decuman's. There are two versions of what happened later: in the first, and probably more likely version, the sexton heard some small noise from the 'corpse' as he closed the vault door, and found the lady beginning to stir in the coffin. In the second version Lady Florence awoke when the sexton attempted to cut off her fingers to get at her ring, and thus revived, she made her groggy way past the petrified sexton to nearby Kentisford manor house. Here she presented herself before her terrified family, who at first thought that they were seeing a ghost. Almost immediately afterwards she gave birth to a son, John, from whom every subsequent family member descended. It does not take much to imagine that this event, of which there is more than likely an element of truth, was viewed as a true 'miracle', happening as it did in a church.

IN THE REALM OF MIRACLES

It is clear that the theme of devotion runs deep in Somerset folklore, and next we look at the events that were reliably recorded in their own time as true 'miracles' — actual instances where God intervened directly and showed the people of Somerset a 'sign'.

Sometimes the providence of God was recognised in what might otherwise have been considered a bizarre — but natural — event. During the reign of King Edward IV a landslide caused by heavy rain flattened and obliterated the ancient chapel of St Mary le Cliff, between Blue Anchor and Chapel Cleeve. The only thing untouched by the devastation was the altar of the chapel and its image of the Virgin. In recognition of this 'miracle', in 1466 the king granted a charter establishing a market and a fair. Although the new chapel was not built on the old one, for many generations pilgrims made their way to the new chapel, which was later incorporated into the modern mansion now known as Chapel Cleeve.

Legend tells us that angels have appeared in Somerset. As early as AD 794 King Offa of Mercia beheld an angel as he tried to sleep on a couch while staying in Bath. At the time he was lamenting the assassination of a political rival, and the angel firstly admonished him and then ordered him to search out the remains of St Alban. The great Oliver King, ordained Bishop of Bath and Wells in 1495, is also held to have had a revelation imparted to him by an angel while sleeping in that great town around 1500. He imagined, as he lay meditating in bed in Bath, that he saw the Holy Trinity, with angels ascending and descending a heavenly ladder. Near this was an olive tree, bearing a royal crown, and a voice echoed in the room, 'Let an olive [Oliver] establish the crown, and let a king restore the church.' This he took as a sign to support Henry Tudor and restore Bath Abbey. These images are depicted on the West Front of the abbey.

One of the most familiar miracles in Somerset history occurred in Wells Cathedral in 1596 and hints at something even more marvellously supernatural. The congregation within were fearful of an immense thunderclap outside that sounded two or three times, and when lighting appeared to flash within the cathedral they fell to their knees in terror. Afterwards, although no one was hurt, the marks of the cross were found to have been imprinted on the shoulders, breast, back or other body parts of those

Wells Cathedral.

assembled. Among those afflicted by this wondrous phenomenon was the wife of the Bishop of Wells, John Still, who exposed part of her body to show her husband that the mark had imprinted itself upon her skin. Afterwards the bishop was amazed to find the mark of a cross upon his own arm. The bishop, who died in 1608, related the marvel to the Bishop of Ely, who in turn recounted the story around 1610 to his friend and scholar, Isaac Casaubon 'in such a manner, as forbade me [Casaubon] to doubt of its truth.'

MARTYRDOM

It must be observed that as well as the many miracles and saintly connections that Somerset boasts, the area has seen its fair share of martyrdom – those who suffered the ultimate penalty for the depth of their faith. Miraculous circumstance sometimes accompanied such outrages. Saints Indract and his sister Drusa were supposedly martyred *c.*710 at Shapwick in the Polden Hills, after travelling from either Rome or Ireland on their way to Glastonbury to pay homage at the tomb of Saint Patrick. On the road the procession filled their sacks with millet and seed, but perhaps on account of their carrying staves tipped with brass, it was thought that they carried gold on their person. At this time King Ina was holding court nearby and a party of his servants, headed by one Hona, resolved to ambush the holy procession and steal the 'gold'. This they did at Shapwick, stealthily entering an inn and murdering the sleeping Indract, Drusa and the entire retinue in their beds by cutting their throats. The corpses, of which some say there were 100, were cast into a pit, but the site was illuminated by a heavenly white light that shone for three nights, and

St Decuman's Well.

King Ina had Indract and Drusa reburied at Glastonbury Abbey, Indract being deposited in a stone pyramid on the left side of the altar. Another story says that the murderers went into a frenzy after the funeral, tearing the flesh from their bodies with their teeth and so killing themselves. The story is a little confused; Indract may, in fact, have been an abbot of Iona who lived during the following century, and he may have been buried at Shepton Mallet.

The church on the south-east edge of Watchet, on the north coast of Somerset, is dedicated to St Decuman. The remarkable story here is that Decuman was a Welshman who sailed across the water to Somerset on a bundle of rods, or alternatively a cloak, and lived a hermit's life of devotion in a cell near the site of the church. His closest companion, so they say, was a cow who accompanied him everywhere and sustained him with her milk. Around AD 706 a pagan inhabitant cleft Decuman's head from his shoulders as he was at prayer, but this did not dissuade the holy man; he took his head in his hands and found his way to a spring (the site of St Decuman's Well, or Sacred Spring), where he washed his head. Some say that he placed his head back on his shoulders, others that he swam the Channel back to Wales with his head under his arm. The most likely suggestion is that his head and body were interred near here, but presumably by Decuman's followers and not by the headless man himself, as was often said. His festival was celebrated on 27 August.

The theme of martyrdom runs strong throughout Somerset. In 1083 the unthinkable happened at Glastonbury when the autocratic Norman abbot, Thurstan, finally lost patience with the monks in an argument over the replacement of Gregorian chanting. Norman archers forced their way into the locked church, killing three monks on the steps of the altar as they prayed, and wounding a further 18. The monks, however, retaliated and, in their fury at the desecration of Glastonbury, killed two of their attackers and ejected the rest from the minster. A furious William the Conqueror ordered Abbot Thurston back to France.

There are Somerset connections with the most famous English martyrdom of them all: the murder of Archbishop Thomas Becket, who was slain in 1170 at Canterbury by four knights acting on a frustrated harangue by King Henry II across the Channel in Normandy. The chantry chapel at Williton was built by Robert, brother of Reginald Fitz-Urse, the leader of the assassins. The vestry of the church at Sampford Brett contains the recumbent effigy of another assassin, Richard le Bret, or le Brito.

Richard le Bret's effigy.

Woodspring Priory, on the windy, desolate land north of Weston-super-Mare, was built in 1210 by a descendent of William de Tracy (another of the assassins), and dedicated to St Thomas the Martyr; a granddaughter of le Brito came forward as benefactress. From here the Kewstoke Rhyne leads to Kewstoke, on the northern fringe of Weston-super-Mare, and here in 1852 a bloodstained wooden cup was discovered in the church. This cup is widely held to have been the one that caught blood pouring from Becket's wounds, and this priceless (if it is what tradition says it is) relic now resides in Somerset County Museum in Taunton.

Back at Glastonbury, the abbey — after having stood in some form for at least 1,000 years — finally fell victim to the legally sanctioned plunder known as the Dissolution of the Monasteries in 1539, a shameful time in English history, which deprived the land of some of its finest buildings. Along with two of his monks, the last abbot of Glastonbury, Richard Whyting, met his end after being accused of 'robbyng the Glastonburye church' of its treasures before the king's agents could get their hands on them. It seems that the auditors found Glastonbury largely stripped of its jewels, plate, ornaments and relics upon their arrival. Although the implication is that most of it was recovered 'with vigilant labour', the bishop's actions have led to a long-standing wishful belief that many of the holy relics kept at Glastonbury were safely spirited away and escaped government detection. Wherever they ended up, if they still exist they would by now be utterly, incalculably priceless. Abbot Whyting was executed on a charge of treason on 'the Torre Hill', with his body being quartered to Wells, Bath, Ilchester and Bridgwater and his decapitated head stuck upon the abbey gate at Glastonbury. It is sometimes difficult to take in the magnitude of events that are said to have shaped the now-silent ruins of Glastonbury; suffice to say that, when all is taken into account, Glastonbury will probably remain one of the most fascinating places in Europe.

In times of conflict the ordinary clergy were always at risk. The Royalist zealot Sir Francis Dodington perpetrated such outrages during the Civil War that after the conflict both sides refused him an amnesty and he was forced to flee to France before returning to his manorial seat at Dodington Court, Dodington, on the northern fringe of Shervage Wood. Among his crimes was the slaying of an 'honest minister' on the road near Taunton. Sir Francis bellowed at him, 'Who art thou for, priest?' To which the reply came, 'For God and the Gospel!' Sir Francis shot the man dead there and then. Bristol has its martyrs too; in the chaotic aftermath of the Siege of Bristol in 1645 Parliamentary forces took over the Bishop's Palace and violently ejected the bishop, Thomas Howell. Howell had only been consecrated Bishop of Bristol that April. He died two weeks later in January 1646, his wife having already died in childbirth, after being exposed to wind and rain when the roof was plundered of its lead during the conflict. Howell was buried at the entrance of the choir from the south aisle in the cathedral, under a plain stone bearing only the word 'Expergiscar', meaning 'I shall awake'.

The Dean of Wells also met a violent death. Dr Walter Raleigh was removed from his position during the Commonwealth because of his support for King Charles I, and was subsequently stabbed to death by David Barret, his gaoler at Wells, on 10 October 1646 during an argument over Raleigh's personal correspondence.

'AND DREAMED THAT I WAS AT GLASTONBURY...'

In 1750 the declaration of a 60-year-old yeoman from the parish of North Wootton called Matthew Chancellor evidences the powerful effect that Glastonbury still held over the local people, despite its having already stood in ruins for 200 years by that time. Chancellor had suffered from asthma and other painful illnesses for 30 years, and in October 1750 he suffered a violent fit before falling asleep and dreaming of Glastonbury. In his dream, he found himself on a horse track 'some way above Chain-gate', where he saw before him a pond of water by which horses meandered and paused to drink. The water was the clearest Chancellor had ever seen, and he fell to his knees to partake; when he stood up he perceived 'a person' beside him who told him that in order to cure his ailment he should fast for seven Sundays in a row, except for partaking of a glassful of water from the 'freestone shoot' in the morning. Then, Chancellor was told, thus cured he could announce the miracle to the world on the seventh Sunday. Of the spring, he was informed, 'This water comes from out of the holy ground, where a great many saints and martyrs have been buried.' Chancellor was then told something regarding the Saviour's baptism in the River Jordan, but could not remember it when he awoke.

On the first Sunday after his vision Matthew Chancellor made his way to Glastonbury and did as he was bid, although he found that the spring was not so plentiful as in his dream and it took him three scoops to fill his clean glass. This he ascribed to the fact that it was autumn and very dry. But he persisted with the ritual, and gradually his ailments cleared.

When news of this 'miracle' was broadcast it created enormous controversy in Somerset and, subsequently, the capital, when reports of the marvellous healing water were circulated in *The Gentleman's Magazine* in 1751. By this time people were travelling in their thousands from as far away as Bristol and Bath, and rumours were sweeping the county that the spring could cure blindness. A pump room was set up at the site, but the excitement soon wore out. This was partly due to charlatans peddling ordinary water in bottles in London and claiming it to be the pure healing water of Glastonbury; but it was also due in no small part to an 80-year-old Glastonbury woman, who dismissed the 'miracle' as nonsense and claimed that she could remember thousands being convinced that cow muck collected freshly from the cattle at St James' Park effected the same type of cures.

By 1752 the tourists were dwindling and it is sad that Matthew Chancellor was remembered less seriously in Glastonbury. He died in 1765 and the parish registers for St John the Baptist Church recorded, 'Burials 1765 August 24th, Matthew Chancellor, the dreamer.'

HOLY STAFFS AND HEALING WELLS

Apart from the fabled Glastonbury thorn or St Decuman's Well, there were other natural landmarks that possessed miraculous qualities or links to the saints. In 1892 E. Stanford, in *A Mendip Valley*, stated that the dead trunk of an enormous yew tree within the grounds of St Andrew's Church, Congresbury, had sprung from the staff of the aforementioned Saint Cungar, and that the swampland hereabouts had been turned into 'flowery meads.' Locally, they said that the Saint had not left for Wales, but that his body lay beneath the yew trunk in a golden coffin.

The Victorian Bristol folklorist Joseph Leech observed something similar in his *Brief Romances From Bristol History* (1884). In College Green, at the west end towards the entrance to College Street, there was a remarkable tree, taller than its neighbours and always the first in leaf. The story was that a monk from adjoining St Augustine's had requested that he be buried there and that the tree be planted to mark the spot, thus accounting for its prodigious appearance and the beauty and abundance of its foliage. The man buried was in fact the abbot, John Strete, who had died sometime in the late 1200s after being worked to death by an emissary of the Bishop of Worcester, himself concerned about falling standards at St

Augustine's. Leech wrote, 'As the tree grew it inclosed the coffin in its roots and drew such sustentation and nourishment from the decaying body of the fat Abbot, that, enriched by his remains, it soon surpassed its sylvan neighbours...'

There was also the Ilminster Thorn, which, according to the story, grew spontaneously and very quickly from a thorn procured by a pilgrim from the Holy Thorn at Glastonbury. A contributor to *Notes And Queries* in 1893 recalled that the Dillington Estate, near Ilminster, used to possess the Thorn and that the cattle knelt down in front of it as though in veneration. This was supposed to happen at midnight on 'old' Christmas Night (i.e. before calendar changes). The contributor to *Notes And Queries* observed, 'It used to be said that there was scarcely a gentleman's park in Somerset which did not contain a plant grown from a slip of the Glastonbury Thorn.' One such can, these days, be found in the grounds of Glastonbury Abbey Barn, seen from Bere Lane.

There were also wells of 'holy water' famed for their 'healing properties', and in defence of Matthew Chancellor (see above), there does seem to have been an actual 'holy well' at Glastonbury. Around 1825 a party searching the abbey grounds found 'a flight of winding steps leading to a subterraneous recess.' Deep beneath the surface was found a pavement and a well, protected by an arch and served by a sophisticated drainage system, which fed the water northwards under the pavement of the chapel crypt. It was supposed that pilgrims entered via a now-blocked doorway in the southern wall of the chapel. But what was interesting was that this find backed up an old legend of a secret chamber and a sacred well at Glastonbury whereby miraculous cures were occasioned from 'holy water'. Until the discovery of the crypt, no known evidence existed to support this story. It is now designated St Joseph's Well.

Many such sites as this, however, exist throughout Somerset in general, and are listed by Charles Hope in an 1893 work on the subject. The well in St Anne's Wood, Brislington, was sought out every 26 July, as its water was believed to cure eye diseases; similarly, Bully Well at Chew Magna. At Ashill it was believed that St Nipperham's Well bubbled the first Sunday in May, and this agitation could help the sick and the lame. The curative properties of the spring below Wembdon Hill, Wembdon, were discovered in 1464, and the spring was then known as St John's well, and later as Holy Well or Holowell. The well head was restored in 1855. Hotwells in Bristol has obtained its name from the hot springs that bubble up through the rocks of the Avon Gorge at the Clifton Suspension Bridge, which became the site of a spa in the Georgian era — the water being said to cure consumptive illnesses. Dunnick's Well near Latcham, by which there was a pool, was said to have effected a cure in an infected eye as recently as 1945.

THE POWER OF PRAYER IN BRISTOL

Chambers' *Book Of Days* relates the marvellous effect that the pulpit orator the Reverend George Whitefield had on the 'savage colliers of Kingswood' at Rose Green in Bristol in 1739: '...soon he saw white gutters made by the tears which plentifully fell down their black cheeks — black as they came out of their coal-pits.' The fervour he awakened in Bristol was extraordinary, and thousands gathered in weeping hordes to hear Whitefield preach in scenes that must have been remarkable. But Bristol's most astonishing story of faith occurred the following century.

A.R. Wallace's *Miracles And Modern Spiritualism* (1896) refers to a Christian evangelist in Bristol named George Muller, who had for decades lived, raised a family, survived and subsided on nothing but the power of prayer. He had, moreover, also established a charity that had aided the education and partial support

Ashley Down orphanage in Victorian times.

of some 4,000 children over the last 30 years. Muller had been born in Prussia and arrived in Bristol in 1832; by 1836 four houses, including his own on Wilson Street, accommodated more than 130 orphans.

What was remarkable about all this was that since October 1830, when he married Mary Groves and began to raise a family, he had never asked for any donations, handouts, or had any income whatsoever and had yet managed to feed, clothe and educate not only his own family, but a burgeoning swell of Bristol orphans that began over time to number in the hundreds. Yet he and his charges never went without, despite a sometimes precarious hand-to-mouth existence. Over the decades Muller's one and only recourse was constant secret prayer, and despite often not knowing where the next meal might come from, gradually his institute's coffers began to grow so that he could support an ever-growing number of orphans. He read the Bible daily and literally prayed for everything he needed in the sincere belief that God would provide. A.R. Wallace observed that Muller's own 'financial records' were logged annually in a book entitled *Narratives Of Some Of The Lord's Dealings With George Muller* (1860), which clearly evidenced that he had no discernible income. Receipts were simply forwarded to donators for any sum submitted, no matter how tiny. Even the architect who designed the new, larger orphanage building at Ashley Down is held to have requested that he might do so for nothing.

A.R. Wallace could only conclude in amazement:

The perfect simplicity, faith, boundless charity and goodness of George Muller have enlisted in his cause beings of a like nature; and his mediumistic powers have enabled them to work for him by influencing others to send him money, food, clothes &c., all arriving, as we should say, in the nick of time. The numerous letters he received with these gifts, describing the sudden and uncontrollable impulse the donors felt to send him a certain definite sum at a certain fixed time, such being the exact sum he was in want of and had prayed for, strikingly illustrates the nature of the power at work.

Muller died on 10 March 1898 and was buried in Arno's Vale Cemetery, where a tombstone erected by some of his orphans (of whom he had ultimately helped some 10,000) partly read, 'He Trusted In God With Whom Nothing Shall Be Impossible.'

Today the George Muller Charitable Trust is based at Muller House, Cotham Park, Bristol. Records of all the children who passed through the orphanage are held here, and Muller's evangelicalism is sometimes referred to as 'The Bristol Miracle'.

CHAPTER 3:

SUPERNATURAL EVIL

INTRODUCTION

On a very gloomy day in January 2010 I cautiously pushed my way through the gate that leads to one of the most mysterious places in Somerset. Here, in the open land behind Stanton Drew Court, Stanton Drew, can be found three separate prehistoric stone circles. These prehistoric patterns consist of The Great Circle, the smaller North East Circle (not far from the bank of the River Chew) and the largely separate South West Circle. To wander among these great stones, or megaliths, is like stepping back in time, and the village of Stanton Drew quickly fades into the background as one takes in the puzzle of these gigantic landmarks, their surfaces pitted with moss and algae, and tries to fathom just why they are here. For these megaliths form what can loosely be described as a site of social and religious life that clearly held enormous significance for prehistoric man. The stone patterns have been dated to between 4,000 and 5,000 years old, although quite why the forgotten tribesmen went to the trouble of creating this awe-inspiring structure is uncertain. The place must have, at one time, been very important to early Bronze Age man, and trying to understand the reason for such structures is like groping in the dark. The tribes who once made pilgrimages here are now like ghosts: we know they existed, but as to their superstitious or communal motives for erecting the Stanton Drew circles, we will now forever be unable to see what their meaning was.

One of the stone circles at Stanton Drew.

The sense of mystery here is exaggerated when you learn that this site was only originally noted in 1664 by the famous antiquarian, John Aubrey, by which time the place had been abandoned for millennia. William Stukeley made the first plan of the megaliths in 1776, but for the most part the stones are understudied and very little understood. Three other large stones, called The Cove, are found in the garden of The Druids Arms pub, and a further stone called Hautville's Quoit can be found on the other side of the River Chew. They are thought to be part of the same complex. Their isolated location, and the absence of any real information, has generated a very famous county legend as to how they came to exist. On a Saturday eve long ago a wedding party was taking place here, but as the hour approached midnight the merriment came to a halt when the fiddler announced that he would play no more. The bride, in no mood to stop dancing, 'swore an oath that she would go to the unmentionable regions to find a fiddler.' Presently an aged man with a long beard appeared on the scene with a fiddle, offering to play, but when he did it was a slow and solemn strain, not a dancing melody. The bride scolded the fiddler and demanded that he play something faster so the party could dance; this he did. The music got faster, and the guests danced faster and faster, round and round, until they found that they could not stop, and as midnight passed into Sunday the aged gentleman resumed his proper form – that of the Devil. He watched the party of dancers whirling round and ignored their cries of terror while he played his fiddle. The spinning dancers were reduced to a ghastly troop of dancing skeletons. C.H. Poole writes that the following morning, 'the shrill sound of the cock warned the unwelcome fiddler to depart, which he did, saying "I leave you as a monument of your wickedness and my power." The villagers in the morning found the meadow strewn with stones, and the wedding party transformed into a sterner substance.' A contributor to *Notes And Queries* in 1856 provided the detail that the pious fiddler, who had set events in motion by refusing to play, was found lying under a hedge, half-dead with fright, having seen the whole spectacle. Interestingly, Poole notes that the stones were called Dawn's-men (i.e. dancing stones), their circular nature indicating to many that they were deliberately erected for the purpose of dancing round. The legend of the petrified wedding party likely grew out of that belief. Perhaps it is the reddish tinge that some of the stones display in places that has led to the stories that they are petrified people, once of flesh and blood. Today, there are strange stories that people who try and count the stones are frequently put to flight by thunderstorms that whip up out of nowhere, and there is one story from the early 1950s that speaks of the stones being struck by lightning in the presence of an antiquarian and enveloped in a strange light that gave off no heat.

Worryingly, there are many places in Somerset that folklore has linked to the Devil. Some of the stories are popular superstitions, but some of the tales are strangely compelling. This is perhaps on account of the Somerset landscape itself in places.

One such location is within what an outsider might term 'deepest darkest Exmoor'. Between the villages of Liscombe and Hawkridge, near the Devon border, an unclassified road takes the driver to the very edge of the River Barle, where there are fords and a clapper bridge called Tarr (or Torr) Steps. This is a man-made construction that some claim to be pre-historic, although this is debatable. Some, however, ascribe these great flat slabs of stone a more supernatural origin. The common version of the story is that the Devil built the Tarr Steps in a single night and claimed the causeway as his own, stating that anyone who tried to cross it would be torn limb from limb. The people of Exmoor tested this by sending a cat across, but although the cat was torn to pieces, a local parson felt that this had undone the spell and bravely stepped onto the stone crossing. Satan met the parson halfway and an unseemly slanging match ensued, with language so foul emanating from the parson that the Devil eventually took to his heels and vanished. Other elements of this story concern the Tarr Steps being created by the Devil cutting the apron strings of a mason carrying stones across the River Barle to assist the construction of a church; if the church concerned was St Giles at Hawkridge, then presumably it was thought that these events happened around 1,000 years ago. John Page's *An Exploration Of Exmoor* (1890) explains that he was told 'by a woman in the cottage above' that the steps had never been properly finished on account of his Satanic majesty's own apron strings snapping and thus depositing the final load of stones near the river – several of which were to be seen in an adjoining plantation. These deposits of scattered out-of-place boulders were called the Devil's Lapful, and it was thought that they could not be moved since whatever stones were hauled off by day were supposedly replaced by night. Although Page considered these stories 'absurd', he acknowledged that, 'There is not an atom of cement in the structure' and it is perhaps this reason why the 'Devil's Bridge' attracted such conjecture as to its origins. It really does seem almost beyond human capability to build such a structure, particularly when I visited it in February 2010. The weather was atrocious, and the journey to the landmark along the lethally steep, thin and blind-bend roads, where the trees gather overhead and almost block out the daylight, was almost like driving into the bowels of the earth. When I visited Tarr Steps there was not a soul about and the water of the Barle rushed but a few inches beneath the green moss on the sides of the flat stone slabs, which in themselves looked dangerously slippery with the rain. I have to say that under conditions like this the old story of the Devil being responsible for their construction seems almost plausible, and I was glad to leave.

In fact, there are almost too many places to recount in Somerset that have been visited by the Devil...

The Tarr Steps.

WHEN THE DEVIL VISITED SOMERSET

The Devil went by many names in Somerset: Old Hornie, Nick, Old Nick, Old Scratch (pronounced skraafsh), Old Harry, th' old fellow, Old Tantarabobus, Old Vengeance and so on. His name found its way into all manner of everyday similes – tough, knotted wood, for instance, was as 'twizzly as the Devil'– and many superstitions were aimed at appeasing him. It was thought that crowing cocks frightened the Devil away in Somerset, and this is frequently lauded as an explanation as to why so many of the county's churches supported weathervanes made to look like the bird. If an infant screamed during baptism, it was thought that this was the Devil leaving them; this implies that babies were thought to be born with Satan watching over them, but their crying drove him away. At Langford Budville the bells of St Peters Church were rung on Midsummer night, tolling out from their lofty position overlooking the Vale of Taunton Deane, in order to scare the Devil into Thorne St Margaret; at Thorne the bells were rung on St Margaret's Day to frighten him back into Langford. Even into the Victorian era, clergymen might be called to bless the herd of a parishioner who believed that 'the Devil was very strong upon his cattle.'

Superstition has attached satanic legends to many landmarks like Stanton Drew. A long stone-littered barrow east of Rode earned the name the Devil's Bed and Bolster, supposedly on account of it being the spot where Satan would lay down his head for a nap. There is a strong tradition that attempts to disturb the chambered tomb here are thwarted by sudden, ferocious outbreaks of bad weather. And at Wraxall, the one now in North Somerset, there was once to be found a pair of great standing stones hidden in woodland called the Sidelands. These were known locally as the Devil's Seat, and supposedly marked the entrance to a subterranean tunnel. Elsewhere the stone that at one time lay on the western side of the road, just south of Staple Fitzpaine, bore the name the Devil's Stone, or the Sarcen (Saracen) Stone, on account of it being lobbed by the Devil during the construction of Norman-era St Peter's Church. The Devil had hurled it northwards from the motte-and-bailey Castle Neroche, of which only wooded earthworks can be seen now, and left his fingerprints in it. Locally they said that the stone bled if chiselled, and the stone is one of a number that peppered the land hereabouts. The Devil was also rumoured to hop from one stone to the other, but now he no longer can – the 5ft-high and 6ft-long block was removed and placed in Taunton Museum.

Where the road called Gibbet's Brow joins the B3134 near Priddy there can still be seen a 'swallet hole' in the side of the hill called the Devil's Punch Bowl. There is another Devil's Punchbowl to be seen from Winsford Hill, a circular, yawning chasm or combe in Exmoor near the Devon border. There is no suggestion of an associated legend in either case here, but some locations have more specifics as to their satanic place names. In 1908 *Folklore Vol.19* recorded the legend that Cheddar Gorge was carved out of the land by the Devil, who wished to spoil the beautiful Mendip landscape (he failed – the gorge is widely regarded as a British national treasure). The hill fort at Cannington, away to the west, was situated on a rounded mountain of limestone that had been dropped there by the Devil's spade when he cut a swathe of devastation through the Mendips. Other spadefuls created the islands of Flatholme and Steepholme, off Weston-super-Mare, and the Iron Age hill fort at Brent Knoll. As he was on his way to bury Watchet and Minehead, he slipped as he jumped the River Parrett and his basket of soil spilled its contents all over.

The Devil also seems to have had a penchant for throwing stones about. In the 1800s it was repeated that two enormous stones and a third smaller one, lying at the roadside between St Decumans and

Williton and nearly concealed by brambles, were lobbed from the Quantocks by the Devil and a giant engaged in a competition. One stone that leant against a hedge bore 'the print of Satan's hand', according to John L.W. Page in 1890, and it had been toppled some 40 years earlier by young men anxious to disprove the legend that it was immovable. The Whit Stones, two 4ft-high megaliths standing in the heather of Porlock Common, are reputed to have been thrown by the Devil engaged in a competition with either a giant, a saint or a mysterious person called Doctor Foster. These stones were thrown from Hurlstone Point at Porlock Bay.

These landmarks were, in the minds of the superstitious, physical evidence of times when the Devil set foot in Somerset, but some tales concerned his actual appearance rather than its aftermath. A famous tale explains that he appeared dancing before Saint Dunstan at Glastonbury upon the assassination of King Edmund I, Dunstan's patron, in AD 946.

In 1698 the traveller Celia Fiennes visited Glastonbury Abbey's ruins, and at 'ye cellar or vault' she was told that if she were to cast a stone downwards it made a clanging echo. The explanation was that the Devil was hidden away down there, sat on a tonne of coins, and the echo was the sound of the stone bouncing off the coins.

Uttering rash comments could put you in a very dangerous situation, as an old story told in *The Quantock Hills* (1904) explained. At Keenthorne, where the Fiddington road joins the A39, the local smithy worked, and a long time ago he boasted that he would dare shoe the horse of the Devil himself. At midnight a huntsman on a great black horse turned up, but the smithy saw a cloven hoof protruding beneath the huntsman's clothes and realised what had happened. On some pretext he darted into the village and sought out the parson, who told him that he must re-shoe the Devil's horse, but on no account must he accept payment, as this would allow Satan to claim him. By this ruse Satan was thwarted, despite repeated offerings of a handsome sum of coins to the blacksmith. The incarnation of the Devil as the leader of the Wild Hunt, or Demon Hunt, is a common one, and more of this later.

As late as 1875 it was said of the Orchardleigh Stones on Murtry Hill that locals of the parish still gave them a wide berth, as it was believed that Pagan rituals, in which Satan himself may have taken part, had occurred there in the past. The Devil's last appearance (they say) was in Wiveliscombe during the construction of St Andrews Church between 1827 and 1829, when he made a spectacular appearance on the back of a dragon and yet was confined to throwing rocks at the builders. St Andrew himself materialized and drove him away from Wivey before he could do further damage.

Ruth Tongue, the Somerset folklorist, was told that 'the Exmoor forest demon' haunted an old ruined chapel at Dunkery, in the shape of a ram or a stag. She was told in 1902, by a Miss Achland, that the rector at Luccombe was forced to hold the Sunday services in the afternoon because the parishioners would not traverse Dunkery Hill after dark. After all this, perhaps it is merely wishful thinking to take for granted what they say about the Devil having left Somerset now – although some affirm that he froze to death one night in the hills near Windwhistle along what is now the A30, and he has been buried there ever since…

TAKEN BY THE DEVIL

Halsway Manor, originally built as a hunting seat north-west of Crowcombe by Cardinal Beaufort, has a number of curious gargoyles – the most remarkable representing the Devil seizing a lawyer. Although only a depiction, perhaps the stonemason had in mind one of the disturbing number of instances where Satan himself is whispered to have whisked some poor unfortunate away from Somerset, never to be seen again.

The theme is an ancient one in the county. Elphege, a 10th-century anchorite from Weston living in a hermit's cell near Bath Abbey, who had risen to the position of abbot there, is said to have seen a diabolical event one night. A growing community of monks, inspired by Elphege's piety, had settled around him, but among their number was one who lapsed into sin – and so met a sudden and unnatural death. Following the monk's burial Elphege was disturbed from his prayers by unholy noises, and in a room adjoining his own cell he saw a horrific sight. The dead monk's body had been unearthed and lay on the floor; demons surrounded him and lashed at the corpse with scourges and taunted him in Latin: 'Nec tu Deo, nec nos tibi.' Fiery serpents darted out of the melee to bite the twitching corpse before withdrawing back among the demons. Elphege sadly withdrew – it was clear that the unfortunate monk was being 'taken', and the following day he gathered together his brethren and related what he had seen in an effort to get others in a likewise situation to confess before they met the same fate.

Most people in Shepton Mallet are familiar with the name Nancy Camel. Her story is one that generations of children have grown up with, although it is not clear when the event related to her took place; some have heard it to be at the height of Shepton's silk stocking industry in the later Middle Ages or early Tudor era. Some think that it took place later, during the great storm of 1703, but J.E. Farbrother, the Shepton Mallet historian whose 1859 survey is among the first to note this tale, concluded that the story was so old that its origin could never be clear. Nancy Camel was a woman who lived alone, shunned by most Sheptonians, in a dismal shelter in woodland north of the town. Eking out a living making stockings by hand (when the rest of the town had started using looms), she was hated and feared by the local populace, who considered her at best a wise woman, and at worst a witch. The latter was confirmed one night when Shepton Mallet was overtaken by a tremendous thunderstorm, the likes of which no one could remember and which enveloped the town in black clouds, pouring rain and lightning flashes. While residents peered nervously through their windows into the darkness, there was to be heard, against the backdrop of the pitter-patter of the rain, a tremendous shriek, followed by the sound of a whip cracking and the rumbling, creaking noise of wagon wheels passing through the dirty streets. Calm returned the following morning, but Nancy Camel was found to have vanished in the night. To the townsfolk, it was clear what had become of her.

Nancy Camel's Hole, or Cave, can be found in Ham Woods. Mysterious marks on the stone before her cave were believed to be tracks burned into them by the fiery wheels of the Devil's wagon. Mysterious marks 'upon the roof in front of the cave' were thought to be the marks of the Devil's hoofs, according to C.H. Pope.

Another Somerset folk tale tells how, way back in history, a ploughboy lashed out at a horrible creature that attacked him on Croydon Hill, Rodhuish; the place had long been rumoured to be haunted by a ghastly horned creature that many supposed was the Devil himself. In fact, the 'creature' had been a mischievous butcher boy who had donned a bull skin, including horns, to play a prank. His victim had lashed out with his plough blades and fled in terror; the next morning the bullskin was found with a great slash cut in it, but of the slain prankster there was no sign. Locally, it was believed that the real Devil had taken him, and Ruth Tongue, in recounting this legend, wrote, '...when the Devil rides over Croydon Hill the butcher's boy is among the souls that follow him.' Ms Tongue also recorded the 'faintly-recalled' story of the Devil being caught in a salmon net in a tidal bore in Clevedon, a transgression for which he drowned the foolish fisherman.

A Tudor pamphlet tells a nightmarish story. On 24 May 1584 Margaret Cooper had to be restrained in her bed at the family home in Ditcheat, a spacious affair with at least four upper chambers. She was raving about the Devil coming to get her, and in view of six or more persons there was heard a noise from the street before a horrible apparition that looked like a bear, but without head or tail, burst into the room. The woman's husband struck this monstrosity with a stool, although it felt as though he had struck a feather-bed. It grabbed his wife and thrust her head between her legs and rolled her about like a hoop, before rolling her through the house and down the stairs. Those assembled thrust cloth and napkins to their faces, as the whole scene was accompanied by an awful smell and crackling flames, but they dared not chase Margaret, merely hiding on the landing or praying at the side of the bed. The woman was kept prisoner by this creature, assumed to be the Devil, for 15 minutes before it apparently let her go and left the premises.

One of Somerset's most famous mysteries is the disappearance of Owen Parfitt in Shepton Mallet. Parfitt was a tailor by trade, but by 1768 he was old, infirm and a cripple, living with his elder sister in a cottage facing the turnpike road to Wells. Early one evening in June the immobile cripple was carried downstairs from his bed, placed in a chair at the door to his cottage (that fronted directly onto the highway) and left in the warmth of the afternoon sun. A quarter of an hour later, when his helpers looked for him, he was gone, and he was quite simply never seen again: he had vanished in broad daylight, in view of a public highway and other nearby cottages. The alert was given by his sister, Susanna Snook, who, from upstairs in the cottage, heard a noise from the front porch, and subsequently found the chair abandoned with her brother's greatcoat hung over it.

At a house named Board Cross, some 150 yards away from the site of Parfitt's disappearance, a skeleton was discovered in November 1813. It was found 2ft under the ground, buried in a 'confused heap', but although the place had belonged to a female relative named Lockyer, there was no suspicion attached to her, and the skeleton was never proven to be Parfitt's. The aura of mystery has clung about this odd episode since then – why would a passing traveller kidnap (if that is what happened) an elderly, crippled tailor? Were his family somehow involved in some conspiracy to kill him and conceal the evidence? If so, to what end? No one profited, and Owen Parfitt was a threat to no one. In fact, his 80-year-old sister lost the little money that the parish afforded her for looking after him. If the skeleton in the garden of Board Cross was his, how had it been disposed of without anyone seeing, and so quickly? The garden was, after all, a front garden that faced the road. And in 1814 a Dr Butler, who examined the discovered skeleton, concluded that the bones were of a young woman, not old man, who had been murdered 30 years before, and of whose death local people had been suspected at the time.

Owen Parfitt was described by neighbours as 'a quiet, sober man, middle height, and stout made.' He was perhaps about 65. But maybe Parfitt had a past that no one knew about, a past that had caught up with him. Some claimed that he was sometimes violent. In 1867 the journal *Once A Week* carried a number of first-hand statements with Sheptonians who had witnessed the searches and who had told their stories in the early 1800s. Village rumour suggested that Parfitt had been a pirate in his younger days, and had seen Africa and consorted with necromancers. The journal noted, 'We must remember that in 1768 the people of Shepton were removed only by a few years from the days when their town had rather an evil reputation; witches were not uncommon, and the Devil had a good many friends and acquaintances there…the common talk of the town was that the Devil had carried off old Owen Parfitt.' After all, it was observed that the day had been fine and bright, but after the alarm had been given a tremendous thunder and lightning storm occurred and the search was conducted in pouring rain…

Finally, consider the following atmospheric story. In 1839 a labouring man took his net down to the edge of the Barle near Perry Farm, at Exebridge on the Devon border, to catch some fish. Suddenly, there was an enormous commotion in his net; he had caught something, something huge that was thrashing about, and the poor man caught a brief glimpse of a cloven hoof before he was launched off the bank and dragged into the water. Whatever was caught in the net dragged the fisherman across the river before he let go and frantically swam to the shore. Scrambling up the bank, he ran home in a state of terror, where his wife called Dr Collyns. The fisherman stammered, 'It was the Devil, zur, I do know it! I seed his cloven foot!' The fisherman initially refused to believe the creature to have been anything other than 'Old Hornie' himself, and had to be shown tracks at the edge of the water by Dr Collyns, who explained that the thing must have been a stag that had hidden in the water underneath the roots of an overhanging elder tree. F.J. Snell's *A Book Of Exmoor* (1903) cites this as a rustic example of the ingrained fear of the Devil here – a fear that probably still lingers in the darkest, hidden corners of Somerset.

DEMONIC POSSESSION

There were extraordinary scenes under the roof of Temple Church in central Bristol on 13 June 1788 when an exorcism was performed. George Lukins, a carrier from Yatton, had for the past 18 years, or so he said, been possessed by no less than seven devils, and as a result his behaviour was erratic. At times he was convulsed with fits during which he howled and barked like an animal, blaspheming and swearing in a shocking manner; at other times, however, he was the opposite, singing jovial ballads and hunting songs – although in different voices. Of Lukins himself, we learn that an episode in a shop on the corner of Redcliff Street (during which he threatened to call 'spirits from the vasty deep') led the proprietor, Mr Bath, to hasten Lukins to Temple Church lest the 'Devil should take it into his horned head to "play hell" among the hardwares and cutlery.'

Seven clergymen were sufficiently impressed by his demonic 'possession' to have him hauled into the vestry of Temple Church, where he was subjected to a ritualistic exorcism. The seven clergymen (one for each demon) succeeded in expelling the evil creatures from Lukins' person, with one later 'returning publick thanks in Yatton church for the success of their endeavours, and the happy delivery of their patient.' Lukins was noted as a psalm singer, actor and ventriloquist in Christmas plays and mummeries, and his exhibition may have been an act, the only truly remarkable thing about his performance being that it fooled so many. Whatever truly plagued him, it was observed that he was still alive in 1804, by now a gentle, polite and cleanly-dressed old man; whether it was diabolical possession, acting or insanity, his 'high spirits' had, at any rate, truly departed and left him in peace.

Temple Church (so-called because it stood on the site of the oval church of the Knights Templar, and also called Holy Cross Church) still stands off Temple Street, although it is now a mere shell, having been mostly destroyed during a German air raid on 25 November 1940.

Temple Church, Bristol, in 1887.

THE WITCH OF WOOKEY HOLE

The legend of the witch of Wookey Hole is one of Somerset's most famous, and she is now a major institution at these famous subterranean caverns in the Mendips; the hiring of an actress to represent said witch has recently made the headlines.

The story is an old one, perhaps best illustrated by writings from an era when to visit the caves was a rare honour, rather than the family-orientated day out that the attraction presents in the 21st century. In 1801 a visitor wrote, 'Here a cavern opens its dire jaws...the interior of which is safely secured, by a door well locked, from the intrusion by the profane.' Led by a lantern-wielding guide, they made their way into a cavern called the Parlour, where the incrustations had been given a variety of names: the pillar of salt, the enormous petrified kidney, a dog, a flitch of bacon and an old witch (there was also cheese, grid-irons, stools, tables and a train of cats, all supposedly part of the witch's surroundings). The guide explained that the caverns had had but one occupant, a wicked old witch who had been turned to stone by a parson while she was cooking a child stolen from the village in a pot in her 'kitchen'. The guide remembered well his own grandmother saying that her father remembered the witch: she would maim cattle, bewitch the local maids and torture the old people with 'cramps and twitches.' The visitor, William Clarke, wrote, 'Fortunately for the lovers of legend, the tradition related by my guide has been rescued from the insatiable maw of oblivion by a modern poet, who has drawn out the oral tale into vision, and secured it to posterity by an elegant verification, the beauty of which will ensure its duration.'

This is certainly the case: everyone knows about the witch, but the allegation that she lived only three generations earlier is a surprising one, for the story is generally supposed to have taken place much earlier, way back in the Dark Ages. An archaic reference by the third-century scribe Clement of Alexandria in *Stromata* refers to a cave in Britain in which the wind produced a noise like the clashing of cymbals, and this cave is generally supposed to be Wookey Hole; this would indicate that the cave always had a reputation for strange phenomena. Although the story of the 'witch' developed in the 18th century, as far back as *c.*1470 William of Worcester gave an interesting depiction of the caves, with their pools and stalactites. He visited the place and wrote, 'There is a certain narrow entrance [into the rock] where at the beginning is an image of a man who goes by the name of the porter, and it is the duty of the people who desire to enter the hall of Woky to ask permission of the porter...The hall is about as large as Westminster Hall, and there hangs from the vaulted roof wonderful pendula of stone.' He observed, 'the figure of a woman is there clad, and holding in her girdle a spinning distaff', although he did not suggest that she was supposed to be a petrified witch. The first allusion to this that I can find is among the writings of the famous traveller, Celia Fiennes, who visited the caves in 1698: 'They fancy one rock resembles a woman with a great belly which the country people call the Witch which made this cavity underground for her enchantments. The rocks are glistening and shine like diamonds...' But there is no background story noted. She calls the place Oakey Hole, and notes that two of the rock formations were said to be petrified babies.

The legend as known today appears to have begun in 1748 with the poem written by Dr Harrington of Bath, which featured in Bishop Percy's *Reliques Of English Poetry* (1756). The story took place in 'anciente days' and a pastor from Glastonbury finally ended the witch's reign:

He chauntede out his Godlie booke;
He crost the water, blest the brooke;

Then – pater noster done;
The ghastly hag he sprinkled o'er;
When lo! Where stood a hag before;
Now stood a ghastly stone.

But the witch left a curse on the area that depleted the region of its menfolk, much to the distress of the young women:

Shall then such maids unpitied moane?
They might as well, like her, be stone...

The word 'witch', or 'wych', in former times meant a hole or break in the rocks, and until the 1800s the older inhabitants referred to the cavern or basin out of which the River Axe flowed as the 'Wookey-Hole-Witch'. The story may, in fact, be due to a combination of unrelated factors, but for lovers of the old tale, it would appear certain that the story dates back to a period earlier than 1748, if William Clarke's guide was telling him the truth in 1801. Or, to put it another way, the story was not an invention by Dr Harrington and was at least based on a local tradition. We can generally suppose then, that the story came about thus: the caves, as befitting such a place, historically had a strange reputation, and that the formations within earned names, including the 'woman'. The local terminology naturally bred a story of the stone woman being a witch, which was fleshed out in the 1700s by Dr Harrington and fed by foggy memories of village stories that perhaps even concerned a real local woman in the 18th century who was supposed to be the 'village witch'. The age of the cave, and Harrington's poem, now leads people to date the story to the early years of the founding of Glastonbury. *The Sporting Magazine's* take on the legend in 1804 was that the witch lived in the caves in the time before Christ, and upon hearing of the birth of the Saviour she resolved to turn herself to stone, but before she did this she turned all the furniture and animals about her to stone. She then 'threw away her stopper', and – helped by an evil spirit – it landed at Glastonbury and from this grew Glastonbury Tor. The fact that there appear to be two wildly different versions of the witch stone's origin is evidence, in my opinion at least, that the story has roots certainly older than 1748.

In 1912 the archaeologist Herbert Balch discovered the almost-complete skeleton of what was judged to be an elderly woman near the entrance to the hole, together with the remains of two goats, a dagger, an alabaster ball (her 'crystal ball'), a pottery 'milking pail' and other relics. She is estimated to have lived between 900 and 1,000 years ago, and although she was in all probability nothing more than an Anglo-Saxon goatherd, she has now earned the nickname 'the witch', and the tale is now generally dated to the time when she would have been alive, although some estimate that she is older than this and Romano-British. Now an integral part of the witch mythology, the skeleton (at the time of writing) resides within the Wells and Mendip Museum, Wells, although the caves are attempting to have her returned to her 'home'. Perhaps this is only fitting. There is another dimension to this story, too. There are gruesome suggestions that skulls that were unearthed in the waters upstream from the Witch's Kitchen in Wookey Hole from 1946 onwards belonged to victims from the Romano-British period who were sacrificed in front of the 'witch stone'. Their decapitated heads were tossed in the river. Folklore has it that some may have even been tied to the witch stone outcrop to be slain. Although it is more likely that there was a specific

The Witch of Wookey Hole.

burial ground in the caves, the suggestion that even in pre-history the witch stone exerted some supernatural power over the primitive British tribesmen has, nonetheless, captured the public's imagination. She is also blamed in modern folklore for the deaths of cave-divers and potholers and other accidents at the site.

Whatever the truth behind her story, the legend of the witch is now one that centuries of children in Somerset have grown up with. An astonishing 25 caverns have been discovered at Wookey Hole, and the curious can now find the witch for themselves. At the bottom of Hell's Ladder, in the bone-chilling cold of the Parlour, the stalagmite alleged to be her petrified form glares at the subterranean River Axe – supposedly the direction she was looking in when the eponymous holy man appeared in his little boat to confront her all those centuries ago…

THE AGE OF WITCHES

In 1603 King James VI of Scotland was also crowned James I of England. In July 1597 the king had published his *Demonologie*, which condemned all magic-workers as guilty of sins against God – and although witchcraft allegations were hardly unknown in England, King James' accession to both thrones brought a new perceived urgency to the threat. His ferocious desire to crush the scourge of witchcraft spread south of the border with a ruthlessness that lasted for decades, and left a legacy that lasted for centuries.

Somerset and Bristol were frequently touched by the hysteria generated during those fear-driven times. In 1612 the inhabitants of Hinton petitioned the Somersetshire Quarter Sessions to apprehend and punish Elizabeth Busher from Glastonbury, a wife and mother of several 'base children', who was apparently the Stuart equivalent of a problem neighbour – 'the disturber of her neighbour's quietness' – but also blamed for the deaths, through bewitchment, of numerous people whom she hated.

Two witches were executed in Bristol in 1624, and in 1653 many witnesses averred that their livestock suffered the murrain, or that their beer turned sour following a visit by Elizabeth Castle. When refused goods, she threatened one woman with the words, 'I have seen the fall of thee already', and her cat was rumoured to have been seen cavorting with a gigantic black toad – presumably the Devil in one of his manifestations.

Sometimes the judicial process found the accused not guilty: Dorothy Chapple of Ivelchester was acquitted on 19 April 1653 at the General Sessions for the Public Peace, being 'a fit object of mercy and to receive pardon for life.' But the accusations were usually heard nonetheless, and 'gaol deliveries' of suspected witches are recorded at Wells and Taunton into the early 18th century. Many accusations appear to the modern reader to stem from petty neighbourhood rivalry, although we know that accusations of witchcraft were judged seriously by the magistrates, and it is clear that circumstances could often slide out of control frighteningly quickly. In many ways we just cannot understand the era, as Wallace Notestein observed in *History Of English Witchcraft* (1911), 'It is quite impossible to grasp the social conditions, it is impossible to understand the opinions, fears and hopes of the men and women who lived in Elizabethan and Stuart England, without some knowledge of the part played in that age by witchcraft.'

THE PERSECUTION OF RICHARD JONES, AGED 12

In 1657 Somerset's most famous witchcraft case occurred. On 15 November Jane Brooks, of Shepton Mallet, gave the 12-year-old son of Henry Jones an apple and passed her hand up the boy's right side. Upon returning home, the boy, Richard Jones, complained of pains in his side, and after roasting and eating the apple, he became chronically ill. Suffering from fits, bouts of speechlessness and blindness, he intimated to his father that Jane Brooks had given him the apple. Things turned ugly, and the boy's furious father scratched the woman's face violently to draw blood, an act believed to deprive the witch of her power.

The boy recovered for some eight days before again lapsing into delirium; on one occasion he cried out that he could see Jane Brooks 'on the wall', and so a cousin called Gibson lashed out with a knife and shortly thereafter Jane was found to have her hand bandaged, which she attributed to an accident with some pins.

On 8 December Jane Brooks ended up before Mr Robert Hunt and Mr Cary, Justices of the Peace, at Castle Cary, together with a woman called Alice Coward, Jane's sister, against whom similar accusations were levelled. Richard Jones was rendered speechless in court by the mere appearance of the two women. During another examination on 17 February at Shepton (before a great number of gentlemen and ministers), the boy collapsed into a man's arms during another appearance by Jane Brooks, and for a while it was feared that he had actually died. Jane was ordered to touch him; he instantly sprang out of his catatonic state. The boy was blindfolded, and a succession of people touched him, but only when Jane Brooks did so did he go into convulsions. Other 'tests' were performed, and witnesses were paraded before the justices. By far and away the strangest accusation came from a married couple named Isles, who said that in the garden on 25 February, not two yards from them, the boy was seen to rise up into the air before being carried – airborne – for 30 yards. He was dropped at the door of a neighbour called Jordan, and for a while he was thought to have died. When he came to, however, he told the couple that Jane Brooks had taken him by the arm and lifted him into the air, although they had seen no one else in the garden. It was also alleged that many persons heard a noise emanating from the boy like a toad croaking, with the words 'Jane Brooks, Alice Coward...' being repeated.

On 10 March 1658 the two women were finally thrown into gaol (the boy, much wasted by his fits, now began to improve), and arraigned on 26 March. Jane Brooks was condemned and executed at Chard the same day.

JULIAN COX'S REIGN OF TERROR

In 1663 a poor old woman, aged about 70, named Julian Cox appeared before Judge Archer at Taunton County Assizes to hear charges that she was a witch responsible for a reign of fear.

The accusations against her were remarkable. The first witness was a huntsman who claimed that he had gone out with his hounds to hunt a hare, finally running one speedy animal to ground behind a great bush near Julian Cox's house. The huntsman, however, found not a hare, but the old woman herself, with her 'head grovelling on the ground' and her 'globes upwards.' The hounds backed away from the old woman, and the huntsman, stammering and with his hair on end, managed to ask what business brought her here, but she was so out of breath that she could not answer.

The huntsman believed that he had witnessed a witch who had just transformed, and returned home 'sadly affrighted.' As naïve as this sounds, other accusations were no less outlandish: one witness had been forced to chop up an enormous toad that attacked him while he was 'taking a pipe of tobacco', and although it was in pieces, it somehow made itself whole again. Another victim's cattle began to bash their heads against trees, bellowing dementedly, and the owner was forced, upon seeking advice in such matters, to cut off the afflicted cattle's ears and burn them on a pyre. Of course, Julian Cox appeared as though bidden to pick them out of the flames. One woman had even seen the accused fly into her own bedchamber window.

When paraded before the court, the old woman admitted her guilt. While walking about a mile from her house, she averred, she had been approached by three figures who rode broomsticks about 1.5 yards above the ground. Two she recognised as a witch and wizard from the locality who had been executed some years earlier, but the third was a man in black who persuaded her to sell her soul to Satan with promises of revenge against her enemies. Once persuaded, this strange man pricked her finger and wrote Julian's name in blood to seal the contract.

This much Julian Cox admitted, and in Judge Archer's eyes it proved the testimony of one witness, a 'young maid' who had refused the old woman alms. This girl had begun to suffer seizures, claiming during her convulsions that it was Mother Cox who was responsible, despite those present being able to see no one else in the room. The judge and jury delivered a verdict of 'guilty', and four days after her trial Julian Cox was hanged.

THE WINCANTON COVEN

The aforementioned Justice of Peace, Robert Hunt, was a zealous witch-hunter. In Taunton in 1664 he presided over what amounted to a purge of some 25 suspected witches who appear to have formed two distinct covens. In overseeing the examinations, Hunt heard confessions to the most surreal, supernatural and nightmarish charges ever brought before a Somerset court.

Joseph Glanvill's famous study of such phenomena, *Saducismus Triumphatus* (1681), tells us that in January and February Hunt heard the confession of Elizabeth Stile (or Style) of Stoke Trister. She was a member of one coven to the east of Wincanton. In about 1654 the Devil had appeared before her in the guise of a handsome man, and later a black hound. In return for her soul, Satan promised that she would 'live gallantly' for 12 years; it took four attempts, but finally Elizabeth Stile gave in, and Satan, to seal the deal, pricked the fourth finger of her right hand between the middle and upper joint. With the blood that dripped, Ms Stile signed a contract with an 'O', and the Devil gave her sixpence before vanishing with the contract. Usually in the guise of a dog or cat, he frequently appeared in her meagre rooms at four in the morning to painfully suck her blood.

In return for this, Elizabeth was granted a spirit named Robin, who wreaked havoc on her behalf when she said the words 'O Satan give me my purpose!' Together with her confederates – Ann Bishop, Alice Duke and Mary Penny – the coven met at 9pm with a 'man in black clothes' at Trister's Gate, before whom they curtsied, and whom all listening agreed must have been the Devil. Dancing, feasting and drinking accompanied this meeting, but the merriment was merely part of a ritual: a wax likeness of one Elizabeth Hill was subjected to a mock baptizement and then stabbed full of pins. The words 'A pox on thee, I'll spite thee' were chanted.

These meetings occurred every so often, with another luckless villager in Wincanton being selected each time for misfortune. Before the meeting, the women would anoint their foreheads and wrists with a green oil given by the demon, Robin, using a feather, and chant, 'Thout, tout, a tout, tout, throughout and about.' There were often other attendees: John Combes, John Vining, Richard Dikes, Thomas Bolster, Thomas Dunning, Thomas Bush, a lame man, Rachel King, Richard Lannen, a lady called Dunford and one Christopher Ellen. All grovelled and fawned at the feet of the man in black – he being the only one that was present at all of the meetings. The mysterious man in black sat at the head of the table, Ann Bishop next to him, speaking in a barely audible voice. Sometimes he played the pipe or cittern, and he wore 'a band', although what this signifies is unclear. When they separated afterwards they would say, 'Rentum Tormentum', or more jovially, 'A boy! Merry meet, merry part!'

It seems that the bewitchment of Elizabeth Hill, the 13-year-old daughter of a Stoke Trister yeoman, was what brought the affair to light. Screaming that she was being attacked by Mother Stile, Elizabeth described during these fits the clothes that Elizabeth Stile was wearing, although she was nowhere near the girl at the time. Upon inquiry, the description of Elizabeth's clothing proved correct, illustrating to the magistrates an incident of divinity or clairvoyance on the girl's part to ward off a supernaturally evil attack. This was in November 1663.

Two of the other women, Ann Bishop and Alice Duke, were ensnared by the Devil a year earlier than Elizabeth Stile, when they performed a night-time ritual at St Peter and St Paul's Church, Wincanton. Walking backwards round the exterior, they found that they were suddenly accompanied by a man in black clothes; on the second occasion a monstrous black toad leapt up at Alice Duke's apron; on the third they were joined by a monstrous animal, something like a rat, which subsequently vanished. Alice Duke, the examinate, gave way to the pressure and persuasion in much the same way as Elizabeth Stile, and for the most part the pattern was the same, except that her demon was a dun cat that suckled at her breast when she sometimes fell into a trance at around 7pm. Various witnesses were paraded before the magistrates, all claiming that the bitter misfortunes that befell them were the work of this coven, but in the end it appeared – at least in Alice Duke's case – that Satan had tricked the women: '…she should want [for] nothing, but ever since she hath wanted all things.'

The trial records appear lost, so the fate of the accused is unclear, although Glanvill (who based his writing on Hunt's depositions) recorded that Elizabeth Stile died in gaol before being executed, her guilt proved. It was Ann Bishop who appeared to be the leader, however, and her fate is unknown. Alice Duke may have, in fact, still been living in Wincanton in 1670, her escape perhaps indicative of the fate of the others.

In addition, 11 others, both men and women whose names were also recorded, were dragged into this madness and accused of complicity in another coven. These 11 formed a coven at Brewham, of which there appeared no immediate connection to that at Wincanton, other than the general location (North Brewham and South Brewham are to the north of Wincanton.). The Brewham coven was examined by the indefatigable Robert Hunt at the Somerset Lent Assize in Taunton in the April to June following the examination of the Wincanton witches.

For the most part, the sequence of events was the same: Christian, the 33-year-old wife of Robert Green, was introduced to the Devil in 'Mrs Hussey's ground in Brewham Forest' one noon, where he took the form of a man in blackish clothes. The finger-pricking, the promises of wanting nothing, the pressing of money into the initiate's hand, the demon (this time it was a hedgehog) that suckled at the newly-initiated witch's breast, the wax images of enemies stuck with thorns all happened as it had at Wincanton. The difference was that the Brewham witches had a number of deaths linked to them. Margaret Agar and Catherine Green, other members of the coven, had bewitched to death the overseer of a poorhouse and the latter's sister-in-law respectively. Margaret Agar is described as a 'rampant hagg'. Catherine, apparently the 'favourite' and instigator, was also blamed for a murrain that swept through the stables of one Robert Walter, killing three of his best horses. The coven as a whole was blamed for the death of one Richard Green, and other misfortunes, illnesses and feverish deaths were laid at their door.

Numerous witnesses appeared at the Assize. On the Thursday night before Whitsunday they called up the Devil by saying the name 'Robin' and thus appeared a little man dressed in black before whom they all grovelled. A woman named Mary Green stated that this sinister little man touched his hat, saying, 'How do ye!' jovially in a low, deep voice. But again the outcomes of the trials are not credibly known. According to C. L'Estrange Ewen, whose authoritative *Witchcraft And Demonism* (1933) was just one of a number of

Victorian or Edwardian books on the subject to note this case, 'The persons named were of the poorest class, and difficult to trace.' Perhaps the implication is that there was at least one local knave in the region who acted as grandmaster of the lodge, and even personated Satan, in order to exploit the lowest sections of society around Wincanton in those years. Apparently Hunt's discoveries were 'stopped by some of them in authority.' But E. Lynn Linton's *Witch Stories* (1861) supposes that Margaret Agar, at least, was hanged from a gallows tree: '...no great loss to the community, but her death placed her among the martyrs to superstition, and left her forever as an object of historic pity.'

REMNANTS OF SUPERSTITION

Accusations of witchcraft continued throughout the century. Richard Bovet's *Pandaemonium* (1684) recounts that he was told, for instance, by 'a lady of the neighbourhood' of Bristol, that the children of a Mr Meredith 'would hang about the walls, and ceiling of the room, like flies, or spiders.' Following the witch trials of the mid-1600s, however, despite there being many arraignments of suspected witches, there appear to have been surprisingly few convictions. One woman, Margaret Coombes, 'died in prison at Brewton [Bruton]' while awaiting trial in 1690 accused of being party to the bewitching of a maidservant called Mary Hill at Beckington. The 18-year-old had allegedly been vomiting crooked pins, pieces of brass, nails and spoon handles for weeks until the arrest of Coombes and two other women. Although witnesses testified to the reality of these seizures, the other two accused women – Elizabeth Carrier and Anne More – were acquitted. But even before this, a strange case had indicated that times were changing.

In 1680, at Taunton Deane Assizes, Sir Francis North tried a man charged with bewitching a 13-year-old girl and causing her to vomit straight pins during fits and spasms. The judge thought it likely that the girl was doubling herself in her fits and taking the pins in her mouth from the edge of her clothing before spitting them out. Upon the man's acquittal, a 'hideous old woman' shouted, 'God bless your Lordship...40 years ago they would have hanged me for a witch, and they could not; and now, they would have hanged my poor son!'

Perhaps it was not the motions of a trial, but the increasing inability of the judiciary to secure convictions that led to the phenomenon continuing longer than it perhaps ought to have done; and perhaps why attacks on suspected witches carried on. In 1694 proceedings were initiated against three men who had taken part in the 'swimming' (ducking) of Margaret Waddam of Rode in a nearby river, during which she nearly died. *The Gentleman's Magazine* for 1731 records that in 'September last' some 200 cheering rioters subjected an old woman to a ducking, or ordeal by water, at Frome on suspicion of witchcraft. The woman had been blamed for strange fits that the son of a man named Wheeler had been suffering, and the mob dragged the old lady two miles out of town to a millpond, where they stripped her, tied her legs together and – with a rope tied around her waist – threw her in. She 'swam like a cork', despite being repeatedly pushed under, and was eventually thrown on a heap of litter where she died an hour later. The coroner, although aware that some 40 people had actively participated in the murder, could get no one to announce who the ringleaders were, and in the end they were only able to charge three who appeared principally guilty with manslaughter.

In the church at Monksilver, beneath the yew tree, is buried Elizabeth Conybeer, who was brutally murdered aged 88 in June 1773 in her Woodford home. The killer used a pair of tailor's shears to commit the crime, and it has been suggested that the true motive was not robbery but an attempt to 'blood' a suspected witch that got out of hand, in an attempt to break a spell that had been cast. The violence had somehow escalated and Elizabeth's two daughters, Sarah and Anne, were also butchered. According to the *London Magazine*, the women seemed to have been surprised at breakfast after the youngest daughter, in her 40s, had been followed home from the butchers. There were cuts to the eldest daughter's forehead and the other daughter had had her cheeks cut. The house had not been ransacked, and the arrest of two people very quickly, with a third suspect identified, suggested a village conspiracy. We learn that a man named Smith was acquitted for the murders.

Such violence is partly explained when we also learn that the 'threat' of witchcraft persisted much longer than we might suppose. *The History Of The Abbey Of Glaston* relates that the practice of 'overlooking' – the evil eye – was still feared in Glastonbury in 1826: 'The superstition consists in attributing to the eye of some particular person or persons; by which, when they are inclined to exercise it, through anger, revenge or malignity, they can fatally affect the mind, body, and property of the unhappy victim, on whom the baleful gaze is cast.' Page's *An Exploration Of Exmoor* (1890) certainly indicates that belief in 'witchcraft' was current in his time, it being believed that drawing the blood of the witch was a charm against all her powers, including the 'evil eye', and the peasantry would sometimes resort to nailing a sharp piece of metal near a witch's house in the hope that she might step on it. In the Quantocks, at a village 'within a few hundred yards of the matter-of-fact railway, the voice of whose iron steed is usually sufficient to frighten away superstition for evermore', there was an old woman who was believed to possess the ability to turn herself into a black dog that prowled a particular lane at night. When she fell ill, she was unable to secure the assistance of a nurse because of this. Page also tells of the belief that witches could transform themselves into hares, and that one such animal had been chased from the window sill of a sick man and struck on the head by its pursuers. Not long afterward the village witch, 'old Sally', was found to be bleeding from a head injury. Even by the later Victorian era 'certain ancient dames' in Withycombe were thought to be capable of turning themselves into white rabbits. C.H. Poole in 1876 cites an edition of *Notes And Queries* in which exactly the same story was told – first-hand – to the vicar in Bridgwater: 'The old woman, whom all suspected, was laid up in bed for three days afterwards, unable to walk about: all in consequence of the kick she had received in the shape of a white rabbit!' Also, witches – when in church – literally could not sit, nor even face the altar, remaining standing throughout the entire service. These women exercised great power over their husbands, and one story concerned the sorry fate of an erring husband summoned magically back to his home in Exmoor, who left a trail of bloody footsteps through the village: his wife had compelled him, through a spell, to run so hard back to her that not only had his boots worn out, but also the very soles of his feet. Village rumours also had it that witches sent forth toads – their 'familiars' – to cause their wicked mischief, and a witch could not die so long as her toads still lived. F.B. Kettlewell's *Trinkum – Trinkums Of Fifty Years: Village Life In Harptree, Somerset* (1927) implies that one ill witch in Chew Stoke committed suicide by pointing at each of her toads in turn, ordering them to 'die', before then expiring herself.

'EVIL MEN', OR CONJURERS

There were also wizards, or 'evil men', prevalent in western Somerset, although these were not so much in evidence as witchcraft, and they appear to have been less malicious and kept a lower profile. John L.W. Page was told of 'a farm with which I am very familiar', where one of the employees was an 'evil man', who – badgered by his rustic workmates – proved his wizardry with a dramatic performance. In the barn during a rainstorm, and holding a rote (a reed used for thatching, that seems to have been an ingredient of the spell) 'this terrible personage ascended towards the cobwebby rafters, until his feet dangled', before he was dragged back to the floor by one of the workmen more braver than the rest. Page wrote of this in 1890 as though it were recent history.

These folk were sometimes called 'white witches', and were often the first port of call to reverse 'spells' cast on village livestock by actual witches. In Bridgwater, for instance, an archaic ritual to help a bewitched pig involved lancing each foot and ear of the animal and allowing the blood to run on a piece of 'common dowlas', which was then stuck through with two pins and tossed onto the fire under some turf. The whole charm was performed in silence except for when the dowlas was burning, when verses were solemnly read from the Bible. *Notes and Queries* observed that this ritual not only worked, but also drew out the suspected evildoer to see why her spell had been broken. One story from Waterrow tells how a witch appeared to waste away and die in the most bizarre fashion after being 'punished' by a conjurer hired by a desperate farmer. The witch 'pined and pined until she was no otherwise than skin and bone hanged up agin' a wall.' She was often carried out the house as though dead, or else found collapsed in the road, whereupon she would 'start up and spin round and round like a whirligig.' Eventually, one day she just recovered, and although the farmer was never again troubled, perhaps in this instance the witch and the conjurer were in cahoots, splitting the fee paid by the tortured farmer.

These 'evil men' were in residence in Somerset by at least 1890, although they were generally considered more helpful and less malicious than their female counterpart, only resorting to harmful tricks in order to prove a point. They relied on 'certain books [in manuscript], inscribed with mysterious and cabalistic figures.' One of Page's acquaintances sought one out at one time, and was told to select and touch a numeral in one of these cabalistic books, being told afterwards, 'That's a lucky number; you'll come to no harm.' And, indeed, the man escaped illness and accident, and in Page's time was still living in West Somerset and in his 80s.

The men could be dangerous when circumstances demanded, however: in 1823 one Dorcas Holman, aged 12 and suspected of theft, was found drowned in a well on her father's property in Crewkerne. The inquest was told that the victim of the theft had consulted a wise man and paid him to put a 'curse' on the thief prior to her death. When personally offended, the conjurers would make people pay. In Stogumber a man who mocked the local 'evil man' at the inn felt mysteriously compelled, upon leaving the inn, to pick up and carry an enormous stone he found by the roadside. This he did, only finding himself able to drop it when he reached home, aching and bent double with the effort. Another story tells how sometime around the mid-1800s a certain 'well-known village character' cursed a tavern after being refused admittance by the landlord – who promptly found that his ale in the cellar barrels had turned sour. C.H. Poole ascribed this to the weather, an observation he might not have bothered to make unless he considered the story to be based on a factual event. I suspect that these types of folk were still in evidence well into the 20th century, and perhaps there are those alive today who actually remember these 'evil men' from a time when the pace of life was slower in Somerset.

DEATH BY WITCHCRAFT

The awesome grip of fear in which the county was still held in this era by witchcraft is perhaps most disturbingly illustrated by an incident that occurred around the end of the 18th century in Wellington. *A Cabinet Of Curiosities* (1824) observes that in the region it was often the practice to obtain traditional remedies in the event of illness, rather than consult an apothecary, with the result that many fakers peddled 'charmed powders and mystic lotions' to the desperate and gullible. Sometimes these remedies were of such a poisonous nature that the recipient died, yet still the superstitious kept coming back to these 'conjurers' again and again. Some were merely fraudsters, like Richard Baker of Westleigh, who died in 1819 aged 70 having made much money from the gullibility of the peasantry. This 'heartless villain' was consulted by a woman from Wellington concerning her daughter, and informed her that the girl had been 'over-looked' by a witch; to this end he prescribed some powders, which poisoned the child to death, although he does not appear to have been arrested for this. The superior attitude of the reporting periodical is a stark contrast to the ongoing belief in the phenomenon of 'witchcraft' that clearly still existed in 19th century Somerset.

In 1823 an employee of Lord King 'at Ashley Lodge in the parish of Porlock' hanged himself in the hay-house. The inquest heard that 48-year-old John Jones had committed suicide in the sincere belief that he had been bewitched. Even as late as 1892 the threat of bewitchment was still considered very real. Presiding over the inquest into the death of a young woman at Lufton, near Yeovil, the coroner Mr Fuller heard that the girl's parents genuinely thought that the cause was a spell, or a 'bad wish', with the girl having been 'overlooked' (bewitched by the evil eye). White witches had been fruitlessly employed to try and reverse the 'spell', but to no avail, and *The History Of The Parish Of Selworthy* remarks, 'In this 19th century, with all the educational advantages in the county of Somerset, the belief in witchcraft appeared more

The Somerset Levels, from Burrow Mump. Ruth Tongue learned in 1959 that an evil spirit in the waters of the nearby Parrett took, in turns, a man, a woman and a child.

extensive than he [the coroner] could credit. There is no doubt whatever that such superstitions are very largely believed in by the country people of this county...' In 1890 a woman in Bridgwater excused herself from an assault charge by claiming that she had been 'overlooked' by her victim.

It was also in the 1890s, according to E.O. Begg (who provided evidences of witchcraft in Exmoor to *Folklore Magazine* in 1945), that the Sloley family held a grip over Porlock: 'About 50 years ago a family called Sloley lived in the Porlock district; two sisters and a brother, and all were credited with being witches and having the power of the evil eye.' Among the 'great wickedness they did', one sister, upon being scolded for stealing cakes at a village fete, simply turned to her accuser and said calmly, 'I've marked you down.' The man thereafter grew ill and quickly died.

F.J. Snell's *A Book Of Exmoor* (1903) records a curious anecdote concerning a farmhouse 'near the north coast of West Somerset', where there lived a farmer, crippled, infirm and slow-witted on account of a wrangle a few years before with a witch during which she had levitated him to the ceiling in retaliation for his dogs being set upon her. But, for the most part, the age of superstition appeared to be coming to an end. Snell commented, 'Are there yet witches left in the Exmoor country? Fifty years ago, it is said, the region was full of them. Now it might cost a stranger some research to find them; but it is safe to answer that there are. Unless the writer has been misinformed, an old lady bearing this character resides in Dulverton.'

Although written over 100 years ago, I do wonder whether this is actually still the case across Somerset generally these days. Pauline Clements' *The Somerset Book* (1982) mentions the story of 'the Roadman', which contains many of the elements of the witch mythology that we have already seen, only giving them a modern setting. A witch somewhere on the eastern side of Exmoor cursed the Roadman in the early 1900s and his sons died in the trenches in the Great War while his daughters went to lunatic asylums. In revenge, the Roadman shot the witch in the guise of a hare, using a blunderbuss filled with silver sixpences, killing her. He inherited her power but, in his bitterness, used it unwisely and was just as bad as the witch. The Roadman was cursed again, this time by an Exeter wizard, with the result that his daughter and grandchild committed suicide in 1925 and he lost power. I wonder how much of this is true, or at least based on a real sequence of events. Possibly, it was how the person who told Ms Clements the story interpreted the sad history of the eponymous Roadman.

In October 2010 I learned of the story of a trio of tourists from Lincolnshire who had driven to Glastonbury where, on Wearyall Hill, two of the occupants had spotted by the roadside what they took to be a sheep. Neither said anything, but within a split second the sheep had gone only to be replaced by a white cat. The third occupant only saw a white cat, and the discrepancy only came to light when one person tentatively queried of the others, 'Did either of you see what happened to that sheep?' I suggested – tongue in cheek – that they might have seen a local witch 'shape-shifting': after all, 500 years of superstition eradicated fully from every village and hamlet would be remarkable, and even today some of these beliefs may still survive in certain remote and isolated areas of the county...

CHAPTER 4:

CURSES, PORTENTS AND SUPERSTITIOUS BELIEF

INTRODUCTION

As we have seen, witches were supposed to 'overlook' their victims with the evil eye, and wise men were reputed to be able to 'curse' people, for a price. But the true nature of a 'curse' is really something else entirely, with a long history, and more supernaturally divine than the result of witchcraft. At Bishops Lydeard you could actually 'curse' someone yourself. Near St Mary's Church can still be sought out the Devil's Wishing Well, the Devil's Whispering Well, or simply the Cursing Well. Here, they say if you curse your enemy in hushed tones then some misfortune will befall them.

At Bath, during the Roman era, people would come to worship the goddess Sulis Minerva and throw thin, rolled-up pieces of lead inscribed with curses full of venom into the springs beneath the King's Bath. The curses, in threatening language and sometimes written backwards, invoked the goddess to wreak terrible vengeance on the wrongdoers: 'May he who carried off Vilbia from me become as liquid as the water', or 'I curse him who has stolen, who has robbed Deomiorix from his house. Whoever stole his property, the god is to find him. Let him buy it back with his blood or his own life.' One particularly vehement curse reads, 'I curse Tretia Maria and her life and mind and memory and liver and lungs mixed up together, and her words, thoughts and memory; thus may she be unable to speak what things are concealed…' I wonder what the results were…! We can never be sure if such a practice was simply ritualistic, or whether it was believed to actually work, but apart from providing a valuable insight into the lives and petty grudges held by the people of Bath 2,000 years ago, these curses remind us that people across the county in general believed that they could shape their environment, either by curse, superstitious ritual or even portentous observations.

The theme of divine retribution is a common one in Somerset; typical is the story of John of Saxony, who in 888 acceded to the bishopric of Athelney and, as he prayed at the alter, suffered an assassination attempt by two servants hired by a certain priest and deacon. Crying out, 'These men are devils, and not men,' he was rescued, and it is recorded that 'the doers of the ungodly deed were punished by God in an awful manner.' Sometimes divine retribution was observed in weather extremes or some other natural cataclysm: the Bristol Channel flood disaster of 30 January 1607, in which houses and villages along the Somerset coast were swept away, was claimed by one William Jones in his *God's Warning To His People Of England* to be the last of three divine judgements on the sinfulness in the county. The others had been the Gunpowder Plot in 1605, and the plague of 1603.

As this implies, some believed that they had the gift of prophecy, and this chapter is also concerned with those who professed to have this skill. Some sought to blame God's wrath on entirely human tragedies: it is likely that the 'monstrous childe born at Taunton' on 8 November 1576 was in some way blamed locally on the sins of the mother or the desertion of the father.

A portent was something different, however; the superstitious belief that a certain event foretold bad news, or was even a death omen, and one did not need to have a special skill to understand the meaning

The Gorgon's Head, Bath: a powerful symbol of the goddess Sulis Minerva.

of the portent. Such omens of doom ranged from the natural – anyone who encountered a white leaf on their beanstalk was doomed to die (John L.W. Page heard that this had happened recently in Watchet) – to the wholly supernatural, where observations of ghosts were sometimes believed to be fatal. Door knockers rapping without anyone being at the door, for example, were thought to foretell a family death, and Page had indeed heard testimony from a yeoman and churchwarden who had been sat at table near the window and heard the door knocker strike three times. The aunt of one of those present had died thereafter. This 'death knock' was also believed to be heard at the bedhead of the sick, each rap a few seconds apart, and signalling an imminent bereavement. There are also numerous accounts of ghosts appearing to some relative on the point of a family member's death, or else it was actually considered fatal to the very person who observed the ghost.

Sometimes it was believed that it was a place that brought ill-luck or was cursed. At Beckington, for example, it is reckoned that attempts to move the stones at the chambered tomb known as the Devil's Bed and Bolster, near Rode, are met with gloomy weather and sudden rainstorms. Above all, this chapter deals with all manner of superstitions, including those designed to bring good fortune, avert bad luck or even find love. All the beliefs, in fact, that folk in Somerset swore shaped their very lives – and, in some cases, even allowed them to control it.

PROPHECIES AND SEERS

One of the earliest instances of a prophecy being made by one with the 'gift' of second sight is outlined in Geoffrey of Monmouth's tome *History Of The Kings Of Britain* (c.1136). It covered a time period that began centuries before Christ up until the year AD 800, and told the story of how refugees from Troy fled to the British Isles, guided by the goddess Diana. There, they defeated a race of giants that inhabited 'Albion' and set up a capital at 'New Troy' (modern London), spawning generation after generation of rulers, both legendary and factual. At one point, at the behest of Alexander, Bishop of Lincoln, Geoffrey deviates from his story to tell the 'Prophecies of Merlin', a long and dire sequence of woe for future Britain, supposedly imparted by the famous wizard in the Dark Ages, which included this prediction: 'The baths shall grow cold at Bath, and its health-giving waters shall breed death.' This information was allegedly imparted to the 5th-century warlord Vortigern, but was perhaps based on Geoffrey of Monmouth's own observation of the decline of Aquae Sulis following the Roman withdrawal from Britain. Clearly, the prophecy did not see into the future as far as the Georgian restoration of the town.

Joseph Leech's *Brief Romances From Bristol History* tells of another prophecy made during an argument between Robert, Earl of Gloucester, and Abbot John of Tewkesbury, which occurred around 1129 when St James Priory was being built simultaneously with Bristol Castle, which was being refortified with stone. Only one stone in 10 was being set aside for the priory, and so Abbot John made a dismal prediction for the castle's future: that when Earl Robert's 'proud fortress is levelled with the ground' the priory would still stand. A furious Earl Robert replied that maybe it would, but by that time the priory itself would have ceased to function as a Benedictine house of God. And so it came to pass that in 1654 Oliver Cromwell ordered the castle to be demolished, just as Abbot John had prophesied – but, of course, by this time papal authority had long since ceased to be absolute in England, with abbeys and priories falling victim to the Dissolution of the Monasteries, although the nave of the priory continued afterwards as an Anglican parish church. Both the Earl and the Abbot had been proved right during their bitter argument in the castle grounds all those years ago; ironically, Earl Robert's tomb is said to reside in the church of St James.

According to folkloric belief, however, we all may possess a degree of psychic ability that affords us vague premonitions of ill luck, for Snell's *A Book Of Exmoor* (1903) tells us that, in Somerset, to dream of eggs, copper pennies or the parson in church with his surplice on was very unlucky. If a lady dreamt of a viper, this meant that she had a secret enemy conspiring to do her harm.

WHEN TWO SUNS SHONE

A contemporary text, *Mirabilis Annus, Or The Year Of Prodigies And Wonders, Etc*, documents the following amazing event: 'About two miles from Chard…on the 12 July 1662, being Saturday, towards the evening, were seen by many credible persons, two suns together in the firmament. They were both so high that they could not discern which was the false sun, till after a while it had continued, it disappeared, and the true sun went on its course.' This was just one of a long list of 'prodigies' observed as dire portents of doom in a nation recovering from the Civil War – another being a disastrous fire that swept through Ilminster in the spring of 1661 and burned down the centre of the town. Another observation similar to that at Chard is even weirder, although perhaps it is a misreporting of the same event. On 19 June 1662 between Trent and the Comptons, just east of Yeovil on the Dorset border, the sun was seen to unexpectedly break through the darkness of dusk at a time when it ought to have been setting. It took on a blood-red, fiery hue, casting such a strangely-coloured light 'upon a town called Bing-weston' that people there thought that the place had been set ablaze. After this it shone very clear and bright, as in daytime, and here the story enters the realms of the fantastic. In the sun a 'man on horseback' could be discerned 'very perfectly.' In a short space of time there appeared another sun 'on the north side' of the first, about two yards distant as it seemed to those on the ground. A second man on horseback could be seen in this other sun…

What could all this portend? Such dire, doom-laden sightings were made in many places and at many times in the 17th century. On 20 July 1674 the people of Chillington, between Chard and Crewkerne, saw a very long cloud of an extraordinary azure colour towards the west, and immediately there emerged from the cloud the 'form of a man with a rod in his hand, and on the top of it there was a thing like a brush; he held it forward in his hand for a little while, and vanished.' From the same cloud then came a man on horseback with a sword, who had a bonnet on his head with a feather hanging down behind him. Then came several companies of horse and foot (two in a row), the footmen being armed with 'musquets', with all subsequently vanishing as they marched through the sky. As they so vanished, others replaced them, the horses being ridden in a 'stately manner' and touching their breasts with their noses, until it became clear that there were two opposing parties filling the sky, one from the west and the other from the east, who then proceeded to charge at each other and engage each other with great violence... Doubtless, at the time this was not written of as merely a simple 'ghost story', but was considered another supernatural forewarning of dire, violent times to come for England.

PROPHETIC DREAMS

One Monday morning in July 1793 the wife of Thomas Walter, a woodcutter, grabbed her husband's arm as he was leaving for work and pleaded with him not to go that day. Asked what was the matter, she stammered that she was filled with an inexplicable certainty that something dreadful would happen to him at work; Walter merely shrugged this off, saying that she should pay no heed to dreams.

That day at work he was engaged in chopping down a large elm tree at Stowey, north-west of Midsomer Norton, when at lunchtime he and his colleagues broke off, leaving the tree half-felled. While they were away, a boy – for a dare – finished their work for them, cutting the roots of the tree so that it was effectively felled, but still standing. The joke backfired badly though, for when the workers returned to the tree, a gust of wind toppled it and Thomas Walter was crushed to death.

Mrs Walter's melancholy and unaccountable premonition had been proved correct, and the details of the inquest were published in the *Sherborne and Yeovil Mercury* on 15 July 1793.

Frederick Hancock's *The Parish Of Selworthy* (1897) notes a bizarre instance of what seems to have been another portentous vision by a lady of that part of Somerset. She had one morning come down to breakfast much distressed, telling her family that she had repeatedly experienced an awful vision during the night (presumably dreamt), in which she saw her favourite brother floating face down in water with slimy seaweed clinging to him. Her brother was a midshipman, and a few weeks later news reached the family that on the very night of his sister's vision he had toppled overboard and been drowned.

BROWN'S FOLLY AT BATHFORD

There is a well-known legend, collected by folklorist Robert Patten in the 1970s, connected to the square tower on Bathford Hill, Bathford, known as Brown's Folly. The tower was built around 1845 by a local landowner called Wade Browne, and affords magnificent panoramic views of the surrounding countryside, although it is currently closed to the public. There have been questions over its safety in the past, it being proposed in 1938 that it be pulled down; happily, it has survived this and may one day be accessible to the public, although presently it is heavily obscured by foliage.

Originally known as Wade Browne's Tower, the longer it stood the more it gained a reputation as a 'folly' and hence its new moniker, and with it, apparently, came an attendant legend. Robert Patten was told that Browne had built the tower to protect his daughter after someone prophesied that she would die on a specific day. Food was winched up the steep side of the tower in a basket to the girl, but one day (the very day Browne was told his daughter would die) the basket was hoisted down untouched. Browne stormed up the steps of the tower, only to find that his daughter had died from a snake bite.

There is a similar story about Cook's Folly, a castellated building looking out on to the Avon Gorge on the Bristol side. It has been re-edified numerous times, and was originally built in imitation of a small castle in 1693. *The Gentleman's Magazine* in 1814 notes the 'ridiculous story' invented by the peasantry, who appreciated neither the building's architectural enrichment of the area, nor the owner's desire to see all the way to Wales. Cook, they said, had dreamt that he would die of a viper's bite, and so confined himself to virtual imprisonment in the folly; but as he sat by the fire 'a viper sprung from some faggots', bit him and so killed him. I cannot help but wonder if this is where the story about Brown's Folly actually originated.

LEGENDS OF BELLS

A Book Of Exmoor explains that in one parish – where is not stated – when the church bells tolled, every old dame could be found on her doorstep, straining her ear to discern whether the bell tolled lightly or heavily. 'No-one but an old lady who has been cradled among the heatherbells' was able to explain exactly how, but certain tones in the tolling foretold an imminent death in the parish. A gloomy picture is painted: 'There is always a certain disappointment in the old crones' faces if the bell has no evil omen in its sound.' It was not an exact science, for apparently they would even begin to argue among themselves, with one often claiming that the bell tolled for the other!

There is also a story which I have been told concerning the bells that were being taken from the ruins of the old Augustinian Priory of St Nicholas, the remains of which are now incorporated into Barlynch Farm in Barlynch Wood, east of Dulverton. The priory was dissolved *c.*1536 and as the Great Bell was carted away by oxen to Exeter, it allegedly produced one last resoundingly dismal peal as though it did not wish to leave its location, which it had inhabited since the 13th century. The Reverend Gresswell wrote in 1905 that attempts to ring it at Exeter produced one sonorous note so awful that it turned all the cream in Devonshire sour! The story I was told was that, 'once they took it to Exeter Cathedral, it cracked and the pieces shattered on the floor: everyone in Dulverton knew that the bell had "died" and therefore this meant very bad luck.' Quite what that 'bad luck' constituted I am unable to find out.

CURSED AND UNLUCKY LANDMARKS

It is perhaps the mystery surrounding the stones at Stanton Drew that has led to a local supposition that to try and count them brought bad luck and was dangerous. Some even went so far as to say that if you counted them correctly then you would be struck dead, and there are other landmarks here that have attracted such dire warnings. At Castle Neroche, a Norman-era motte-and-bailey castle built on the site of an earlier hill fort, a mound on the northern side was traditionally thought to be the marker for treasure that was buried beneath. In 1854 the *Proceedings Of The Somersetshire Archaeological And Natural History Society* related a strange story concerning one of the groups of people who periodically invaded such earthworks with spades, 'urged on by the love of filthy lucre.' Before they had found a single coin, all were gripped with a strange panic and, dropping spades and pickaxes, they fled the site. Within one month they were all dead, some by illness, some by accident and some by mysterious fevers. This supposedly happened in the 1750s. F.W. Matthews' *Tales Of The Blackdown Borderlands* (1923) tells the story of a bunch of diggers who actually hauled out a treasure chest – but when one of them swore, the chest slipped back into the mound, and in the chaotic attempt to recover it some of the men suffered injuries. Finally an immense thundercloud darkened the sky over them and they fled 'Castle Rach' (as it was known locally) in the rain, convinced the Devil himself was after them.

Proceedings also noted in 1875 how the parish vicar would recount that the larger of the two Orchardleigh Stones on Murtry Hill, Buckland Dinham, had been excavated and found to go at least 10ft – its own height - into the ground. Folklorist Ruth Tongue, having been informed of the story in 1909, elaborated on this belief when she wrote that one of the stones had toppled and crushed a digger, before righting itself once more. Another well-known – but non-specific – story of this type concerns an Exmoor family upon whom misfortune after misfortune was heaped, the cause of which remained a mystery until the parents discovered a gold-handled sword in their son's bedroom. He confessed that he had been digging at an ancient tumulus in the district and found it; here was the cause of the family's trouble.

SUPERSTITIOUS RITUALS AND BELIEFS

In times gone by, a ritual carried out by county folk consisted of raking the ashes level on the hearth before retiring to bed, and then making the shape of a cross in them with the finger. This was designed to ward off fire, thieves and illness until daybreak. One of the commonest superstitions in Exmoor was that chopping into the elder tree meant extremely bad luck, and woodsmen would not touch this tree in the belief that if they did, all their cattle would die. The explanation for this was that the Lord's cross was of elder. Even the famous Punkie Night ceremony, with its hazy origins, in Hinton St George can be seen to have some added ritualistic significance aimed at procuring good fortune for the village.

Traditionally, the custom originated centuries ago thanks to the womenfolk of Hinton and Lopen (for Lopen also claims the event) hollowing out mangolds, lighting a candle within and using these as beacons to help their drunken husbands to navigate their way home in the dark from Chiselborough Fair. They apparently also went from door to door begging for money and candles to assist their enterprise. Nowadays, on the last Thursday in October the children parade the village streets with 'punkies', or lanterns made from hollowed-out mangold-wurzels containing a lighted candle, singing, 'It's Punkie Night tonight, Punkie Night tonight, give us a candle, give us a light, it's Punkie Night tonight.' There are variants on this, one being 'give us a candle, give us a light, if you don't then you'll get a fright', implying an element of ritualistic avoidance of bad luck. Some say that the origin of this is that the drunken menfolk got lost in the fields and ingeniously hollowed out turnips to make lanterns to navigate their way home to their worrying wives; therefore both men and women are claimed as the originators of this traditional event, so choose your explanation! Whatever its origin, the Punkie Night procession is now famous across the county.

Some of the most charming rituals concerned affairs of the heart. Would-be housewives, if shelling peas, would hang any pod containing nine peas over the doorframe. Thus, any man who entered the house after that was destined to be her husband. In Exmoor, the maid would lay a table for supper, open all the doors and sit and wait until midnight. When the clock chimed, the ghostly shade of her future love would enter the house and ravenously attack the food!

Another strange love ritual involved the young maiden going into the churchyard on Midsummer Eve with a handful of hempseed. She threw this behind her and, without looking back, she sang, 'Hempseed I scatter, hempseed I sow; he that is my true love, come after me and mow.' She then ran from the church and, before she got to the gate, she could look behind her – if she was brave enough – and see the ghostly wraith of her intended pursuing her with a scythe! No second glance was permitted, or the ghost of her lover would scythe her feet from under her as she ran. It is certainly my own belief that some of the rituals must have been observed to work to one degree or another in order to have persisted for so long...I cannot help but wonder how many lineages exist in Somerset today thanks to these strange – and slightly disturbing – love rituals. But the unmarried maid should beware stepping over a broom; this meant that she would bear a bastard child.

Superstitious belief was part of everyday life in days gone by, although most of it portended bad luck. For instance, the discovery of a double-yoked egg somehow foretold a hurried wedding due to pregnancy. Snell's *A Book Of Exmoor* (1903) provides many examples of omens of impending death: the howling of a dog at night, fruit trees or broad beans blossoming twice, a white bean being found growing in the garden or a bee suddenly dying. At funerals, those gathered had to walk in couples, as a person walking in single file was judged very unlucky. It was also an ill omen to return to the house after starting a journey, although this could be tempered by 'sitting down again' before setting off once more. In some parishes it was thought that if a clock chimed in the church while the text was being delivered then a death could be expected very soon. I wonder if this actually had a bearing on the timing and length of church services in past times.

And, of course, the port of Bristol had many superstitions, a curious example being that thunderous weather could be expected if, before the vessel passed Lundy Island, the ship's cat stretched so that its paws touched.

In the islands of the Bristol Channel it was believed that if the cream-coloured Burnet Rose (*Rosa pimpinellifolia*) blossomed out of season, it foretold a shipwreck. One has to wonder what repeated combination of circumstances brought about these beliefs, which were so thoroughly regarded as truisms in their time and went unquestioned.

SIGNS OF GUILT

In former times it was believed that a corpse would bleed in the presence of its murderer, and there was supposedly an instance of this actually happening at Wincanton. In 1730 a traveller named Sutton had made the mistake of announcing that he had a great deal of money and important documents on him during a spot of respite at a tavern in Castle Cary. When he left he had attracted the company of a local troublemaker called Jack White, and the pair apparently began fighting at the junction just south of Bratton Seymour, a little way out from Wincanton, after White made an inebriated pass at two women along the way. Sutton was left slain by the roadside by the fleeing bandit, his head bashed in and one of his eyes gouged out by his assailant using a piece of wood.

When Sutton was found, his corpse was taken to the inn at Wincanton where it was laid out on a table. When Jack White came to look at it with the rest of the neighbourhood, his guilt was betrayed by a thin trickle of blood that began to seep from the cold wound on the body. Others saw this and accusing eyes began to turn in White's direction; he promptly fled, but was quickly caught and dragged back to the

inn, where he was physically forced to touch the corpse. At this the wound began to bleed more plentifully, and in the minds of those present White's guilt was proved.

He was subsequently hanged on 19 August, his body then being encased in a metal gibbet cage and hoisted up at the crossroads – which to this day bears the name Jack White's Gibbet. The story is a well-known one today, with many people able to repeat versions of it in some form – the most commonly-cited 'fact' being that White was caged while still alive and simply left to starve to death. Of course, the ghosts of White and his unlucky victim are said to haunt the crossroads.

Guilt has quite often been betrayed by supernatural judgement. In 1646 the sister-in-law of David Barret (the murderer of the Dean of Wells) had 'her mouth drawn back to her neck in a most frightful and dismal manner' in Wells; this she blamed on her soul being damned because her brother-in-law had coerced her into saying at the trial that the Dean had provoked his own murder by striking Barret. This was a lie, she explained, before she died on her deathbed.

During the Monmouth Rebellion the task of dipping the corpses in pitch before they were hung fell to a man from Chedzoy called Napper, later nicknamed 'Tom Boilerman' by villagers who began to turn on him in the aftermath of the battle. Some years later he was killed when he was struck by lightning at North Petherton – no doubt villagers saw this as divine retribution.

The *Sherborne Mercury* of 21 April 1741 reported that nine men had appeared at Taunton Assizes charged in connection with the murder of a glover. All were sentenced to death, with one poisoning himself before he could be executed. The man who appeared principally guilty stated that if he were the criminal, then might his legs rot off. His legs 'actually rotted off at the small' and he had to be carried on a chair to receive sentence of death.

The hand of divine justice – or perhaps even a curse – might have been observed once again in 1824. That January three men named Moon, Beard and Lewis led a man named Wyatt from a tavern to a field near Marksbury, where they robbed him and beat him so badly that he died. Lewis turned king's evidence and escaped, while his two companions were sentenced to death. In a shameless display designed to pass the blame, Lewis returned to Weston, where he and another ne'er-do-well hung Moon and Beard in effigy. On the day that the pair were executed at Ilchester, 5 May, however, and almost at the same time as the execution, Lewis collapsed with some sort of brain inflammation and died shortly thereafter.

A curious story with a similar theme was written of by Milborne Port historian Emma Pitman in 1883, concerning the days when there was a workhouse there. The story was pulled from a local newspaper of 1813, outlining how one of the female inmates had stolen a garment belonging to another woman in the house. The woman was charged with theft, but vocally claimed her innocence, declaring that God might strike her deaf, dumb and blind if she knew where the garment was. Later that evening she ate her supper as usual, after which her speech became a mere mumble before she closed her eyelids and died there and then.

FATAL BLASPHEMING

In 1857 two labouring men were moving cinders near the railway station at Glastonbury. An outraged lady requested that the pair moderate their language, as they were turning the air blue with their swearing. One man, the worst of the two, stated that he was cursed anyhow, so why bother. At that point his horse ambled onto the railway track, the man attempted to push it off and out of nowhere a locomotive slammed into him, killing him instantly. The story featured in *Word-Lore: The Folk Magazine* in 1928, drawing upon an article in the *Taunton Courier* of 22 April 1857. It adds the grisly detail, 'And what is most affecting to relate, the aged man, his companion, stood over his mangled corpse as insensible and unmoved as a stone' – an allegory, perhaps, designed to conjure up an image of being turned to a pillar of salt in the mind of the reader.

Black's *Guide To Somerset* (1904) refers to a curious landmark 'at a small bridge a little to the right of the railway…a stone called "The Naked Boy", which people here declare to mark the highest point' of the Brendon Hills. This stone is still there, between Naked Boy's Bridge and Sminhay's Corner, a strange, pointed affair by the side of the road within sight of a couple of others, its surface green with lichen. The railway referred to was the now-dismantled old Mineral Line to the west, the bed of which is still apparent and in some places converted into a public right of way, while in others traversing private land. The stone(s) may have been linked to the tumuli that are scattered hereabouts, but as to the name the 'Naked Boy Stone', the story is that youths of a certain age many centuries ago were thrashed, beaten or chased naked around this stone in a kind of ritual designed to forever imprint on them the fact that this was the boundary of their parish, lest they stray too far. Some say that the stone is in fact a petrified drunkard who passed this site, marking as it did two of the hill parishes and what became the Trevelyan estates, who was turned into stone for his wicked, drunken transgression. Every night his ghost emerges from the stone to drink from the nearby Beverton Pond. Quite what this signifies, I'm unsure, but the story – much like the one before it – appears to contain a message of morality.

GHOSTS AS PORTENTS OF DEATH

J.J. Hissey's *The Charm Of The Road* (1910) notes that the link between ghosts and imminent death was a strong one in Somerset. Hissey was told that if you stood in any churchyard where you had a relation buried at midnight on a specific date of the year (he forgot the date, but it may have been St Mark's Eve), you would see the ghost of your deceased relative rise from the grave and go into the church. If two spirits rose from the ground then the watcher himself was doomed. The woman who told Hissey this was too afraid to try the ritual herself, but she said, 'Other folk I know have, and have seen the souls rise out of their graves, so it must be true.' It was also believed that on Midsummer Eve the ghosts of the living could be observed by those hidden in the church grounds at midnight; this was called 'spirit watching', and the phantasms of all those in the parish drifted into the church. Their hands and faces were transparent and their garments seemed woven out of mist; even the parson and the clerk drifted past, as insubstantial as the rest. From behind the sturdy church door, those hiding outside could discern weird and mournful organ music and the low murmuring of voices. At length the ghostly congregation would begin to depart the church; those that remained inside were those destined to die, and Exmoor historian Frederick John Snell was told of one case where a 'spirit watcher' had gone insane after witnessing his own daughter's ghost fail to reappear from within the church. The sexton found him sitting gibbering in the porch,

Crowcombe's church, where 'spirit watching' was practised.

screaming idiotically 'Lucy! Lucy!' for his doomed daughter, for he alone knew her fate. This supposedly happened some time before 1870, when the anecdote appeared in the *Argosy*. According to Ruth Tongue, this ritual was being carried out at the Church of the Holy Ghost, Crowcombe, in the 1870s, when this story dates from. John L. W. Page recorded in 1890 that there was a church in Exmoor where 'a few years ago so many were affected with this morbid curiosity, that a gate, studded with nails on the top and still in existence, though no longer in situ, was erected to keep them out.'

Page also observed that a tailor had recently entered into an argument over the tardiness of some work he was doing on a customer's clothes, justifying his lack of enthusiasm by saying to the customer that there was no point, as his client would be dead in 12 months. This comment identified him as one of those who still practised this superstition, despite its having largely disappeared by Page's time.

A variation on this theme at Selworthy in the 1800s concerned the belief that ghostly figures hovered near the bier cloth in the church, as though to announce that it would soon be in use and a death in the parish was imminent. One sexton in that parish, according to writer Frederick Hancock in 1897, even believed that he heard 'loud calls' in the evening before discovering the next day that a member of his flock had died during the night.

A similar belief concerned actual, identifiable phantasms – often of those living but on the very point of death. An example of this occurred in Selworthy, when a loud and continual tapping on the door of a house one evening announced a visitor; the occupants found no one on the threshold, however, and only learned later that at the time that this happened their son was passing away in his lodgings in London. In fact, there is a strong tradition of ghosts appearing at the point of death within sight of puzzled witnesses, who only realise later that what they saw was a portent of that person's actual demise. Frederick Hancock's *The Parish Of Selworthy* (1897) notes some fairly recent instances in that place, including a landlord's wife who encountered their lodger rushing silently past her and entering his room one night; the following morning she learned that he had never even been home, for he had been killed in an accident at work in a quarry the previous day.

There is a strange story from Taunton, to the effect that in 1828 a group of men drinking at the White Hart Inn clearly saw the landlord, a man called Baldwin, walk into the room, past their table and out again. He rudely ignored their cheery 'Hello's and requests that he join them for some cider. Somewhat annoyed, they first ordered the serving boy, and then Baldwin's wife, into the room to ask them what the man's problem was. Both stated categorically that Baldwin was at that precise time in Bristol on business and it could not have been him they saw. The arguments raged, with the old women in Taunton beginning to say that Baldwin had been killed in Bristol and his ghost had been seen. A short time later, however – much to his wife's relief – Mr Baldwin returned from Bristol, and amidst all the relief at seeing him alive the mystery of the matter was forgotten. Within a year, however, Baldwin had died, and the old dames of the town clucked and said that the wraith had been an omen of the landlord's impending death.

Another legend with this theme concerns the murder of Sir John Dinely Goodere, who – owing to squabbles with his brother over money – was abducted by two ruffians on College Green, Bristol, as he made his way home following a lunch during which the brothers had apparently reconciled. The baronet was dragged to the *Ruby*, a man-of-war lying in King's Road. Here he was strangled, with his treacherous brother, Captain Samuel Goodere, standing sentinel before the vessel, sword in hand, should the sounds of struggle be overheard. The crime was brazen, and the captain and his two accomplices – Irish crewmembers called Mahon and White – were quickly arrested. Four months later on 20 April 1740 'the wretched fratricide was executed within sight of his own ship…an attempt at rescue having been frustrated.' At the exact time of the slaying a strange incident happened: the victim's nephew, Samuel Foote, was kept awake at his father's house in Truro, Cornwall, by the softest and sweetest strains of music he had ever heard, and which came from no traceable source. Foote clearly equated the strange melody with his uncle's ascension to heaven, a ghostly portent of death heard by him only.

GHOSTS THAT ARE FATAL TO ENCOUNTER

In other instances, however, ghosts were themselves fatal to encounter. Briggs' *The Fairies In English Tradition And Literature* (1967) tells us of an awful ghostly visage that haunted moorland on the outskirts of Taunton. This wraith was called the One with the White Hand, and it supposedly rose from oak trees or a scrub of birch at twilight to drift after travellers. Her clothes rustled like dead leaves and she was as pale and skeletal as a corpse, with her hand outstretched as she pursued her terrified quarry across the moors. If this dreadful creature caught up with you she would touch your forehead and send you mad, or else touch your chest and kill you. People found on the moor in this condition supposedly had the outline of a white hand above their heart, and this ghastly vision continued to haunt the area around Taunton until she was banished by a brave man performing an exorcism ritual with salt. Horrific as this was, it is not the only rumour of ghosts that brought death with them in Somerset.

In Wellow it was rumoured that a demise within the Hungerford family was imminently announced by the appearance of a ghostly 'white ladye' at St Julian's Well, who appeared as though in mourning by the stream. The Hungerfords were the Lords of the Manor, and following their fall the evil omen was never seen again. This simple legend, noted in *Rambles About Bath* (1848), illustrates that in days gone by ghosts were not only seen as mere phantasms of the dead: on occasion their appearance was portentous of forthcoming disaster.

Brockley Combe, south of Nailsea, was found by the folklorist Ruth Tongue to be haunted by the ghost of an old woman, whose appearance foretold insanity and death to anyone who glimpsed her. She allegedly appeared every 26 years, having been seen by the cousin of Ms Tongue's informant in 1912 – presumably the cousin had met an unfortunate end. This would make the evil old woman's next appearance due in 2016. Brockley Combe is indeed very haunted, as we shall see.

I have been told (although not by anyone living there) that there is meant to be a phantom coach and four horses that was once glimpsed, or heard, pulling into Gaulden Manor on the evening before a death at this proud Elizabethan pile, now famous for its gardens. The manor is south-east of Tolland and allegedly has other ghosts – notably a phantom Grey Lady who materializes on the stairs, although she is supposed to be harmless. It is with these eerie stories in mind that our tour of mysterious Somerset leads us into the realm of ghosts and haunting…

CHAPTER 5:

GHOST STORIES OF SOMERSET

INTRODUCTION

Just shy of the Dorset border can be found the village of Chilton Cantelo, a truly isolated place north of Yeovil that consists of a smattering of farms and Chilton Cantelo House, an 18th-century manor house built by the Goodford family that now functions as a small private boarding school. There is no public house, nor post office, but there can be found the fantastically-prominent St James' Church, which seems far too big for the place, until you learn that the Goodford family enjoyed great prosperity and had a great many employees in the years following the Napoleonic Wars. The church is of Norman origin (it still contains a Norman baptismal font), although it was largely restored in 1864 when parts of the building began to slip due to roadworking.

Opposite this landmark can be found Higher Farm, formerly Higher Chilton Farm, an impressive building in its own right owned by the Kerton family for many-a-year, which now functions as a bed and breakfast. Tucked away inside this building there is a curiosity that forms the basis of one of the best-known legends in the county.

Much has been written of the skull that resides within Higher Farm, but the basis of the story follows these lines. Theophilus Brome died on 18 August 1670 aged 69, having retired to Somerset and having taken an active part in the Civil War in support of Cromwell. Brome was a Warwickshire native who went into semi-exile upon the Restoration of the Monarchy in 1660, and upon his death his will stated that he wished his head to be hidden within Higher Chilton Farm, while the rest of his body was to be committed to the ground in the adjacent church. This was because Brome feared that, as a sympathiser of Cromwell, his body would be dug up and his head decapitated and taken to London to be stuck on a pike at Traitor's Gate; such barbaric treatment had been meted out to Cromwell himself post-mortem, and others too. This wish was adhered to by Brome's sister upon his death in 1670.

John Collinson's *History And Antiquities Of Somerset* (1791) is the first to make reference to the tradition that Theophilus Brome's unearthly spirit would return to haunt the farm should the skull be moved from its hiding place. Collinson wrote, '…the tenants of the house have often endeavoured to commit [the skull] to the bowels of the earth, but have as often been deterred by horrid noises portentive of sad displeasure.' The last attempt to bury the skull with the rest of the body had occurred *c*.1770, and the attempt was aborted when the sexton's spade broke while digging up the body. The sexton 'uttered a solemn asseveration never more to attempt an act so evidently repugnant to the quiet of Brome's head.'

And so the skull still resides here, hidden in the farm. On 2 February 2010 I visited Higher Farm and was told by the long-time owners, Mr and Mrs Kerton, that in 1820 labourers making additions to the 'old' part of the 17th-century house had re-discovered Theophilus' skull in the wall along with the will that his sister had acted upon all those years ago. There is some suggestion that the workmen used the skull for drinking out of (according to ghost hunter Christina Hole in 1940), but nonetheless the skull was not buried with the body in St James' Church after its rediscovery. It was placed reverently in a specially-made cabinet at the end of the hall beside the door to the sitting room. The will that was discovered is also still with the Kerton family, although it is in such a fragile condition that it cannot be displayed.

The farm exterior bears a coat of arms dated 1826, which would have been crafted when this event happened, and it is here Theophilus has lived ever since, tucked away in his little cabinet in the alcove above the low door to the cider cellar.

By the late Victorian era the skull was popularised as having caused much terror and trouble in bygone times, with folklorist T.H. Thiselton-Dyer observing that, '…buried it will not be, no matter how many attempts are made to do so.' The skull is now often referred to as a 'screaming skull' or 'cursed skull', although this is considered unfortunate by the Kerton family; they have never known Theophilus to be troublesome, and consider him (or rather, his skull) a friendly benefactor. Upon being shown Theophilus' skull, I was curious to see that his lower jaw was missing and that he appears at some stage to have been varnished. It is true that my camera, newly fitted with fresh batteries, refused to work upon attempting to take a photograph of this heirloom and yet worked once more outside of the farm; however, this cannot be attributed to any supernatural intervention since I simply obtained another camera, which worked without any problems.

It seems that the story of the skull screaming, or even dismally moaning, if taken out of the farm is folklore and, in Mrs Kerton's words, 'pure nonsense.' At one point Mr Kerton moved to pick up the skull as though to handle it, but then explained that although he did not mind moving the skull within its recess for me to observe it, he would not take it from its cubbyhole; however, this appears to be merely reverence

Theophilus Brome's skull.

to an age-old family tradition founded on Theophilus Brome's own wishes and not because of any superstitious reason. The reason for Theophilus Brome's desire that his head be hidden was very natural, given the era in which he died, and his tomb in the church is concealed beneath the church wall nearest the farm — meaning that his head and body were buried apart, but as near to each other as was possible under the circumstances.

In many ways, tales like this are archetypal of the traditional Somerset ghost story; they have a beginning, middle and end, occasionally a moral, and just enough historical, factual elements to make it seem almost possible that it could have happened in the way we are told. The legend of Chilton Cantelo's skull has certainly fascinated generations for decades, and no doubt will continue to do so. But although ghost stories in this day and age do not seem to conform to miniature stories as often as they once did, it would appear that many of Somerset's oft-told ghostly anecdotes from the past are more than mere folklore, for they range from the barely-believable and poorly-evidenced to the fascinatingly credible, and it is clear that in the Victorian era the advent of a more sophisticated media did not kill off the phenomenon of 'ghosts'. In fact, it encouraged it. This chapter lays out a selection of some of Somerset and Bristol's well-known (and not so well-known) ghostly encounters from days gone by for the reader to ponder.

'SNIPT AND SLASHT'

As if to evidence that contemporary reporting of supernatural phenomena is not a modern development, Joseph Glanvill's remarkable *Saducismus Triumphatus* (1681) chronicles many a strange tale told to the writer, not least a bizarre phenomenon in North Cadbury related to him by 'a reverend and learned friend of mine.'

A girl in the village, for some months, found that she could not put on 'clean linen nor holiday-clothes, but they would be snipt and slasht full of holes.' Quite what was behind this is unclear: Glanvill interpreted it as witchcraft, but it sounds like the behaviour of a particularly nasty poltergeist, assuming that a human factor was not to blame.

'CURSED HIM BY CANDLE, BY BELL AND BY BOOK'

Page's *An Exploration Of Exmoor* drew upon an 1889 account featured in the *West Somerset Free Press* concerning a famous ghost to the west of Minehead, at Porlock. The ghost was of a man named Lucott, whom Page describes as a 'wicked boaster', but whom other retellings have as a pirate or buccaneer. A week after his death Master Lucott was seen causing trouble in ghostly form at Porlock Weir, and 12 parsons were employed to banish the ghost; however, only 11 could be found and at the exorcism in St Dubricius' Church the ghost was not troubled at all. Those assembled performed the ritual and used bells, candles and books, but it had little effect. Lucott stood and watched the proceedings, his pallid face grinning with malicious delight, before boldly walking into the holy men and sending them running. After this a 12th parson was secured from the parish of St Decuman, who squared up to the ghost and dared it to eat a consecrated wafer. Lucott did, and immediately became obedient to the priest's orders. The ghost dumbly climbed a horse and rode eastward to Doniford.

Along the way the ghost assaulted an open-mouthed bystander near Watchet, knocking the fellow's eye out for staring at him. But for all intents and purposes, the ghost had been exorcised, and allowed its essence to enter a little box that the priest then hurled into the sea. The story's origin is unclear, but it would appear that these events are supposed to have occurred some 450 years ago.

Porlock Weir c.1890, haunted by Lucott's spectre. Drawn by Alfred Dawson.

MADAME CARNE'S GHOST

It certainly seems that ghosts were a lot less shy in days gone by. A brass preserved in the vestry of ancient St Nicholas' Church at Withycombe, south-east of Minehead, announces that Madame Joan Carne was thrice married: first to John Newton of Sandell, then to Charles Wyndham and lastly to Thomas Carne of Ewenny, Glamorgan. She died in 1612 and was duly buried in the parish church.

Joan Carne resided at Sandell (Sandhill) Manor, the home of the Wyndhams and now a farm. Page describes the place as 'a fine old house, [which] retains some wood-framed windows and oaken-wainscot bearing the date 1588.' An upper room was said to be haunted by Madame Carne's ghost in Page's time, for locally she was supposed to have been a witch who had done away with all three of her husbands and taken control of the Sandell estate. The most well-known story about her was that following her funeral the cortege returned to Sandell manor, only to find the widow's ghost frying eggs and bacon in the pantry. As old as this legend is, the Somerset folklorist Ruth Tongue heard variant details, as told to her in 1959 and published in *Somerset Folklore* (1965). Madame Carne was banished to a pond by a priest brought from Watchet, but she is – supposedly – returning to Sandhill Farm at the rate of one cock-stride (a very short distance) a year. I understand that when she eventually reaches there, a disastrous fire will overtake the place…

ONE COCK-STRIDE A YEAR

Wellington was the ancient seat of the Popham family, and it seems that one of their number – Sir John Popham – left a strange legacy in the area. Sir John was Lord Chief Justice from 1592 to 1607 (the year of his death), but despite his high standing in Elizabethan England, history – or gossip – has been less kind to him. John Aubrey wrote of him, 'I have seen his picture; he is a huge, heavy, ugly man…he lived like a hog.' Rumour had it that Popham had acquired Littlecote House, Wiltshire, upon corruptly acquitting a relative named 'Wild Will' Darrell, who had been accused of tossing a newborn into the hearth of a fire to die in the flames. The crime certainly occurred, but Popham may in fact have found his ability to impose a stiff penalty on Darrell restricted by the latter's position as a great man and court favourite, and it is entirely possible that Littlecote was acquired legally. But Aubrey related that both Popham and his wife died of the effects of gluttony and a profligate lifestyle, heavily in debt and accusing each other of acquiring their various properties illegally. There was even a scandalous allegation that Popham himself had thrown a newborn babe to its death out of an upper window at Kimbolton Castle, Cambridgeshire.

It seems strange that Sir John Popham left such a questionable reputation behind him when he died on 1 June 1607 – his will dated 21 September 1604 provided an infirmary and education for the people of Wellington. Perhaps it is the fact that he was the richest lawyer of his time, having an income of £10,000 a year, that made him unpopular. Popham's residence here was the now-defunct Wellington Court House, and the parish church, dedicated to St John the Baptist, contains a beautiful monument to Sir John and Lady Popham. Here he lies buried, although according to tradition, his soul still wanders...

One of the earliest references to Sir John's restless spirit appears in *The West Somerset Word Book* (1886), which records that his ghost was reputed to haunt 'a certain spot in the parish of Wellington, on land which formerly belonged to him, but now forming part of the estate from which the Duke of Wellington takes his title.' Popham was whispered to be making his way into town 'by a cock-stride every year.' Sir John is supposed to have been thrown from his horse and into a pit at a combe just west of the 175ft-tall Wellington Monument at Higher Ash Wood, where he either drowned or broke his neck. This gully was called Ouelscombe Bottom (or Wilscum, or Wilscombe). The pit within was believed to be the very

Sir John Popham and his wife in Wellington church.

entrance to Hell, or the Red Sea, where the wicked were banished, and where Sir John's ghost languished until New Year's Eve 1607, when the fervent prayers of his wife Amy (who died in 1612) managed to free his trapped spirit. Since then, it has been making its way back to St John's Church in Wellington at a cock-stride a year. Some say that his journey is beneath the ground, and when he passes under dwellings subterranean noises and poltergeist activity is experienced. On 23 June 1909 the *Wellington Weekly News* carried a letter from Mr F. Milton, a local naturalist, in which he explained that, according to his father, in *c.*1859 some men employed in cutting down trees were forced to temporarily abandon their work because one of the trees cried out piteously, as though in distress. The implication was that Popham's ghost was at that time within the tree, using it as a temporary abode on his long way back to Wellington.

The vice-chairwoman of Wellington Museum told me that there were 'various legends about his [Popham's] death and subsequent walking', but of these she could not – or would not – comment. Whatever the cause for this reticence, it indicates that the strange legacy of Sir John is a well-known one in Wellington, and until fairly recently it was common for the phrase 'er's as bad as Popham!' to be used to describe someone unpleasant. After 400 years, perhaps the ghost of Sir John now has Wellington within reach; after all, his task is not entirely impossible, unlike some punishments meted out on evildoers and the wicked in folklore.

MRS LEAKEY'S WHISTLE

The story of old Mother Leakey's ghost is a very famous one. The parish register records Susannah Leakey's death on 5 November 1634 at the home of her son, Alexander, in the old seaport town of Minehead. In her lifetime Mrs Leakey was considered of amiable and friendly disposition, and her son drove a considerable trade between Minehead and Waterford in Ireland. Quite what it was that had insulted, offended or even possessed the elderly widow as she lay on her deathbed, however, seems to be unknown, but she announced that she would return after death 'in the Divell's likeness' and there would be trouble.

Within six weeks of the widow's demise and burial in the church at Minehead, Alexander Leakey's dwelling was subjected to furious knocking and crashing noises in the chamber and about the bed, which came from no visible source. After 12 months of this, 14-year-old John Leakey – Susannah's grandson – died of a progressive illness, claiming that he could get no peace on account of the racket. Worse, before he died he shouted that he could see the Devil in the room, and after death some observed strange black marks – like bruises – about his neck. At Easter 1636 Susannah's daughter-in-law, Elizabeth, was making her way to bed, a candle in one hand and a book in the other, when she was shocked to see Mrs Leakey herself sat in a chair in the parlour looking at her. After some minutes the apparition turned its head and groaned dismally before disappearing. The ghost began to appear regularly in a physical form, but only before Elizabeth Leakey, until one day in November 1636 Mother Leakey appeared before her as she was dressing herself and this time spoke to her, demanding that Elizabeth go to Devon and recover a gold chain and deliver a bond to a relative. A curious observation was made that the apparition's eyes did not move. Further instructions were given that were to be passed on to another of Mother Leakey's relatives in Ireland. When asked whether she resided in heaven or hell, the ghost groaned so loudly that the maidservant downstairs heard the noise, and the apparition vanished.

The instructions to be taken to Ireland were not to be made public and were for the ears of King Charles I only. There was a delay in Elizabeth leaving Minehead, however. This, it seems, angered Mother

Leakey, and her son Alexander subsequently began to suffer losses at sea, a circumstance that was blamed on his dead mother's supernatural wrath.

All this we learn from an official inquiry into this bizarre melodrama, which is likely to have been taken so seriously because of rumours of witchcraft. The inquiry was conducted by the Bishop of Bath and Wells, Paul Godwin, and Sir Robert Phelipps, hearing the evidence of 'Mr Byam, a grave Minister neere Minehead' and Mr Heathfield, Curate of Minehead.

The whole affair seems to have petered out after being dismissed as nonsense by the investigating magistrates. They concluded, 'Wee…doe believe that there was never any such apparition at all, but that it is an imposture, devise, and fraud for some particular ends, but what they are wee know not.' The report is dated 24 February 1637. From C.H. Poole in 1870 we find that in Minehead this story took on many dimensions of its own: Mrs Leakey appeared to many persons, in houses and fields about Minehead; her ghost somehow kicked a doctor for failing to assist her over a stile; and that she was wont to appear at the quayside calling for a boat. Here, she whistled whenever she saw one of her son's vessels off Blue Anchor Bay and this whipped up terrible storms and caused great damage to shipping. She even seems to have ordered her daughter-in-law to go to an Irish bishop and threaten him with hanging unless he mended his ways, to which the profligate bishop replied that if he was born to be hanged then at least it would spare him from being drowned. As late as 1890 John L.W. Page recorded the belief that an 'evil spirit' – supposed to be Mrs Leakey's – still haunted Culver Cliff, at the back of Minehead Quay, and Warren Point. On one occasion he saw two children flee from here, spooked by the 'imaginary presence.'

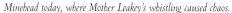

Minehead today, where Mother Leakey's whistling caused chaos.

ECHOES OF THE BATTLE OF SEDGEMOOR, 1685

To the north of Westonzoyland, on the edge of Bussex, can be found a small parking area and hoardings depicting images from the 'last time Englishmen took up arms against fellow Englishmen.' To the west, a rough track leads one away from the edge of the village and further out from civilization into the flat, wet and gloomy moors. Along the track known as Langmoor Drove, heading in the direction of the King's Sedgemoor Drain, can be found the lonely memorial to a disastrous conflict that haunts this region still, in more ways than one. By the trackway stands a grey tombstone-shaped granite monument depicting the epitaph 'To the glory of God and in the memory of all those who doing the right as they gave it fell in the Battle of Sedgemoor 6 July 1685 and lie buried in this field or who for their share in the fight suffered death, punishment or transportation Pro Patria.'

The story of the battle is a well-known one, even today. On 6 February 1685 the Catholic Duke of York acceded the throne as King James II upon the death of his brother Charles II. On 11 June, James Scott, the 1st Duke of Monmouth and Buccleuch and the 36-year-old illegitimate son of Charles II by his mistress Lucy Walter, landed at Lyme Regis in Dorset with three ships and some 80 men to take the crown from James II and restore Protestantism to England. Monmouth embarked on a campaign through the West Country – a predominantly Protestant region of England, where many peasants, artisans and yeomen rallied to his cause, fortified by small victories in clashes with local militia. A 1680 pamphlet indicates that Monmouth was already a highly-regarded figure in this area, his royal legitimacy implied by the 'miraculous' curing in 1680 of one Elizabeth Parcet, who suffered from the King's Evil. She managed

The Sedgemoor memorial.

to touch Monmouth at the 'White Lodge, Henton Park, Somerset', her recovery being witnessed by many; it goes without saying that this 'cure' was only thought possible when practised by a ruling monarch.

Monmouth's army carried four light field guns and some 1,500 muskets, but as the ranks swelled, there were more of the army that were armed with pitchforks and sharpened farming implements like scythes than with the artillery of a true fighting force. Monmouth's intention was to take Bristol by force, while an anti-Catholic rebellion swept parts of England and Scotland. Despite having himself symbolically crowned king at Chard, however, the duke's expected support struggled to materialize and Bristol was too well defended by Henry Somerset, 1st Duke of Beaufort, and the Gloucester Militia. Although Monmouth had, by this time, rallied some 4,000-5,000 men to his cause, they also found Bath too well defended, and a violent skirmish with the forces of the Earl of Feversham forced the rebels to chance their arm and march eastwards towards Wiltshire. By the time they were forced back to Wells on 1 July (where they looted the cathedral of lead to make bullets and stabled their horses in the nave), morale was low. News had reached Monmouth that a rebellion by the Earl of Argyll in Scotland in support of his cause had collapsed north of the Clyde, and by now Monmouth had taken to repeating that Charles had secretly married his mother and he was no bastard son – he was, in fact, England's legitimate heir.

The Duke of Monmouth's forces were pushed back into the Somerset Levels, to Bridgwater, where they sought to fortify the town as their base. Feversham's army was by this time camped behind the Bussex Rhyne at Westonzoyland, and at about 10 o'clock on the night of 5 July the Duke of Monmouth took the decision to break out of Bridgwater and launch an assault on the enemy encampment. A local farmer's servant led the ragged army in the direction of Bawdrip, and then southwards in the direction of Westonzoyland and into the open, desolate Sedgemoor marshes. It was during this night-time march that a small encampment of Feversham's scouts were startled by the near approach in the darkness of Monmouth's forces, despite the duke ordering the entire march to be undertaken in utter silence. A warning shot was fired by the sentries and one of their number galloped off to alert Feversham and his second, Major-General John Churchill, and in the gloom of the darkness all hell broke loose at Sedgemoor.

The clash occurred between 1 and 2 o'clock in the morning, and lasted about an hour and a half. It was a difficult site for a battle, as much marshland as firm ground, and crossed by dangerous rhynes and ditches. Feversham's men outnumbered Monmouth's in terms of foot soldiers, horsemen, artillery and arms, and outdid them in professionalism; Monmouth's men were blocked and the carnage inflicted on them was fearful. In fact, although there were deaths on the king's side, Monmouth's men were systematically annihilated by a much better-trained and equipped professional fighting force in the moonlit darkness of that fateful night.

Many are believed to have died along Moor Drove Rhyne. At the end of it all, 16 of the king's soldiers lay dead. These were given a Christian burial in St Mary's Church, (one allegedly with his chest obliterated by a cannonball). More than 100 soldiers were also badly wounded, and scores more died of their injuries after the event. Some 500 rebels were arrested and imprisoned in the church, while many others were hunted down and summarily executed when found in their hiding places. Of the rebels, some 300 fell on the battlefield, five of the wounded perished within the church, which was being used as a temporary gaol, and in frantic skirmishes around Westonzoyland a further 22 were hanged by the king's soldiers. Four of these were hung in 'gimmaces' – a Somerset expression meaning hung in chains. This, of course, does not take into account the hundreds so barbarically punished at the subsequent Bloody Assizes. Other retellings speak of 300 soldiers being slain by the Bussex Rhyne, and the battlefield being littered with the carcasses of 1,000 rebels. One account even speaks of 2,700 dead.

The duke himself escaped the battlefield, but did not last long as a free man. This disastrous battle – and its brutal consequences after the fact – is legendary in Somerset, and there are those among the older generations in this region who even today harbour contempt for the Royalist forces of the Stuart dynasty, proclaiming the king's forces to be 'much worse than Cromwell ever was.' Such comments as this I have heard with my own ears. The carnage has also imprinted itself on the psyche of the people in the region in other ways though, and quite naturally Sedgemoor is supposed to be haunted.

In the immediate aftermath of the clash, when the king's soldiers were pitilessly rounding up Monmouth's shattered army and sympathisers, there were several legends generated. A contributor to *Notes And Queries* recalled that one of his ancestors, Richard Alford, was churchwarden during the rebellion and a Monmouth supporter. He escaped interrogation, however, by presenting a party of the king's men with a jug of cider bearing the king's image. Others are said to have not been so lucky.

One of the most famous stories concerns a young Somersetshire man famed for his swift running, who was rounded up. Feversham promised the captive his freedom if he could outrun one of the wild marsh horses that populated the area. A halter was attached to the man's neck and attached to the horse, while a soldier sat atop the beast to spur it on. The spectacle was meant to be some ghastly death game to entertain the king's bored soldiers, but for three quarters of a mile from Bussex Rhyne to Brentsford (or Brintsford) Bridge the half-naked runner frantically kept pace with the wild horse. It made no difference: an enraged Feversham had the heroic runner instantly strung up and hanged. This is a very famous story, and it is said that the thundering hoof beats and furious snorting of an invisible horse can be heard, accompanied by the frantic cries of strained effort that are supposedly his human competitor. At Chedzoy they tell me that the runner's name was Samuel Sweet, and his story features in a locally well-known poem by Charles Causley, *The Ballad Of Samuel Sweet*. The ghost of the runner's heartbroken girlfriend is also believed to haunt the area of Lang Moor, after drowning herself in the River Carey. Another legend speaks of an athlete named Swayne being run to ground near Moorlinch. Here he was made to leap for his life, and three enormous bounds took him to the edge of Loxley Wood – into which he promptly vanished. *All Year Round* (1869) remarks that three stones marked the site of this prodigious leap 'on the Shapwick estate', which were called Swayne's Jumps in memory of this event. These stones can still be sought out via a public pathway and signpost that directs one into the woodland from the extremely busy A39.

The day following the battle the dirty road between Westonzoyland and Bridgwater (now the A372) contained 20 gibbets, and from each swung the corpse of a rebel. The atrocities would likely have continued, had not – according to tradition – the Bishop of Bath and Wells, Thomas Ken, informed Feversham that such behaviour on his part constituted murder and the rebels were entitled to a fair trial. This set the scene for the equally infamous sequel to the battle called the Bloody Assizes.

At the Sedgemoor Inn in Westonzoyland there are also alleged to be ghosts linked to the uprising. The white façade of the inn displays an impressive pub sign depicting images of the battle, and inside – on the edge of the inglenook fireplace – can be found stonework displaying groves said to have been made by soldiers sharpening their swords. Cannonballs are also on view. It is here that Feversham was awoken at 1 o'clock in the morning by the innkeeper, to be told that the rebels were approaching northwards of Westonzoyland.

The Sedgemoor Inn on a gloomy day.

Phantom footsteps that cannot be accounted for have been heard clumping about in the first floor corridor outside the bedrooms late at night. The fireplace downstairs is haunted by the slight spectre of a young girl sometimes glimpsed fading through the nearby wall. This is thought to be the ghost of Mary Bridge, an 11 or 12-year-old girl who stabbed a Royalist soldier to death with a small sword (taken from his scabbard) when he attempted to assault her mother. The soldier had quartered himself with the family in the aftermath of the battle and Mary was tried under court martial law by Colonel Kirke – who acquitted her and even presented the girl with the weapon. This, at least, was the version of the story told 175 years later by one of her descendents in Old Court, Wellington. The sword is currently on display at the Bridgwater Museum.

Folklore, Myths And Legends Of Britain (1973) by the Reader's Digest repeats the now well-known story that in the late 1700s a farmer making a night-time sojourn across the levels was subjected to the cry of 'Come over and fight!' in the near distance – a call which he took to be the voice of a drunkard whom he could not see in the fog. This is believed to have been the despairing cry of Monmouth's poorly-armed men from the other side of the River Carey (the King's Sedgemoor Drain was engineered in 1795) as they were being slaughtered by musket fire and cannonballs from long-range, and forms the basis of many a legend here now.

For many years the exact location of the slaughtered casualties was unclear. The bodies of the peasants had been buried *en masse* somewhere on the battlefield, under a gigantic mound of earth raised above the burial pit, which over time was ploughed flat. In *c.*1860 an antiquarian found, however, that the site

These grooves on Chedzoy church are thought to have been made by local rebels sharpening their weapons.

advertised itself by discoloured, darker-tinted grass that grew above the graves, and later unearthed bones some 2ft down: 'Thus the darker-tinted grass is a more lasting memorial than many which man places to mark the burial of his dead.' Around this time Sir W. Boyd-Dawkins was told by a villager that his great-grandfather had been part of a group of men employed to dig trenches in the moor and cover the bodies over with sand obtained from Bussex Farm.

The memorial was erected in 1927 to commemorate the battle. Today, according to this memorial, the slain still lie submerged in the ground of the Somerset Levels hereabouts. There does not appear to have been any attempt at cultivation. When I visited this site, passing by only a couple of dog walkers, it was very overcast and starting to rain. The village of Westonzoyland suddenly becomes very far off, and out here it is not difficult to imagine the ghost of the Duke of Monmouth surveying the scene of his misguided insurrection on a gloomy day. The duke was, incidentally, arrested huddled in a ditch, disguised as a shepherd, two days after the battle. He was carted off to London, where his execution was brutally, barbarically botched: an event that has in itself become part of London folklore. I have heard it said that his ghost — a solitary figure, seen from far off, but recognisable by its long, fashionable locks and wide-brimmed hat — can be observed on either the anniversary of the battle or the anniversary of Monmouth's own death on 15 July. His ghost also supposedly haunts the remains of the castle by the River Parrett in Bridgwater, despite this having been destroyed before Monmouth's time. Furthermore, a headless ghost that was often seen in a field between Catcott and Edington was also thought to be Monmouth's.

Of the battlefield, *The AA Illustrated Guide To Britain* (1971) observes, 'Ghosts are said to haunt the battlefield — vague, shadowy creatures which loom up over the marsh and quickly vanish again. At night, green blobs are said to glow over the battlefield, representing the unquiet spirits of Monmouth's slaughtered army.' The traveller J.J. Hissey explained in *The Charm Of The Road* (1910) how he was told by a parson during a visit to Somerset that older cottagers would swear that they could hear thundering hooves on a certain night. A farmer had recently heard the sounds of galloping hooves rushing past the lane where his cottage stood one winter night, and was told by an older parishioner, 'We always listen for them on that night and always hear them.' I also remember hearing a story about a London reporter nearly colliding with a mysterious horseman who appeared out of swirling mists one night in the 1930s, before vanishing back into the gloom across a small bridge. The mystified pressman is said to have pulled over by the road, wondering why the horse's hooves had made no noise, before realising, as the fog lifted a little, that neither bridge nor horseman could be observed anywhere. I was told that this was 'supposed to be the duke's ghost fleeing the battlefield.'

Fiona Shearer, the proprietor of the Halfway Inn on Westonzoyland Road, Dunwear, told me, 'There are many tales of sightings of "ghosts" in this area, in particular soldiers from the battle. In the surrounding fields there is meant to be a mass grave where the Royalist soldiers, having imprisoned them overnight in Westonzoyland Church, took around 250 rebels into a field, shot and buried them.' Sedgemoor has an atmosphere of its own, inspiring neither feelings of horror nor triumph, merely evoking a sensation of pity and sadness at the slaughter of the misguided and overwhelmed ragged army that had allied itself to Monmouth. The reason why this one event has firmly entered the hearts and minds of the populace is that so many countrymen died here. In many ways, however, it was the atrocities of the aftermath that have stamped the so-called Duking Days into the collective consciousness of Somersetshire folk.

THE BLOODY ASSIZES

In 1856 a contributor to *Somerset Notes And Queries* pondered over the curious name locally given to a 'building standing over an archway, which crosses the road near the parish church' in Langport; this, he learned, was called 'the Hanging Chapel', but none knew the reason why.

It is highly likely that this place was (or was thought to have been) the site of an execution of one of Monmouth's supporters following the series of trials under Judge George Jeffreys that even in its own time was referred to as the 'Bloody Assizes'. In the autumn of 1685 Judge Jeffreys made his way into the West Country, guarded by a party of Colonel Kirke's soldiers, with the first of the trials occurring at Winchester. Others followed at Salisbury, Dorchester, Exeter, Wells, Taunton and Bristol. In many ways, the ruthless treatment of Monmouth's supporters after the battle is even more notorious than the event itself. *Somerset Notes And Queries* wrote of these events:

> When he [Jeffreys] proceeded to Taunton and Wells, such was the effect of his menaces that the juries gave their verdict with precipitation, and numbers of innocent persons were in consequence confounded with the guilty. Almost every market town and village in the county was the scene of these iniquitous executions. The rights of sepulchre were denied to the sufferers; their heads were stuck on the tops of houses and of steeples, and their mangled limbs were hung on trees, in sight of their lamenting relatives and friends. Even those who escaped the penalty of death were obliged to submit to the extortion of fines, which reduced them to beggary, and where they were already too poor to pay, they were sentenced to be whipped and imprisoned.

Some 350 died under these circumstances. It is no wonder that the legacy of the Bloody Assizes has left such an impression upon this area, nor is it any wonder that there are many stories of ghosts linked to these times.

The land was festooned with the carcasses of rebels swinging from the boughs of trees, and what a ghastly sight the Somerset countryside must have become, for many were drawn and quartered or disembowelled as part of the punishment. Many corpses were also dipped in boiling pitch to preserve them – this last being Col Kirke's idea. John L.W. Page found that a specific tree on the southern side of the Dunster to Timberscombe road (A396) had accommodated the corpses of three rebels, and could still be pointed out by 1890. The owners of Temple Farm, Chedzoy, told me in August 2010 that Slape Cross, off Chedzoy Lane, was supposedly named after a 'Colonel Slape' who had dangled there. At Wells, the gallows was erected on Jeffreys' command in the south-west of the city, at a site ever after called Gallows Close; it was still employed over a century later when a man named Tucker breathed his last on it for a murder committed at Ansford. The gallows was dismantled sometime in the early 1800s, with the upright post being incorporated into the door frame of a house in Southover. At Cothelstone Farm Colonel Bovet and a man named Blackmore were hanged on the outer gateway, and tradition declared that their blood ran all the way to Bishops Lydeard. This aside, quite naturally many of these sites are meant to be haunted: the Heddon Oak at the crossroads near Crowcombe is believed to have been a gallows tree, and on windy nights the clanking of chains and the agonised choking of dying men can apparently still be heard. The road that runs past the George Inn at Nunney, within sight of the ruined shell of the 14th-century castle, is another site that holds this tradition.

Fugitives were also run to ground in the aftermath of the insurrection. Near Weston-super-Mare there is a well-known story that a Monmouth partisan, John Plumley esq, escaped to the seat of his manor at Locking – where his hiding place was betrayed to soldiers by the family's excitable pet dog. Plumley was hung by the neck from a branch in his garden, and after the fact his wife took the dog in her arms and threw herself to her death down a well – a sorry state of affairs said to have been re-enacted in spectral form ever since. Plumley's two sons died on the battlefield and it is thought that he himself managed to evade capture for some time by hiding at various places in the Mendips; one of the caves at Burrington may have earned the moniker 'Plumley's Den' before he eventually thought it safe enough to return to Locking. The site of his capture is supposed to have been a little wood that for many years went by the name of Plumley's Copse, and tales of these ghosts probably began with the parish clerk in the late 1800s.

The most notorious assize was the one that occurred within the Great Hall of Taunton Castle. Jeffreys, it seems, arrived in the town making a veiled insinuation to 'depopulate the place' and we learn that 143 were hanged here. A claim during the trial that some 1,000 soldiers had died at Sedgemoor no doubt fuelled the judge's notorious rage against the insurgents, and it was not uncommon to see the corpse of a man hanging by a rope from a chamber window in the town. The carcasses of some swung from the signpost of the old White Hart tavern, and on the spot where the bodies were quartered the executioner stood ankle-deep in blood. Jeffreys even boasted that he had hanged more men than any judge since the time of William the Conqueror, and it is clear from Humphrey William Woolrych's 1852 biography of Jeffreys that there was not a shred of pity or mercy in the man.

Katherine Briggs and Ruth Tongue's *The Folktales Of England* (1965) tells the story of a young farming lad who was hanged outside the family home in Walton, near Street. After the execution the lad's father slaughtered his prize bull, cut its heart out and hammered nails into it. He then bricked it up in the chimney, and this ritual had a dramatic effect: whenever the fire burnt beneath the chimney, the judge suffered debilitating coughing fits and chronic chest pains. And whenever he suffered this, 'there come a sight afore 'is eyes, no matter whether 'e closed 'em or no – the sight of a 'anging lad.' This was a common tale in Street, where the gallows tree was known as Marshall Elm; apparently it still stood as late as 1946.

The Great Hall of Taunton Castle, now the Somerset County Museum, is reported to echo to the sound of the marching feet of King James' soldiers, presumably as they thrust yet another unfortunate before the pitiless judge. The ghost of Jeffreys himself is also reported to have been witnessed in the hall, looking resplendent in its red-and-white finery and long judge's wig. The Director of the Museum explained to me that, although he had not experienced anything himself – 'having been in the building at all hours of day and night over many years' – he was nonetheless aware of 'periodic stories about the Great Hall being haunted.' It is also claimed that Jeffreys' ghost haunts the rooms he took at the ancient Tudor Tavern on Fore Street.

It is interesting to observe that Jeffreys remains, even among today's younger generation, a demonised figure, with a young woman from Banwell telling me in August 2010 that 'The Ship Inn in Banwell is also said to be haunted. Judge Jeffries used to hold court there, I think they were called assizes courts, and there are gallows in the pub. He used to travel around holding court; apparently he was known for being a ruthless and unforgiving judge. There are dungeons under the house on the other side of the road.'

In 1688 James II was overthrown and forced to flee to France following the invasion of William of Orange. London was in a state of furious anti-Catholic rioting, and Jeffreys, disguised as a seaman and attempting to flee the capital, had the misfortune to be recognised by a lawyer with whom he had once had an argument. It is remarkable that this hated figure was not immediately lynched by the mob, but he was conveyed to the Tower by a strong guard. In due course a remarkable petition entitled *The Humble Petition Of The Widows And Fatherless Children Of The West Of England*, signed by 1,000 women from Somerset, Dorset and Devon was carried to the Tower demanding Jeffreys be brought to book for the Bloody Assizes. While awaiting trial for high treason, Jeffreys died in the Tower on 17 March 1689, of apoplexy, it is said, brought about by his fear of being killed by the mob.

CANNARD'S GRAVE

South of Shepton Mallet, following Cannard's Grave Road leads one to Cannard's Grave – a little place described by Poole in 1870 as then being 'a patch of dreary, woebegone-looking buildings whose best days have passed.' Among these he included the hostelry, a place that he suggested must have witnessed many gambling marathons, much drunken profanity and smuggling plots in days gone by. This tavern dates to *c.*1625 and was until recently the Cannard's Grave Inn – its pub sign displaying a grim representation of a fellow being hanged in Puritan times. It is (at the time of writing) Cannards Well Hotel, and the road that passes by here is very busy nowadays; however, there is a ghostly story attached to the place from long ago, when the place was quieter and all that stood here was a windswept gibbet post placed strategically near the tavern that had, ironically, become a den of thieves.

A 17th-century landlord, Giles Cannard, is supposed to have been a wealthy and devious man, perhaps wont to participate in highway robberies and provide a safe haven for the criminals that gathered at the inn. Some even say that the occasional customer was plied with alcohol and murdered, but eventually Cannard was suspected of forgery and the authorities came to arrest him. He placed a noose round his own neck after inventing a ruse to re-enter the inn one last time, hanging himself from a beam; he had realised that his days were numbered. The Revd H. Allen, rector of Shepton, wrote in 1692 that it was well known that Cannard's ghost could not rest and had taken to frequenting his old tavern.

There are other versions of this legend: that Cannard was lynched by a crowd of merchants who had suffered the abuses of the criminals who frequented his inn, or that his name was, in fact, Thomas Kennard and he was the last man hanged in England for sheep rustling. Despite his place in Shepton's history, some even consider Cannard to have been an entirely fictional character! Cannard is widely held to have been buried at the crossroads, however, where his ghost mingles with those of other felons who ended their days on the gibbet. A pub nearby is called the Highwayman Inn, another memory of those times.

Crossroads were often associated with the burial of suicides or gibbeted murderers, and there are sites in Somerset bearing names related to burials, such as Webber's Grave, south of Wellington. Near Oxenford Farm can be found a crossroads designated Mary Hunt's Grave (where the Dowlish Ford to Cricket Malherbie road crosses the Knowle-St-Giles to Moolham road), south of Ilminster. I have made various enquiries as to why this place is so-called, but have come up with no success as to any historical reason for its name; nonetheless, both these sites are popularly believed to be haunted by the ghosts of their interred namesakes.

BEWITCHMENT AT THE LAMB INN

From an account entitled *A narrative of some extraordinary things that happened to Mr Richard Giles's children at the Lamb, without Lawford's gate, Bristol; supposed to be the effect of Witchcraft. By the late Mr Henry Durbin, Chemist; who was an eye and ear-witness of the principal fact herein related*, we learn of the strange events at the Lamb Inn between November 1761 and November 1762.

Under the roof of the spacious Lamb Inn, it was two of the daughters of Richard Giles, the proprietor, who were the focus of the haunting when it began in the early hours of the morning on 13 November. Molly, aged 13, and eight-year-old Dobby were terrified by scratching noises and mysterious knocking sounds, but soon the whole household became aware that some kind of awful poltergeist-like entity had invaded the premises. Although it started off with the usual kind of random, pointless, attention-seeking pranks associated with poltergeist activity, the haunting grew in intensity and also in violence. The girls, for instance, displayed bite marks and other signs of violence as though they had been assaulted; furniture was violently tipped over and little Dobby one day claimed to have been carried up the stairs by a mysterious 'woman in a ragged dress, a brown chip hat and great holes in her stockings.'

Richard Giles also ran a fly-wagon between Bristol and London, but it seemed the poltergeist wished to ruin him. His horses would suddenly stand still on Kelston Hill, and on one occasion the leading two horses charged back to their stables at Bath – leaving the others stood in the road – when their chain traces unaccountably snapped during one of these episodes. Giles began to fall sick, apparently convinced that a rival waggoner had employed a witch to curse him. He appears to have become a victim of his own stress and fear, claiming on one occasion that he had witnessed a strange woman stood by the side of the road looking at him, just before the harness on his gig snapped and he was thrown into the mud. His condition got worse until he sickened and died on 15 May 1762.

On 27 November a 'cunning woman at Bedminster' (i.e. white witch) was employed get rid of the spirit, and an archaic ritual performed at the Lamb apparently saw it off. Some were hugely sceptical of the whole affair: Bristol historian John Evans observed in 1824 that the two girls were sent to stay with a Mrs Haynes of Wick Court, where the elder of the two was one night found, newly scratched, hiding in an upper room. For this, Mrs Haynes 'directed the natural application of a birchen rod to Miss Molly's sensible posteriors' and thus put an end to the ghostly goings-on at Wick Court. Common sense laid the blame for the whole thing at the feet of Richard Giles' wife and mother-in-law, Ms Nelmes; the whole scheme had been a plot to drive down the value of the Lamb Inn in order for Ms Nelmes to purchase it outright.

But there is a question mark over the whole affair nonetheless. The chemist, Mr Durbin, who logged the events and stayed at the Lamb, found much of it inexplicable, and there is a suggestion that not only he, but also others actually witnessed what they took for supernatural phenomena. For instance, he wrote he had seen a wine glass 'rise from the drawers [on which it had been placed] without hands' before being flung with violence at a wall. Durbin's account was not even published in his lifetime. It was not until 1800 that the public learned fully of these strange events. So it is at least clear that Durbin made no commercial gain by going 'on the record' about events at the Lamb Inn. Whatever was truly going on, the Lamb Inn was demolished in the early 20th century.

THE GHOST OF GALLOWS ACRE LANE

One of the most haunted places in the city of Bristol was Clifton Down, now an area of public space north of the village of Clifton, on the eastern side of the Avon Gorge. At one time Pembroke Road was known as Gallows Acre Lane on account of the gibbet post here, and Joseph Leech's *Brief Romances From Bristol History* (1884) paints a grim picture of the scene in days past: '…a couple of footpads who were caught, convicted and hanged, were dipped in a bituminous composition, engaged in iron basket-work, and suspended from tall poles, thence to dangle and decay away – a terror to…the simple peasants who had to cross the greenward after sundown.' This pair were executed for the murder of Sir Robert Cann of Stoke House's coachman on the Downs, but the gibbet's most famous occupant was one Shenkin Protheroe.

An early 20th-century view of Clifton Down and the Avon Gorge.

Leech describes Protheroe as a 'demon cripple' who walked by his hands using little hand stools, since his legs were useless. He made a living by beggary, but on one occasion – his greed excited by the gleaming contents of a pouch carried by a drover who took pity on him – he contrived an evil scheme. Waiting for the drover to return this way, Protheroe concealed himself in a ditch and called out to the kind-hearted victim as he passed by, crying that he had fallen and could not extricate himself from the ditch. When the drover went to help, the cripple produced a knife and stabbed his victim to death as he leaned over him.

Protheroe was quickly caught (the proceedings of his robbery were found on his person) and hanged on 31 March 1783. His corpse was suspended from the gibbet post, where it decayed and in time presented only a sun-bleached skeleton. Residents hated passing the gibbet, and would form small groups so that they could walk by it *en masse*; there was a tradition that Shenkin Protheroe hung about the Down in ghostly form, and in 1786 one local prankster played a trick on a party passing this way. It was a fearful windy night, and as the group passed underneath the gibbet it all of a sudden began 'dancing', swinging violently to and fro under a shaft of moonlight. As those assembled stood rooted to the spot in terror as a dark figure glided down from the top of the post, moaning dismally and sending them scattering in all directions. Among the group was a young girl named Jenny Rudge, who, in the confusion, escaped her escorts and managed to elope with her lover, a hosier's apprentice named Richard Foyle. Amazingly, the whole thing had been a plot and it had been no ghost at the gibbet, merely a stout-hearted accomplice of the lovers lowering himself down with a rope! When the gibbet was taken down, Foyle made a tobacco box from the woodwork and, since he had married Jenny, carved in the lid: *'To the memory of Shenkin Protheroe, Esq.'*

'CHOPPED HIS BOWELS OUT'

In the past, stories of ghosts and hobgoblins were used as a means of pacifying children, and the memoirs of one Samuel Budgett testify to this. A successful Somerset merchant in adulthood, Budgett recalled how as a child he had been brought up in Wrington, Backwell, Nailsea, and Kingswood. By 1803, when Samuel was seven, his parents owned a general shop at Coleford and young Samuel was being educated by 'Mrs Stone, at the Yew Tree.' One elderly woman here, who taught them how to operate the spinning wheel, recounted an atypical ghost story to terrify the children.

A man 'chopping wood at a place called Goodheavers' accidentally 'chopped his bowels out', by which injury he died. The flailing hatchet was embedded so firmly in the block of wood that it could not be removed and the poor man died in such agony that his ghost was doomed to return to the site ever after. This it did, where it would calmly amaze observers by dipping its finger into the fire before touching its pipe to light it. Then the ghost would descend into a nearby coalpit. This wraith lived in the pit, and two attempts to 'lay' it failed, before a third ritual banished it to the Red Sea, since when it had never reappeared.

Although there is little by way of truth in this, it speaks volumes nonetheless, for it is a good instance of the type of storytelling that many county ghost stories are perhaps founded on. It was certainly striking enough for Samuel to remember it in adulthood, recounting it as he did 50 years later.

THE GUARDIAN SPIRIT OF BROCKLEY COMBE

Brockley Combe is a wooded combe on the southern edge of the village of Brockley (south of Nailsea), that cuts chasm-like into the mountain and winds upwards for a mile and a half. *The Westonian Guide* (1829) tells us, 'Near the entrance of the combe is a picturesque cottage, whither many parties of pleasure resort in the summer season, and where Dinah Swan, the guardian priestess of the glen, has resided for upwards of half a century.' The allusion to the woman being a priestess was a metaphor, although it appears that the ancient Dinah Swan may have had something of a reputation as a 'wise woman'. Nonetheless, when she died in 1833 she was allegedly found in a petrified state of terror, although silent in death, at the gates of Brockley Hall. An inquest suggested that she had been frightened to death, and ever since she is supposed to have haunted the combe – perhaps the 'guardian priestess' in death as she was in life.

Quite what spooked her so badly that she died was never established (she may have been fleeing an intruder in her cottage), but there are other ghosts that haunt this place. In fact, Brockley is considered one of the most haunted sites in the region, with many ghosts: there is a phantom monk wearing a cowl at Brockley Court, and what appears to be the ghost of a Victorian cleaning lady at St Nicholas' Church. With these other ghosts to contend with, there is a tendency for their mythology to overlap; some believe that Dinah Swan may have been trying to escape a phantom coach and horses that was believed to be driven in complete silence by a cadaverous-looking coachman wearing 18th-century clothes from the direction of an old trackway that leads into Brockley Wood near the Main Road junction. I wonder if this is the same awful hearse-like apparition that Ruth Tongue declared in 1965 had been responsible for 'otherwise unaccountable accidents, most of which have been fatal. It was seen fairly recently by a cyclist, a football team and a man who had been a complete sceptic.'

In 1904 another spectral coach and four horses was written of as sweeping along the road between Cutcombe and Timberscombe (now the A396). And, even more formidable, in the 1800s a headless horseman was thought to patrol a particular crossroads in the parish of Selworthy. He could be espied at midnight on moonlit nights and appeared to be guarding the spot.

HAUNTED HILLFORTS AND LANDMARKS

As we have seen, the ancient hill forts, barrows, earth mounds and tumuli of Somerset have many an accompanying legend of Satanic origins, buried treasure or fairy dwellings. Some are haunted, although by more mundane spectres than South Cadbury, where King Arthur's spirit supposedly dwells.

A Book Of Exmoor (1903) tells us that Mounsey Castle, an old British fort in woodland north of Dulverton, by the Barle, was circled on 'a certain night of the year' by a phantom chariot that disappeared off into the cairn in the field below. Hidden away in the Quantock Hills is Dowsborough fort, where it was said that if one dared sit atop the ramparts, the phantom singing of ancient British warriors could be discerned from within the bowels of the hill. Some supposed Dolebury Warren fort, between Shipham and Dinghurst, to be populated by the ghosts of Danish warriors. On the other side of Somerset, at Buckland Dinham, north-west of Frome, locals avoided walking down Murtry Hill Lane on account of a ghostly white lady who would drift about the standing stones known as the Orchardleigh Stones. But perhaps the most remarkable story comes from Exmoor.

At the disused slate quarry near Cow Castle, another fortified Iron Age settlement near the Barle, there stood, at least until 1890, a dilapidated and abandoned cottage by the rapid stream of the White Water. This ruin was feared by all and supposed to be haunted on account of a dreadful crime that had occurred in this vicinity over 30 years earlier, when it had been the dwelling of a man named William Burgess. Burgess' young daughter, Anna, hated the woman he wished to marry, and so to rid himself of this flea in his ear, Burgess killed the girl and buried her upon the Moor. This brutal man was forced to hastily exhume the remains when word got out that two fellows had chanced upon the grave and announced that they intended to remove its contents that night, for they thought that poachers had hidden a dead sheep there. Burgess next threw the body down the flooded Wheal Eliza mineshaft and then fled England for Wales. A strange light is said to have hovered over the disused shaft by night, until eventually it was searched and the girl found. Burgess was later tracked down and met his end on Taunton gallows on 4 June 1859. Of this place, the explorer John L.W. Page wrote, 'Without at the time knowing aught of the tragedy, I experienced a distinct feeling of depression as I climbed the track behind the haunted ruin, through the rain of an autumn evening...' The strange light, apparently, never appeared at the mineshaft after the body was pulled out, but some do say that it has been seen over the poor girl's grave in St Luke's, Simonsbath.

THE SURGEON OF ILMINSTER

James Cox, the Ilminster historian, recorded a bizarre legend in *A History Of Ilminster* (1958). In the 19th century townsfolk told the story of a local surgeon who received the cadaver of a recently executed young man in order to perform medical experiments on it.

As he began cutting, however, the 'corpse' suddenly returned to life, having been improperly hanged and merely unconscious. The surgeon, rather than lose his prize, ruthlessly cut the man's throat, and although it was unclear when this was supposed to have happened, the surgeon lived at the Market Hill, where in the 1800s they said that the victim periodically haunted the place.

THE SKULL IN THE BOX

The *Bristol Evening Post* of 21 October 1967 recalled a fascinating piece of lore passed down successive generations by the owners of Barrow Court, a staggeringly beautiful three-storey manor house (with an adjacent church) west of Barrow Gurney, that was built in the 16th and 18th centuries from portions of a Benedictine nunnery established *c.*1212. It was purchased and restored by Henry M. Gibbs around 1881, and it was he to whom a strange phantom materialized one night.

Henry was standing at the front door, which commanded a fine view of the straight carriage drive that led to the iron gates, when he observed a woman making her way over the grass past a cedar tree in the silence of dusk; she wore a long dress and a high-necked Elizabethan ruff-style collar. This strange woman appeared to vanish through the wall that divided the court from the Church of the Blessed Virgin Mary.

Gibbs wandered over to the place where the woman had vanished and placed a stone there. The following morning he ordered masons to demolish part of the wall and dig beneath, whereupon their spades hit a small box buried in the ground, which was found to contain a woman's skull.

The nunnery's life ended effectively when the Dissolution closed it down on 19 September 1536, with Katherine Bowie being the last prioress. If the appearance of the ghost is anything to go by, however, she was not a nun, and her skull's interment appears reminiscent of the request by Theophilus Brome at Chilton Cantelo rather than being a murder. Whoever she was, Gibbs had the skull buried in the churchyard, which seems to have put a stop to her wanderings.

'EVEN THE WALLS SHAKE AT TIMES'

By the Victorian era, a fledgling newspaper industry and periodicals were latching on to stories of encounters with 'real' ghosts, it being clear that instances of superstition made good copy. Sometimes they were reported in a half-serious, half-sarcastic fashion; the *Bristol Times* observed in 1846 that 'We have this week a ghost story to relate. Yes, a real ghost story, and a ghost story without, as yet, any clue to its elucidation.' This concerned an ancient residence that adjoined and almost formed a part of All Saints Church on the corner of Corn Street and High Street in Bristol. It had been converted into a vicarage house and lately the sexton, his wife, a lodger and his maid had been troubled by mysterious footsteps thumping about the place, a strange light like a flickering candle that spontaneously appeared on the wall and the appearances of a ghostly bewhiskered gentleman who shook the maid's bed during the hours of midnight and 2 o'clock. Interestingly, All Saints Church was for centuries said to have been haunted itself, since the time of the Dissolution, by a black-cowled figure given the name 'the Black Monk'. He is reputed to have appeared on several occasions in the chancel or drifted down the aisle, before disappearing through walls in full view of shocked witnesses.

In August 1868 the *Bristol Evening Post* reported that the house of a Mr Travis in Thorney, a hamlet by the River Parrett south of Langport, was bedevilled by a poltergeist. Some kind of entity had invaded the house that July, opening and closing doors in a forceful manner and whipping pillows and bolsters from beneath sleeping occupants in the bedroom. There is a suggestion that some kind of phantom conflict was being played out: there was the 'boom of many muskets' heard, as well as 'the distant boom of a field piece.' The noises came from different parts of the house and 'it is even said that the walls shake at times.' Scores of people attested that this phenomenon was a real one, affirming that no human agency could have caused the disturbances without being caught. This haunting was also reported in the *Western Gazette* of 31 July 1868 and the *Weekly News & Advertiser* of 21 July 1868, it being a good example of the immediacy with which an increasingly sophisticated media was able to bring such stories to fascinated county folk – reinforcing the general belief that 'ghosts' were real and not just folklore or stories to frighten children.

'TROUBLESOME' SPIRITS: VICTORIAN URBAN LEGENDS

Papers held in the Somerset Archive and Record Service pertain to a destructive haunting in Sidcot, north of Axbridge, around 1780 that centred on the cottage of a deceased 'wizard' named George Beacham, and began on 22 July with the intrusion of a terrified girl named Mary Neads bursting into a Quakers' meeting and shouting, 'For mercy's sake, do ye come out, or old Joany Beacham's things will be all broken to pieces!' It seems that the ghostly activity stemmed from the conjuror's desire to be buried in his own garden and not in consecrated ground – a wish that his widow, Jone Beacham, did not adhere to. Mendip historian F. Knight commented in 1915 that 'no explanation was then or at any later time forthcoming.' This incident is only one of many ghost stories from Somerset; there are in fact almost too many too catalogue, without even including those that appeared in the popular press, and there is certainly enough material in letters, pamphlets, diaries, periodicals and studies of witchcraft to suggest that the phenomenon was thought a real one, greatly feared by the people of Somerset. *Notes And Queries For Somerset And Dorset* (1895), for instance, tells the story of a mansion near Frome with a haunted corridor. A contributor confessed to being 'petrified with amazement' at the sound of footsteps and a rustling gown that passed beside him and a friend while they held a midnight vigil at the house. And this came from a learned man, not a superstitious villager.

In the later 1800s village gossip had it that the 'great house at Allerford' (probably Allerford House in this village near Porlock, famed for the Packhorse Bridge) was 'troublesome'. *The West Somerset Word Book* (1886) records that the gentle euphemism 'troublesome' was used to personify ghosts, while their inability to find peace was coined 'to go again.' It cites an interesting example: 'The tenant of a cottage [where is not said], whose predecessor had been killed by the fall of a wall, came to my father and said, "I can't never bide in the 'ouse, the poor old Harry's that troublesome; zo zoon's I be abed and the can'l a-douted, he do come and drag my timmern leg all about the chimmer by the buckle-straps."' The wooden-legged victim of this poltergeist was still living in 1885, the book noted. From the same work we learn that in rural western Somerset ghosts were sincerely believed in and referred to as 'bullbeggars', 'galleybeggars' or even 'bogies'.

These bogies and bullbeggars lurked at many a haunted spot in Somerset. In the parish of Selworthy there was a meadow where there stood a post that was haunted by an awful, shapeless thing that would leap out on travellers and rattle its chains. At Muchelney, where can be found the remains of the Benedictine Abbey, they said that the ghost of an abbot haunted the adjacent Priest's House. Henry Alford's poem *The Abbot Of Muchelney* depicts the ghost thus:

> And often, down that dark and narrow way;
> Along the windings of that hidden stair;
> Sweeps a dim figure, as the rustics say;
> And tracks the path even to the house of prayer…

The 'house of prayer' at Muchelney.

Strange chanting in a foreign tongue was heard on the wind, and there is the usual legend of lovelorn strife occurring at this Norman abbey, when a nun and a prior fell in love. She suffered the traditional punishment of being walled up alive by her brethren, he being banished. Elsewhere, at Barton Hall, Bath, in 1868 a phantom is said to have appeared, displaying a human countenance, but devoid of eyes. And phantom ladies are believed to haunt many a site in Somerset; sometimes it is not even known who they are and their identity remains a mystery, with the spectral figure merely being assigned a colour scheme of white, grey or black. At Huish Barton Farm in the Brendon Hills, Page wrote in 1890 that this rambling 200-year-old place was haunted by a 'lady in silk' and there was a door in the corridor that led to the 'haunted room', that, up until the present incumbent, appeared to have been kept locked. Whatever curse was supposed to have visited those who entered, however, was long forgotten by the time the supremely non-superstitious owner allowed Page to poke his head round the room.

Pinkworthy, or Pinkery, Pond – an old and man-made Exmoor lake high on the moorland near the Devon border – was haunted by the 'bogy' of a suicide. The ghost was that of a lovelorn Devon farmer whose hat and coat were found on the bank in 1888, and hundreds of people turned out to watch the pond being dragged and then drained. Page wrote of this, 'Bog-trotting at any time is disagreeable enough, but bog-trotting in the company of a possible ghost does not commend itself even to the mind of the moorman.' The method used to find his submerged body was rather curious, another of those odd Somerset ritualistic practices from days gone by: they lit a candle and stuck it in a loaf of bread, launching it on the water in the belief that it might come to a standstill over the body. Needless to say, the techique failed.

107

Coffins feature regularly in Somerset folklore. The spectral one that appeared before horse-drawn traffic in the middle of a road at North Petherton, south of Bridgwater, also had a phantom man sat atop it. I wonder if this is at all connected to a macabre event in December 1823, when a man from that parish was implicated in an act of grave-robbing from the churchyard and the corpse was supposedly conveyed to a surgeon in Bristol. Another spectral coffin is widely held to display itself in the road between St Audries and Holford, along what is now the A39.

Echoes of creaking gibbets are another familiar theme of Somerset legend. To the west of Nether Stowey in the Quantock Hills can be found Walford's Gibbet, site of the gibbeting of the corpse of John Walford. Walford was a charcoal burner, who loved one girl and yet was forced by circumstance to marry another, until ultimately – exasperated by her slovenly behaviour – he killed her and disposed of the body at the site picturesquely known as Dead Woman's Ditch (although the ditch may have had this name even before the murder). Walford was executed in 1789, but although the gibbet post was taken down in the early 1800s, for generations afterwards it was whispered that the creaking gibbet cage could be heard on blustery nights, and that the awful putrid smell of decomposing flesh could be detected. A woman dressed in black also drifted by the site, according to the writing of Thomas Poole, the valued friend and benefactor of Coleridge in his early days at Nether Stowey.

The theme of violence is common in many of the county's ghost stories. The bar of the George Inn at Bathampton was (and indeed still is) believed to be haunted by the rakish ghost of Viscount du Barre, a French aristocrat fatally wounded during an exchange of pistol fire with an Irish gentleman, Count Rice, on Claverton Down in 1778. The viscount was laid out at the George after his body had lain a full day on the down.

Dead Woman's Ditch.

Rice was, incidentally, acquitted of murder at Taunton Assizes. Perhaps the weirdest story of the era was submitted to *Notes And Queries* by a Mr T. Westwood, who averred that in 1840 he had stayed with a fox-hunting squire in Taunton and learned from him of a dilapidated old hall near the roadside somewhere out in the Somerset countryside. This hall possessed a single window that was always illuminated at night, despite the place being empty and the rest of it being in darkness; one night the squire's curiosity had gotten the better of him and he and a friend forced an entry into the hall. In the lighted chamber they found that nothing accounted for the source of the illumination of the room and the cobwebbed, dust-covered furniture within cast no shadow. This room had a light of its own, and worse, the longer the squire and his colleague stayed, the sicker they began to feel. The squire described the feeling as though his life was being sucked out of him, and the pair desperately staggered out of the place, never to return. After the fact, the squire learned that the last occupants here had apparently kept this specific room locked, never entering it through fear of some fatal supernatural phenomenon that resided within...

THE CRANMORE TUNNEL

There has always been a certain romance about stories of secret tunnels, hinting as they do at lovers' trysts and dramatic escapes. Such subterranean passages radiate out from Southill House, an early 18th-century manor house at Cranmore.

Rumours of secret tunnels linking the house to Doulting were common among the inhabitants there, but the existence of such was proved in the early part of the 19th century, when the new front façade was added. A Victorian servant, Edwin Cox, wrote that labourers working the grounds found an underground passage that was big enough to drive a haycart through. A second tunnel was discovered thereafter, and both led to the cellars.

Cox was himself persuaded by the owners to explore the passageway with the offer of a small sum of money, and so he bravely lowered himself through the opening into the vaulted stone tunnel and dropped 7ft to the floor. This was despite the story that a previous owner had walked dreadfully after death and so 12 parsons had been called to the house to perform a ritualistic exorcism that banished the ghost to the tunnel.

Cox, however, found only furniture and other household debris. In the gloom of the cellar, lit only by his flickering candle, perhaps he dismissed the stories of the ghost; or perhaps it merely lurked in a different part of the underground network. For a larger, labyrinthine network of tunnels was suggested when, in 1998, a cow fell into a third tunnel, and perhaps there are more as yet undiscovered.

'HIS GHOSTSHIP HAS EVIDENTLY BEEN LAID!'

There was much excitement in Shepton Mallet over a ghost, according to the *Western Antiquary* in 1887.

The scare started when rumours spread that a 'ghost' had been seen in the Bowlish Meadows at a point known as the Five Trees. It was being rumoured that over the past week a 'white indistinct object, floating about 3ft from the ground' had been seen by numerous people, including some brewery men whose truthfulness was doubted by those who scoffed at the story. The phantasm apparently moved rapidly and disappeared near a hayrick, but those who saw it searched the hedgerows without success.

Huge crowds began to gather at the meadow, and on the Thursday night there were chaotic scenes when word spread among the crowd that the ghost had been seen to disappear near the hayrick again.

People in the crowd surged towards the hayrick and proceeded to smash it to pieces and the police had to be called to restore order. Some remained until 11 o'clock at night, but the spirit did not materialize again. On the Friday some 200 people gathered, but again the spirit did not appear, and so the local newspaper commented that 'his ghostship has evidently been laid as it did not appear. In all probability the apparition is simply an optical delusion.'

THE UNINHABITABLE COTTAGE

In Frederick Hancock's *The Parish Of Selworthy* (1897) he writes that 'in a hill country parish lying in a fold of the Brendon Hills' there was, in his time, a cottage beside a large wood that was vacated by tenant after tenant on account of strange ghostly phenomena that plagued it. Locally they said that many years earlier a Jewish pedlar had vanished after leaving an inn, and afterwards the owner of the cottage and his wife had obtained an unknown source of wealth. A long time afterwards a quantity of bones were found beneath the outhouse.

Strange and indescribable sounds had prevented many a tenant from getting any sleep, and one observed the figure of an unknown man sitting near the chimney corner who faded from view before his very eyes as he approached. One night, this tenant's wife had unlocked the door, but found that an invisible force from inside held it fast shut, although she knew that the farm was empty. A keeper watching the cottage from the adjoining woodland saw, to his terror, 'a mysterious light suddenly appear, and from the light a figure, huge, white and terrible of aspect, develop, from which the man fled shrieking and demented.'

HAUNTED TOURIST ATTRACTIONS

Some of the county's premier tourist attractions are haunted, often by the great and the good. It is famously repeated that Leigh Woods at Abbot's Leigh — commanding a spectacular view of the Avon Gorge and the Clifton Suspension Bridge — is haunted by the bridge's designer, Isambard Kingdom Brunel. Brunel died in 1859, famously never seeing the completion of his landmark bridge, and now they say that his ghost has been seen on many occasions, his side-whiskered person wearing the clothes that everyone recognises him by: high trousers, waistcoat, high collar, long coat and tall stovepipe hat. They say that he gazes at the bridge, before vanishing as he begins to walk towards it. Incidentally, this spot is also believed to be haunted by the spirit of a mysterious young man who walks sadly through the woodland as though towards the bridge, before disappearing. The bridge, unfortunately, has a reputation for suicides, and it has been suggested to me that the ghost is that of a young man who leapt off the bridge in 1999. One of the stories about the bridge, as told to me by a resident of Banwell, is that more than once in the Victorian era ladies who jumped to their death were saved when the wind caught their dresses and turned them into a 'parachute' that set them down in the mud of the shallows, where officers in rowing boats arrested them. This actually happened; Sarah Ann Henley's life was saved in 1885 when her billowing skirt and petticoat acted as a parachute. In surviving, she set a world record for the longest fall, of 250ft, and received a marriage proposal while recovering in hospital. According to legend, one woman, however, landed forcefully in the mud and sank into it before anyone could reach her, suffocating rather than drowning. These tragedies are supposedly the reason for horrific screaming heard from Leigh Woods, which whistles through the Avon Gorge as though caught on the wind.

An early photo of the Clifton Suspension Bridge.

Elsewhere, at the fantastically prominent Dunster Castle, this woodland-enshrouded and palatial seat of the Luttrell family is home to many rumours of ghosts and underground passages. Its lofty walls are saturated in conflict and history, and in 1869 there was accidentally found within its walls a grim relic of times past: the remarkable 7ft-tall skeleton of a chained prisoner immured upright in a walled-up oubliette within the guardhouse. Quite what his crime was, we will never know, but he was immobilised by chains and iron grips around his neck, wrists and ankles. The writer Eric R. Delderfield wrote of this in *Exmoor Wanderings* (1956): 'It is one of history's well-kept secrets, for nothing more is known as to who he was, or why he had been done to death in such a manner. Other skeletons were discovered nearby. The astounding fact is that the late Mr G.E. Luttrell used to say that every good gun dog he had would always stop in his tracks and make a wagging exploration at the very point where this gruesome discovery was made.' There are numerous ghosts here, including a mysterious man dressed in green sometimes seen in the old stable block, with the King Charles Bedroom being said to be the most haunted room here. Maxwell Lyte, the master historian of Dunster, also noted in 1909 a room called 'the Spirits Room' in the old castle layout, before the Victorian alterations, that was now called 'the Prynne Dressing Room'. He wrote, 'The inventories of 1741 and 1781 alike mention "the Spirits Room" and the latter shows it to have been situated immediately above the little room at the eastern end of the hall. Although the name has survived to the present time, nothing is known about its origin; Dunster Castle has no ghost.' Curious indeed, then, that Dunster is regarded nowadays as one of the most haunted places in Somerset! And this is a phenomenon that continues to the present day, with many parts of the castle said to be haunted or exuding an oppressive or evil atmosphere.

Dunster Castle c.1890

The Director of the Castle Hotel, Taunton, told me, however, that 'no such "fiddler's room" exists', and that the story was an invention.

Colonel Sir William Luttrell gave the greater part of Dunster Castle to the National Trust in 1976. In fact, in 2010 I was kindly informed by the manager of Dunster Castle and Gardens that 'there is an old rumour that one of the first members of the National Trust staff to live here had part of the building exorcised. I can't confirm this, and it wasn't organised by the National Trust, but it does form part of ghost tours which often get highly overemphasised.'

At the equally prestigious Castle Hotel in Taunton, built on the site of one of the outer gatehouses of the castle, one of the rooms is supposedly plagued by the sound of a mysterious violin playing. The phantom behind this mysterious fiddling is apparently a strange woman who has been seen at the premises, although some have it that she is an entirely different spectre.

Some believe that Farleigh Hungerford Castle, on a knoll beside the River Frome, is haunted by the ghost of Sir Thomas Hungerford, who obtained the castle in 1369. Sir Thomas, one of the earliest speakers of the House of Commons, died in 1398 and was buried within the old chapel of St Leonards. And Combe Sydenham Hall, a privately-owned Elizabethan pile situated in a very deep and narrow vale at Combe Sydenham Country Park in the Brendon Hills, was haunted by the ghost of Sir George Sydenham, a Royalist officer who died in 1596. Every night his ghost rode down the combe sometime between midnight and cockcrow.

At Hinton St George, three miles from Crewkerne, we learn that Hinton House – 'a large and splendid edifice, in the midst of noble woods and extensive parks' – came into the Paulet family after the heiress Elizabeth Deneband married Sir William Paulet. The staircase here is traditionally said to be haunted by a Grey Lady, who some believe to be the heartbroken spectre of one of the daughters of the Paulet lineage. She, according to the story, attempted to elope with a lover of the wrong social class, a man who Lord Paulet ran through with a sword when he caught up with them. Traditional stories like this often attach themselves to ancient manorial seats, and the vague version I was told may, in fact, have been woven around the very mysterious death of 29-year-old Simeon Stuckey, a respected builder of Chard, whose killing in 1830 in a wheat field near 'Earl Poulett's Park' excited much speculation and attention in the area. In the past, one of the rooms here was also believed to have been haunted by the troubled ghost of Frederick Poulett, the 13-year-old youngest son of the earl at the time, who died in the room from a five-day illness in 1808.

The list of haunted places goes on and on. There is hardly a site that does not harbour a ghostly legend of one sort or another. What is immediately apparent is that there is often little to substantiate many ghostly spots, other than a local assumption that 'it is so'. The Victorian public were certainly greatly fascinated with the spirit world; T.F. Thiselton-Dyer's *Spirit World* even notes that the phenomenon could be a selling point. A local advert read, 'To be sold, an ancient Gothic mansion known as Beckington Castle, 10 miles from Bath and two from Frome. The mansion has been closed for some years, having been the subject of proceedings in the Chancery. There are legends of haunted rooms and miles of subterranean passages, affording a fine field of research and speculation to lovers of the romantic.'

But here we must leave our exploration of Somerset's old ghostly legends and move into the 20th century.

CHAPTER 6:

MODERN GHOSTLY ENCOUNTERS

INTRODUCTION

The phenomenon of ghosts is a curious one, taking on as many forms as it does. In the past, folklore seems, in many cases, to have 'created' the ghost it wanted, while today's ghost stories are far more likely to be random, meaningless affairs, often not involving actual sight of a spectre. I ponder why people such as Judge Jeffreys are supposed to be doomed to continually haunt the places of their mischief, while there is no suggestion whatsoever that the early cannibalistic settlers of Cheddar still hang about in ethereal form.

These days, stories are more likely to be anecdotes, very often without the ghost itself having a 'back story', an identity or even a visible presence. For instance, the owners of the Camelot pub in South Cadbury told me in March 2010 that the place had seen no direct paranormal occurrences, only the odd and unnerving phenomena that could not be put down to anything definite: names being called, doors being flung open and chairs tipping over without any reasonable explanation. The owner, David Catton, commented, 'all the activity that happens appears to be friendly and is always witnessed by several people, some of which will still not stay after midnight.' This – without sight of an actual ghost – appears to be the trend more often nowadays, evidencing that the phenomenon of 'ghosts' cannot be easily pigeonholed. I happen to believe that the answer to the riddle of ghosts (excluding poltergeists) seems to lie with the person who actually saw it, by which I mean that ghost hunters could set up camp for 100 years at a place where a ghost had recently been seen and still not see anything. The answer lies exclusively with the person who says they saw it: either they imagined it, misinterpreted something else or they invented it, or else they possess a special ability that the rest of us do not. T.F. Thiselton-Dyer's *Ghost World* records of folk in Somerset that 'a child born in chime-hours [that is, exactly at 12 o'clock at night] will have the power to see spirits.' I wonder how many of those who claim to have seen ghosts were actually born at this time. Or else they do not possess any special ability, but happened to unwittingly be in a specific place at a specific time during which an exact set of million-to-one circumstances – atmospheric, supernatural and cosmic – combined for the ghost to be seen or heard.

These personal observations aside, it is clear that death and the afterlife are such a fixture of the popular imagination that the fascination with ghosts is unlikely ever to leave us, the hereafter being the great unknown that it is. This chapter, which deals with the 20th and 21st centuries, illustrates that the 'ghost' – in all its forms – is still in existence in modern Somerset, with remnants of the old-style ghost story still evident, as well as more modern, random encounters, terrifying in their meaninglessness.

There are even rare instances of technology actually appearing to substantiate the phenomenon of ghosts. In 1990 amateur photographer Reginald Wickens took a famous photograph of Morton House in Frome, where Field Marshal Montgomery had his headquarters from June 1940. The photograph, apart from displaying the low wall of Morton House that fronts onto Rossiter's Hill and its impressive floral decoration, captured the shadow of what appears to be a helmeted and goggled motorcycle rider, who almost seems to be swerving to avoid the photographer. The photograph is an intriguing one, since

Westonzoyland control tower. A Bridgwater resident told me, 'There has also been talk of apparitions around the old tower on the old airfield. I believe that in the past interested people have gone to the tower at night to try and film the "ghosts".'

the explanation that it is the photographer's own shadow falling across the frontage of Morton House does not fully explain the mysterious image. The shadow is too large to be the photographer's, indicating something with a closer proximity to Mr Wickens than his own shadow. Added to this, the position of the sun at the time resulted only in minimum shadow, and there is nothing behind the head of the 'person' that could accommodate a shadow. There was no possibility of a double exposure. Motorcycle riders had often been dispatched from Morton House and Mr Wickens learned that, of these, three had been killed in accidents — including one who had swerved into a wall and been killed at the very spot where Mr Wickens had been standing when he took the photograph.

Above all, this chapter illustrates that in Somerset and Bristol some things never change, and the love of ghostly stories is one of them.

PHANTOM FOOTSTEPS AT NAILSEA COURT

In 1916 the romantic authoress Barbara Cartland was living at Nailsea Court, a huge, rambling 15th-century house and gardens south-west of Nailsea itself. The house was very old and contained much antique furniture and panelling, and the writer often observed that as she made her way up the staircase she appeared to be accompanied by the clump of footsteps that either fell on the stairs before her or behind her. No figure, however, was ever seen.

One night while in her bedroom she became terrified by the sounds of footsteps slowly thumping up the stairs as though making their way to the bedroom door. The footfalls sounded as though one of the limbs was injured, and in her terror Ms Cartland began to pray in a trembling voice. At this, the ghostly footsteps halted outside her bedroom door. The notorious Major Wade, who took an active part in the Monmouth Rebellion and proved a false friend to his associates, at one time inhabited the court. But Ms Cartland was later to learn that a wounded Cavalier had supposedly managed to stagger back to Nailsea Court after a confrontation during the English Civil War, where he then died, and this is to whom she ascribed the phantom footfalls. Shortly before her death in 2000, Dame Barbara Cartland granted *The Scotsman* an interview in which she described Nailsea Court as 'the most haunted house in England.' She even went to the trouble of having the house blessed by the local rector during her time there.

GHOST OF A FUTURE KING

At the end of World War One a lady visiting a friend who lived near South Cadbury had a baffling experience. Taking herself for a walk, she had, to her surprise, seen an old and striking house stood alone in the middle of a field, together with a man and a little boy who stood before the building. The pair appeared to be wearing clothes from a different century, although the woman could not decide which era; moreover, strangely the boy appeared to be of higher standing than the man. As she looked at this pair, wondering why she had not noticed this place on previous visits, both the man and the boy simply faded from view, although the building remained.

Later, the lady quizzed her hostess as to possible explanations for this mystery, but received none. Even more puzzling, the next time she visited the field the house itself had disappeared. A subsequent investigation into the archives of the lady's friend's family, however, suggested that during the civil war of 1141-1153 the young Prince Henry had been sent to Somerset for safety. He had stayed with a loyal supporter of Empress Matilda, who had lived near Cadbury Fort, although the actual location of this safe house had been lost to the ages.

For some reason, the woman appeared to have been granted the privilege of seeing not only a ghost – and a ghost of the future King Henry II at that – but also, somehow, the ghost of an entire house as well. The story was told to ghost hunter Christina Hole and featured in her *Haunted England* (1941).

PHANTOMS OF BARDON HOUSE

According to the Somerset Archaeological and Historical Society's *Proceedings (Vol. 92-96)*, whose representatives obtained a visit to historic Bardon House at Washford in 1947, with permission from the owners at the time, Mr and Mrs E. Collier, there were multiple ghosts to be found at this 15th-century building. The Colliers attested that ghosts would emerge at any time and any place, walking through walls, but causing no trouble – for they were the 'phantom replay'-type spectres. One of the phantom manifestations consisted of the delicate tinkling of a piano playing after dark that could not be tracked down, and it was said that this was the ghost of Maria, widow of Robert Leigh esq of Bardon, who died at Taunton in September 1828. Maria Bourget was born a native of Berlin, but married and settled with Robert Leigh in 1770, bearing five sons and one daughter; Maria is believed to have been a very musical lady, often performing for her children. Sometimes, the ghostly music took the form of plaintive harpsichord strains. There was also another ghost here, or at least she was assumed to be a different ghost: 'an old lady with white hair and wearing a black silk dress of an antique fashion appearing in the passages after dark.' She bore a 'sorrowful countenance' and the rustling of her dress identified her presence.

The allegations that Bardon House are haunted go back as far as 1909, when the *Bardon Papers* explained that the ghost of the deceased Sir Robert might be seen wandering about the drive with a head – 'not his own' – under his arm at midnight. The noise of his carriage could also be discerned.

THE GREY LADY OF YATTON CHURCH

Many of the stories in this chapter are little more than anecdotes: brief, fleeting glimpses of some wraith, often without any identification of the ghost, nor any real explanation. It is often the simplest of encounters that impresses the most, the lack of sensationalism somehow creating a weird paradox that makes the 'supernatural encounter' more believable. Within the 14th and 15th century-Church of St Mary at Yatton, with its highly decorated south porch, they say that the ghost of Lady Isobel Newton moves about in the de Wyck aisle in the south transept, where there are two elliptic arches over two ancient effigies of an old man and woman that supposedly represent two of the early de Wyck family. The *Bristol Observer* ran an article in February 1952, in which a parish clerk claimed to have heard footsteps echoing around the aisle, before seeing a greyish phantom woman moving slowly about the white-marble altar tomb.

THE WOMAN IN THE MIST

To the east of Bicknoller, Bicknoller Hill was purportedly haunted by a phantom referred to as 'the Woman in the Mist'. Somerset folklorist Ruth Tongue observed in 1965, 'She has been seen in recent years, and like the Scottish Blue Hag she herds the red deer. Like her, too, she is sometimes reported as an old, frail crone and sometimes as a great misty figure...' This hunched-over old woman was sometimes seen to be gathering sticks, but she always simply melted away in the mist before the eyes of any witnesses. She was seen face-to-face in 1920 and also in the 1950s. Interestingly, Bicknoller Hill is the site of another ancient settlement, known as Trendle Ring, and these Iron Age seats of habitation are often historically supposed to be haunted, or otherwise the subject of other legends.

GHOSTS OF THE ROAD

In November 1966 the *Bristol Post* reported a now oft-repeated supernatural encounter experienced by Jake Thomas and his son, who had been riding a motorbike one night along the A38 south-west of Bristol. As they cruised via the three artificial drinking water reservoirs called the Barrow Tanks (at Barrow Gurney), their headlamp fell on a woman up ahead who appeared to be crossing the road; she stopped in the centre, as though allowing the motorbike right of passage, but then suddenly walked into the path of the bike. Mr Thomas and his son hit nothing, however; they apparently drove right through her! Later, Mr Thomas learned that the stretch of road was haunted by the ghost of a young woman nicknamed the Lady of Barrow Gurney. The speculation was that she had been killed in a motorcycle accident many years before.

The woman is said to wear a white coat, and Mr Thomas' story is atypical of an encounter with this mysterious person; the exact spot where numerous motorists slammed on their brakes to avoid her is rumoured to be denoted by multiple skid marks on the road surface, evidence of many vehicles slewing to a violent halt. Modern folklore, much repeated, has it that this stretch of road, which skirts the northern fringe of Somerset before dipping at Bridgwater towards Taunton, is very haunted. Nearer Taunton, it was a strange grey-haired man in a soaking-wet long, grey overcoat who was reported to be mysteriously appearing in the centre of the road, according to Michael Goss' authoritative book on such phenomena, entitled *The Evidence For Phantom Hitchhikers* (1984). After this spectre had been blamed for a number of near-accidents, and having been seen most recently in 1970, press coverage prompted a lorry driver named Harry Unsworth to reveal his own bizarre encounter with what was presumably the same ghost, only 12 years earlier in 1958. Mr Unsworth had encountered this person on numerous occasions, usually spotting him out in a rainstorm and making his way along the A38 with a torch. He would sometimes give the man a lift for some four miles, but found him dismal company, for the passenger would gloomily recount stories of road accidents, which was not a very cheery topic for a lorry driver at 3 o'clock in the morning, especially when his passenger could barely conceal his smirk. In November 1958 Mr Unsworth again stopped to pick up the man, but after dropping him off was told by the stranger that there was luggage he wished to collect, and then would Mr Unsworth mind taking him to a new destination? Unsworth agreed, but after waiting for the man to return for a while he lost patience and drove off. Three miles into his journey, to his utter astonishment, he encountered the man in the road once more, having somehow traversed three miles on foot in some 20 minutes (Mr Unsworth was sure that no other vehicle could have collected him). This time he refused to stop his lorry for this creepy figure, but was forced to do so when the man in the overcoat made a suicidal leap into the path of his lorry. There was no collision, but Mr Unsworth stopped anyway; in the road he found the man gesticulating as though insane, before the figure then turned away and appeared to abruptly vanish!

I do remember hearing, many years ago now, that a woman was run off the road in the early 1990s at Rumwell by a strange man in a raincoat flashing a torch at her oncoming car, who she could not find when she furiously left her damaged vehicle to remonstrate with him. The story is a classic and oft-repeated modern tale of urban legend proportions, and writer Michael Goss logged another strange case that is now also well known. In 1977 the constabulary at Frome Police Station were forced to concede that, 'We have had people coming here in a state of virtual hysteria,' in connection with alleged encounters with a phantom hitchhiker who rumour said was haunting the area. On 4 August that year it was reported in the *Bath And West Evening Chronicle* that a man in a highly agitated state had recently experienced a bizarre occurrence on the Frome Road, between Nunney and Critchill; he had stopped to give a lift to a youngish-looking man aged between 30 and 40 who wore a checked sports jacket. The stranger accepted the lift, but was little company, asking to be taken to Nunney Catch (south of Nunney); his most telling comment other than this was that it was cold. The stranger was sat in the back seat and the car doors were locked, yet somewhere en route the driver found that a conversation-starter went unanswered and that no one was sharing the car with him. This frightening experience is what led him to Frome Police Station, where he was, understandably, breathalysed with negative results. The man was so worried that his strange passenger had fallen out of the car (although he knew that this could not have happened) that a team of police officers were sent to comb the hedges at the roadside.

The same driver – incredibly – encountered the same man some time after. On this second occasion the driver merely found the hitcher standing in the middle of the road and swerved to avoid colliding with him, crashing his car in the process. Of course, as he staggered from his vehicle the road was now clear...

This 'ghost' had become local legend, even before its widespread publicity in August, when a local building society manager charged with organising Queen Elizabeth II's Silver Jubilee in June 1977 formed vigilante patrols to keep the ghost away from the festivities! The affair was a publicity stunt, the vigilantes finding only a white sheet with a huge, painted grin that had been hung from some trees by local pranksters, but it does indicate why 'the hitcher' is now one of Frome's most well-known ghostly urban myths.

Although this gentleman's appearance would seem to make him a relatively modern ghost, the phantom gypsy girl who I have been told drifts in front of drivers along the A363 at Sally-in-the-Woods, Bathford, seems to be from a different century; at any rate, she is deemed responsible in urban legend for the excessive number of car accidents along this stretch of road. The accident rate is not in doubt, but whether the cause is supernatural is debatable, although the road has been notorious for decades as a black spot. I have also heard that the eponymous 'Sally' was a young gypsy girl who was slain long ago, although there are not really any specifics.

Some may remember that another phantom girl was reported in September 1999 as having appeared on the B3114 in the vicinity of Herons Green Bay, Chew Valley Lake, startling drivers who feared that she would walk in front of their car. A number of people claimed to have seen her, describing her as being about 14 years old with shoulder-length hair and a Victorian-style dress with billowing sleeves. Witnesses observed that the conditions when she was spotted were usually dismal, making it all the more unlikely that this was an actual young girl that was being seen. She has been named the 'Lady of the Lake', due to her appearances beside the waters of the bay. Chew Valley Lake is a man-made landmark, owned by Bristol Water and providing much of the drinking water for the city. The lake was created in 1956, a defunct village called Moreton being submerged by the water in the process, and it is suggested that the young girl was, in life, an inhabitant of that place who is still trying to make her way home after suffering an accidental death some 100 or so years ago at the early Georgian era Stratford Corn Mill.

Perhaps the most unnerving road ghost hereabouts is the one I was told of by a resident of Banwell: 'On the moors near Wick St Lawrence…there is a little bridge that apparently people have seen a body on. They only see the body at the last minute, which makes people crash or stop quickly, and when they get out to see if the person is okay, the body disappears; it happens during the day and at night.'

Strange as they are, ghosts of the road are not a phenomenon that came with the automobile. Frederick Hancock's *The Parish Of Selworthy* (1897) speaks of an incident in the Brendon Hills 'some years ago', in which a woman was being driven home from dinner in a gig late one evening when the party came across a group of prettily-dressed children dancing in the road. It was a bright summer's night, and the gentlewoman pressed her driver to take care when passing the children, but the merry group merely faded away into nothing before the eyes of the astonished lady and her driver, even as he slowed the horses down.

THE PHANTOM MONK OF BRISTOL CATHEDRAL

Curiously, one of Bristol's most famous ghosts is also one of its most mundane; perhaps it is the setting of the magnificent Bristol Cathedral that has led to the spirit capturing the public imagination. The cathedral – more properly, The Cathedral Church of the Holy and Undivided Trinity – is small and low for such a building, its design accordingly described in the 19th century as '…little more than half a cathedral; the nave, according to some, having never been built, and according to others, destroyed and never rebuilt.' This should not detract from the fact that the cathedral is an exceptionally impressive building, which owes its origins to Robert Fitzharding, Mayor of Bristol, who *c.*1148 completed a church and monastery for Augustinian canons on the rising ground near the harbour. This place was dissolved in 1539 and the cathedral as we see it subsequently grew out of the remaining portions.

An early photograph of Bristol Cathedral.

This site is famously haunted by a ghostly monk in a grey habit, who appears to have first been written of by Margaret Royal in a short volume entitled *Bristol Ghosts* (1977). He is now one of the city's best-known spirits, featured in many a ghost hunt. This spectral figure has been seen to make his solemn way to the adjacent library, which was built on the foundations of the ordinary priory, where it dematerializes at the section of wall in the side of the building displaying the clear outline of a long-bricked up doorway. In the library this figure has also been seen in a studious disposition — always at about half past four in the afternoon. Numerous subsequent writers have observed a discrepency in his appearance: the habit of the Augustinan monks was black, and so the Grey Monk of Bristol Cathedral appears not to have been one of their brethren. Six canons were inducted here on 11 April 1148 as the first thereof, but maybe the ghost is that of an almoner, or perhaps a visiting Cistercian or Carmelite friar, or simply an Augustinian monk wearing a different-coloured habit. Or perhaps, down the centuries, he has just 'faded' somewhat!

GHOSTS OF BRISTOL

In July 2010 a resident of Weston-super-Mare posited this all-encompassing statement as a truism: 'Obviously, there will be loads of ghosts around Bristol that relate to the slave trade. Bristol was one of the main ports, the SS Great Britain and the Matthew are based there. I imagine that the SS Great Britain will have some ghost stories.' Bristol, with its population of over one million, is both an ancient and modern city: lively, contemporary, fashionable, and yet still deeply steeped in its own history. It grew up around its harbour on the River Avon and, as a result, from the 10th century onwards it became a flourishing commercial port of such importance that it was granted county status in 1373, becoming distinct from both Somerset and Gloucestershire. Bristol became internationally famous in 1497 when John Cabot – a Genoese navigator who settled in Bristol 10 years earlier – returned in triumph from the lands of Nova Scotia. On 24 June Cabot planted the flag of the Tudor monarch King Henry VII there after an expedition in his ship, the Matthew, to establish new trade routes and seek out new stocks of fisheries. But Bristol has seen it all, from the triumphs of exploration and suspension bridge-building to the tragically dramatic; the year following the city's joy at Cabot's endeavours, Bristol was the scene of mass arrests and burnings for heresy, and the city has also seen shipwrecks, slave trading, piracy, siege and barbaric executions (in 1326 Queen Isabella ordered 90-year-old Hugh Spencer strung up and beheaded, his remains being chopped into pieces so that 'the dogges did ete it', as part of a power struggle with her husband, King Edward II). The great and the noble played out their battles here during the English Civil War; marauding armies ran amok, taverns exploded with appalling casualties, and even the launching of a ship could occasion mass drowning, such as occurred in 1639. Sensational crimes were committed and ferocious riots were fought here, with the city in a state of revolution in 1831. Little wonder that Bristol has so many ghosts.

Clifton is one of the most haunted parts of the city. The Edwardian spiritualist and ghost hunter Elliot O'Donnell grew up here, and his *Confessions Of A Ghost Hunter* (1928) recalls some of the legends he heard during his school years, including the rumour that Durdham Down was haunted by 'the shadowy figure of a white-faced child', as well as weird screaming noises. The ghost was said to be that of Melinda Payne, who had been murdered in the 1850s and buried beside a narrow pathway that led to the River Avon called the Gulley. Of the most haunted places was a vacant house 'in a terrace, not far from the suspension bridge, and it probably dated back to somewhere about 1780.' The last tenant – probably *c.*1900 – had encountered a 'lady dressed all in black standing in one of the rooms. She had her back to him and, obviously unaware of his presence, was arranging her hair under her hat.' She simply vanished before the startled man. His two young sons saw the lady in black standing in the doorway holding the hand of a ghostly little boy on one occasion and a strange ominous cry appeared to pass through a room. Perhaps the most disturbing thing that haunted this building, according to O'Donnell, was 'A strange looking figure [that] was in the act of mounting the staircase leading to the floor immediately overhead. Its back being towards [the witness], she could not see its face, but the thing, as a whole, gave the impression that it was very evil and grotesque, more like some huge, horrible ape than a human being. It went up the stairs two or three at a time, and she heard it open and shut the bathroom door and then bound about all over the floor...'

It is common knowledge that the historic half-timbered Llandoger Trow in King Street, dated 1664 and named after the Welsh barges that docked nearby, is supposedly haunted by the ghost of what is commonly said to be a lame little boy. The tavern was reportedly built with the profits from slave trading, and its picturesque overhanging upper stories hide many rumours of smuggling and subterranean passages reaching to the water's edge. The ghostly little boy appears to be a 20th-century phenomenon, his appearances consisting of dragging and thumping footfalls that make their way up the staircase late at night, and although there is no conclusive indication of who he might have been, his celebrity is such that nowadays the Llandoger Trow is actively sought out by ghost hunting television projects. The ghost hunter Andrew Green wrote in *Ghosts Of Today* (1980) that the little boy used to be seen 'in the yard near a wall, in what is assumed to be his bedroom over the Old Bar, and on the stairs. A couple who used to live in

KING-STREET.

part of the building saw the ghost of the lad slowly moving up the stairway on two occasions some years ago.' He apparently carries an enamel pail or bucket. In 2009, on the occasion of another overnight ghost hunt here, the *Evening Post* of 4 August quoted the receptionist at the adjoining Premier Inn as saying, 'The ghost of the little boy is not the only strange thing around here. The original pub, the Jacobean Room, is really creepy, and so is the snug and the cellar. Upstairs, where some staff members live, people say the electrics are always really funny, with lights going on and off for no reason. The upstairs toilets are a bit freaky too.'

The parkland of the Oldbury Court Estate in Fishponds is believed to be haunted by the ghost of a former Dowager Duchess of Beaufort, who (according to tradition) died after being hit by a bolt of lightning on her horse on Pur Down. The legend declares that she haunts this area, retracing a journey to Stoke House, Stapleton, the historic seat of the duchess, and this ghost was actually witnessed in the park – partially obscured by the treeline – by an 18-year-old ghost hunter in the grounds of Blackberry Hill Hospital, according to the *Bristol Evening Post* of 19 February 1965. Some think that this ghostly lady was, in life, Elizabeth Somerset, who died in 1799, although it is likely that the tradition relates to an earlier duchess. One of the ponds hereabouts that earned Fishponds its name was filled in *c.*1800 by the duchess at the time, after a little girl lost her life beneath the water; perhaps the duchess' pain at the tragedy has caused her to drift this stretch of the River Frome.

At Brislington, the 18th-century folly known as the Black Castle, or Arno's Castle, was completed *c.*1760 by William Reeve, a Quaker copper smelter. This black-and-white 'sham castle' is set near the cemeteries of Arno's Vale, and it was famously written by Sir Horace Walpole in 1776 that 'I took it for the Devil's Cathedral.' Although it may have started out as a stable block, laundry and servants' quarters for the lord of the manor, during its lifetime it has been owned by a member of the slave-trading Tonge family and has functioned as an antiques showroom, a social club and a public house. At the time of writing (early 2009), its future is uncertain. There are reports that its chapel on the first floor of the west tower is haunted by the ghost of a slain nun. According to popular lore, she also haunts the top of the castle's highest tower, and some believe her to be 'headless.' Whoever she is, she has a long history here, but there are other phenomena too: there is a little girl who has been seen to vanish, and the place has also suffered random poltergeist activity that seems removed from these actual 'ghosts'. Nearby, the corridors of the prestigious Arnos Manor Hotel – also Reeve's brainchild – are allegedly haunted by the ghost of a young nun (the same one, I wonder?), who was bricked up in the structure after falling pregnant. This was when the place was a Roman Catholic convent in the mid-1800s and it is repeated that builders discovered her skeleton in the aftermath of a bombing raid by the Luftwaffe on 16-17 March 1941. I have been told that she haunts the place because her bones were simply heaped in with the rest of the debris, rather than being properly interred. The *Evening Post* has reported several investigations here.

Back at Fishponds, the *Evening Post* caused great excitement in late 2008 when it reported 'A phantom nurse dressed in a World War II uniform has been spotted wandering the corridors of an ex-hospital building in Bristol. The spectre – dressed in a white headscarf and with a cardigan draped across her shoulders – has been seen by people at The Vassall Centre...[staff at Aspects and Milestones] claim the spirit moves about the office wearing a white apron with a grey gown and pushing a trolley. They also say they have felt her touching their shoulders and moving diaries around, and have heard her rattling blinds and felt her pushing against doors they are trying to open...'

At the time of writing, it is unclear who this phantom nurse is supposed to have been in her lifetime. Although the *Telegraph's* full report on this story could quote no actual witnesses to her visible presence, many knew of her, and instances were cited of freezing drops in temperature that were supposed to be the work of the ghost. The story is an intriguing one, not least in that it is modern folklore in the making, but it also evidences that, for all its modern trappings, Bristol still loves stories of ghosts and superstition...and who knows, maybe the ghostly nurse will one day appear and be caught on a mobile phone camera, for example, putting everybody in no doubt that she is not simply a modern urban myth.

KING JOHN'S HUNTING LODGE

Axbridge is an ancient town that became a borough before 1066. Its hub is a spacious square, off which there are many small, old streets. The High Street contains several historic buildings, including the white, timber-fronted King John's Hunting Lodge, a mediaeval building that has no confirmed connection with King John – but which does, apparently, harbour an Elizabethan ghost. An entry in the museum diary for 22 August 1978 suggests that a phantom lady was spotted sitting in the famous Stuart-era Mayoral Chair, wearing a striking white Elizabethan-style dress – although how or why she sits in a chair built after her

own era is a mystery. The museum is also haunted by a ghostly tabby cat that has been seen on numerous occasions in the panelled room on the first floor, where it materializes through a closed door and lies down, curling its tail round itself in the normal manner of sleeping cats, before slowly fading from view.

King John's Hunting Lodge, Axbridge.

PHANTOM TRANSPORT

Rumours of phantom transport seem to go back almost as far as transport itself. As long ago as *c*.1895, the area near Porlock called Bossington Three Cross was held to be the haunt of a phantom coach, and another coach and horses was supposed to haunt the lanes about Hartrow Gate on the Taunton road. This was according to folklorist E.O. Begg in 1945, and based on an informant recalling her parents and neighbours talking about the mystery. The coach at Bossington was driven by a headless coachman and it had been spotted by the brother of Begg's informant one night, sweeping past him and disappearing in the lane.

There are, of course, also strange stories of phantom tall ships and galleons that have been glimpsed on foggy days off the coast of north Somerset or in the Bristol Channel. A number of people watched a 'ghost plane' dive into the sea off Minehead in 1965, prompting a concentrated air and sea rescue operation. But nothing was found, and the writer Ivan T. Sanderson noted in *Invisible Residents* (1970), 'It was said that there was "something abnormal about it. It did not seem to be distinct, but had a misty appearance about it." There was no mist or fog about.' This is reminiscent of a bizarre report logged with the Ministry of Defence in 2009 by a witness who saw, in the early hours of 25 June, something very strange over Minehead. The thing 'looked like a highly-lit aeroplane with wings. It was heading north-north-west to south-south-east. It was visible for 20 seconds then changed direction quickly and dropped out of the sky or disappeared…'

So the ghostly vehicle is not a new phenomenon. And, if we can stretch credulity to believe that 'ghosts' are real, then the appearance of inorganic objects in phantom form adds another confusing dimension to the already-multilayered mystery of what ghosts actually are. There is, nonetheless, said to be a ghost train in Somerset. In September 1857 a collision between two steam locomotives on the 'Old Mineral Line' near Watchet killed three people. Apparently (so I was told), if you can navigate your way to the old shell of the winding house, climb atop it and look in the direction of Kentsford Farm (i.e. towards Watchett), you can hear the squeal of screaming brake pads followed by the thunderous sound of a collision.

GHOSTLY THEATRICS

No theatre in Britain is complete without its age-old rituals that superstition says must be performed to ensure a good show. Quite often, the appearance of the famous ghostly lady dressed in black at the Theatre Royal in King Street, Bristol, is judged to be a positive omen – at least there is no suggestion that she is harmful in any way.

The theatre opened on 30 May 1766, with much pomp and ceremony: the first plays were *The Conscious Lovers* and *The Miller of Mansfield*, with the prologue and epilogue provided by David Garrick, the foremost actor of the day. It is claimed that the ghost has been glimpsed from different vantage points in the theatre, even by actors from the stage, and her presence is felt in many places. It is said that she wears a long, black dress with a stiff collar and her hair is pulled back in a bun. Some originally thought her to be the famous 18th-century tragedienne Sarah Siddons, who performed at the Theatre Royal during a spell away from the capital; as early as 1961 it was observed in a theatrical periodical that 'the ghost of Sarah Siddons can still be seen in her old dressing room.' But others now think the ghost to be Sarah, the wife of William Macready, who took over management of the theatre in 1819. In 1824 Sarah Macready introduced three orphans onto the stage while a search was being undertaken for the children's parents, who had fatally fallen into the lock of Cumberland Basin in the dark. She read on stage a poetical address as part of a fundraising event and helped to raise a trust of £500 for the children – no small sum in those days. If the ghost is that of Mrs Macready, then surely she does not leave harm in her lavender-scented wake following an ethereal appearance. Whoever she is, she has been seen and sensed for decades now. Sarah Macready would seem the more likely candidate, given the years of tireless effort she put into maintaining the theatre following her husband's death.

There is a more famous ghost at the Theatre Royal in Sawclose, Bath, however. Here, the ghost is the legendary Grey Lady, supposedly seen on her own in the so-called 'Haunted Box', a misty, grey figure, although distinctive-looking with feathers in her headdress and elegant long, white gloves. Not unlike the ghost of the Theatre Royal, Bristol, she leaves behind a beautiful scent of jasmine and cold chills in the air at various points in the theatre. It is often repeated that Dame Anna Neagle, the popular British stage actress, allegedly saw her during a performance of *The Dame Of Sark* on 23 August 1975, but quite who the Grey Lady is not clear. The theatre's origins date to 1705, during the time of the great Bath 'master of ceremonies', Richard 'Beau' Nash, who transformed Bath into the most fashionable town in England. The gist of the legend is that she was, in life, a married actress who began a liaison with a gentleman who occupied a particular box (the so-called Haunted Box, or Grey Lady Box, where she sometimes appears) while attending her performances regularly. Inevitably, he was slain by the enraged husband in a duel for her hand, and the actress is supposed to have performed one last time on the stage – hiding her anguish – before taking herself to the Garrick's Head Pub next door and placing a noose around her neck. It is either this, or a variation on this theme.

Theatre Royal and Popjoys next door, Bath.

Both the Garrick's Head and the Theatre Royal harbour legends about the spectres of these star-crossed lovers. In truth, the origin of the Grey Lady is as misty as her own appearance and she could be anyone, from a theatregoer, to an actress, to the wife of a former manager. As for the famous 'duel', I cannot seem to pin down a historic reference to it and it appears to be folklore, although this can never be certain. Of duels in Bath, we learn that 'Beau' Nash, threatened by the Public Gaming Act of 1745, which aimed to restrict gambling and gambling houses, attempted to make Bath's betting society respectable. He banned swords and even smoking in some establishments, although we do know that his predecessor as master of ceremonies, a man named Webster, was slain while duelling in the Orange Grove in 1704. Of the Theatre Royal incident, I should imagine that it is possible that the drama on stage gave rise to the legend off it. This is not to suggest that the Grey Lady herself is a myth though – I have been told that the Grey Lady was spotted as recently as the 1920s, by no less a personage than the Russian ballerina Anna Pavlova, who apparently glimpsed her in the box. The theatre's own website actively promotes this ghost.

These days, the famous Ghost Walks in Bath begin and end at the Garrick's Head, where we learn that successive landlords all smelled the familiar scent of the Grey Lady's jasmine in the cellars. On the other side of the Theatre Royal is the famous Popjoys Restaurant, named for a former resident – Beau Nash's beloved mistress Juliana Popjoy. There is a story that just before Christmas 1975 a man alone in the bar upstairs was astounded to see the ghost of Juliana herself walk into the room, wearing the clothes of an elegant Regency lady, and she actually sat down next to him on the settee before disappearing.

GHOSTS OF AQUAE SULIS

Bath is the most complete and best-preserved Georgian city in Britain. It is also one of Britain's oldest cities, famous since Roman times for its warm mineral springs that originate in the eastern Mendips, collecting mineral salts on the way, and reaching the surface again at Bath. The Roman camp established here c. AD 44 utilized these springs and later became a prosperous spa, Aquae Sulis. Visiting the famous Roman baths is a marvellous experience and offers perhaps the best glimpse anywhere of what life might have been like for the well-to-do Roman elite in Britain. The remains are remarkably intact and the life of that Roman community is vividly brought to life. In AD 56 it was written of the West Baths, 'The picture is not complete without some quarrelsome fellow, a thief caught in the act, or the man who loves the sound of his own voice – not to mention those who jump in with a tremendous splash.'

Despite its proximity to Gloucestershire, Bath's countryside identifies it immediately as part of the West Country, with its splendid stone-fronted houses reflected in many of the surrounding villages. It is perhaps no surprise that Bath is traditionally regarded as one of the most haunted places in Britain.

According to folklore, one of the most dramatic ghostly encounters is a spectral replay of events on 18 March 1772, when 21-year-old Richard Sheridan, destined to become one of England's greatest playwrights, collected 16-year-old Elizabeth Anne Linley from 11 Royal Crescent in the dead of night, prior to their elopement to France. Elizabeth was reputedly an extremely beautiful girl and talented stage singer, who was daughter of the Orchestra Director at the Pump Rooms. It was over Elizabeth's honour that Sheridan fought two duels with a contemporary named Captain Thomas Mathews, the second of these at Kingsdown, which saw the two men badly wounded and brawling violently, striking each other with the hilts of their swords, the blades having broken in the conflict. Sheridan was lucky not have been killed in the encounter, and perhaps the romance attached to the saga is the reason why a phantom coach and snorting horses that has been heard – or even seen – in the elegant curve of Royal Crescent is believed to be linked to all this.

There was excitement in 1975 when it was reported that a television rental showroom in Bath might be experiencing a poltergeist. Richard Lever, the owner, told reporters that doors were slamming shut by themselves and the televisions would jump channel or switch themselves on or off – this last requiring the physical push of a button. Lights would also switch themselves off, and electricians were puzzled as to the cause of all this; then Mr Lever found out that a previous occupant named Walker (who had died in the house) had apparently had a mania for saving electricity that extended to switching off unnecessary lights and closing doors. Mr Lever told reporters, 'I don't believe in ghosts, but some force here is doing something.'

Ghost hunter Andrew Green found that in the 1970s the hallway and a bedroom of the Beehive Public House in Lansdown Road (now the Grappa Bar) was haunted by a ghost who was seen so clearly that it was possible to provide a very good description of her: she wore 'a happy expression, a mop cap, a bluish-grey gown to the floor, and black, shining shoes.' Apparently friendly, she was usually visible for a couple of seconds before fading away. York Villa, the Georgian villa off London Road, has a staircase where slow, sad footsteps gloomily clump as though someone with a weight on their mind is ascending. Locally they say that two children died of starvation there during the reign of King George III and these were the children of one of Frederick, Duke of York's many mistresses. She left York Villa to plead with the duke when he ended their romance, leaving the children in the care of servants. The servants abandoned the two children, however, leaving one elderly retainer to check on them a week later; he found that they had both died, and the footfalls ascending the stairs are believed to be his: a phantom echo of the moments just before he opened the door and found the pitiful bodies huddled together. The building later became home to Bath Tramways Sports and Social Club.

Gay Street, which leads from the Circus, has long been the subject of infantile sniggers and, predictably perhaps, is rumoured to be haunted by a ghostly figure who has his hair tied in a ponytail and only appears before young men! But by far and away Bath's best-documented ghost is the so-called Man in the Black Hat, who haunts the vicinity of the Assembly Rooms. The Assembly Rooms were the inspiration of John Wood, an architect whose family settled in Bath in 1727 and whose father, another John, was an architect before him; both are feted with having helped to turn the town into a showpiece of Georgian architecture, and the Assembly Rooms were designed by Wood the Younger in 1769 and built two years later. An elegant complex consisting of four main function rooms, the Assembly Rooms played host to the balls of Georgian Bath, which were prestigious social occasions for the great and the good of the day. Although partly destroyed in 1942 by German bombers, the Assembly Rooms have been restored, and display the huge internal arches, high ceilings and low chandeliers typical of the architecture of the era. Today it is a popular venue for wedding ceremonies. It is in the streets outside the Assembly Rooms – Bennett Street and Saville Row – where the ghostly figure has been seen, however, rather more than in its interior. It is the frequency with which he is seen, combined with the clarity, that makes the Man in the Black Hat so plausible. The ghost has caught the attention of some of the leading ghost hunters of the day, including Andrew Green, Peter Underwood and Margaret Royal, all of whom have found reports of him very credible. A very clear encounter with this ghost in Saville Row was reported in the *Bath And Wilts Evening Chronicle* of 16 March 1950, but he has been seen dozens of times since, and possibly for a long period before this. In general,

The Assembly Rooms, Bath.

he is described as being small, thin and stooped, wearing a large, black hat, variously described as a Guy Fawkes-type affair or a Quaker's hat. Some observe him to have breeches and a black cloak, and he invariably vanishes in the street or at the entrance to the Assembly Rooms, although he has been glimpsed inside the premises on occasion as well.

I contacted the National Trust about all this, and was told by the Roman Baths and Pump Room Manager, a person in a position to know, 'The Man in a Black Hat is often referred to in ghost reports as relating in some way to the Assembly Rooms in Bath or its vicinity. There is no substance to the story, although, like so many ghost stories, it is endlessly recycled…The lack of any sensible basis for it does not seem to deter.' But today this phantom is a favourite of Bath's famous Ghost Walk – a rare instance of folklore being seemingly backed up and corroborated by independent witnesses, who in some four instances even sketched the strange figure after the fact. All four drawings are said to tally remarkably. Despite his sceptical stance, it is clear that my informant was at least aware of the Man in the Black Hat's existence, so you will have to make up your own mind.

CORFE'S CHILLING PRESENCE

In 1983 the B. Family moved into a three-storey, stone-built edifice in Corfe, south of Taunton. The place, rather forbidding in appearance, dated to 1780, and had a new house built onto it in 1886 by the-then Taunton Medical Officer of Health, who used the original part of the building as a dispensary, consultancy and surgery. In those days, a surgery meant what it said, and one can only imagine the agonized suffering and blood-spattered floor that must so often have been the scene in that room. After World War One, a new doctor took over the practice, but – so the family heard – may have become unbalanced and hanged himself in the 1930s.

The place had, by 1983, been developed into three adjoining family homes, with the residence that the family moved into being the original part. The surgery had long been converted into the dining room and they were quick to learn that the place had a 'spooky reputation' in the village, although they never noticed anything out of the ordinary other than that their new dining room was always freezing cold, despite whatever was done to warm it up.

In fact, within a few years one or two people had said that they felt inexplicably uncomfortable in the dining room, the strange chill permanently pervading the place. One female lodger, who claimed the psychic gift, refused from the outset to ever go in the dining room and said she 'knew' something horrible had happened there, preferring to eat perched in the kitchen. In 1998 the family decided to convert part of a top-storey bedroom into an en-suite bathroom, the son having long since left. The husband of the family tells me:

'The bedroom is directly above the ground-floor dining room and is on the third floor. The dining room fireplace chimney runs through the bedroom. The first contractor appointed by the bathroom company lasted one day and left without explanation. A new contractor was appointed and began work. Odd things soon began to happen. Fittings would mysteriously disappear, only to turn up in another room, seemingly hidden, and tools would never be in the place they were left. No one else had access to the house, so we were at a loss to explain it. Then one day the fitter was hammering away and suddenly let out a wail of anguish. I was working in my office at the end of the corridor and ran to see what had happened, expecting to find blood flowing. Instead, he was standing ashen-faced and shaking, unable to speak for a few moments. When he calmed a little, he said he had suddenly felt this extreme cold pass by him, and touch his neck, which felt like ice. He said he had never had such a weird and frightening experience in his life, and could not explain it. After prolonged dosages of warm, sweet tea, he felt able to resume, though with some trepidation and with the reassurance that I would stay nearby. Immediately, we discovered that the hammer he had been using was missing. Neither of us could find it, and I suspect he thought I was playing tricks on him. Another hammer was fetched from the van and, upon his return, we both saw the original tool lying right where he thought he had left it. It had definitely not been there a few minutes before!'

The job progressed smoothly from then on, and since the renovation there have been no further complaints about the uncomfortable atmosphere in the dining room, the husband commenting merely, 'We have concluded that whatever had been in the house, no longer is, having taken exception to all that banging and drilling!'

HAUNTED HOSTELRIES

Pubs and inns containing (and even, it has to be said, publicising) their own ghosts are a cultural phenomenon nowadays, and seem to have filled the gap in the market when there were no longer any stately homes left that were unhaunted. But, as we have seen at the Lamb Inn, Bristol, the haunting of inns is not exclusive to the 20th and 21st centuries. A few miles outside Taunton, at Culmhead up in the Blackdown Hills, can be found a small, whitewashed country inn, the mediaeval Holman Clavel Inn, which historically has been famously haunted by a ghost nicknamed 'Old Charlie' or 'Chimbley Charlie'. The Reader's Digest *Folklore, Myths And Legends Of Britain* tells us that he resides on the beam over the fireplace and that he once ruined a dinner party for a visiting farmer who had dismissed him as nonsense, by putting all the dinner things away even as the maid tried to lay the table! The ghost hunter Joseph Braddock observed in 1956 that he still played his mischief on the-then owners, the Phillips family, with one of his favourite tricks being to take a tablecloth and hide it for five weeks, before returning it to where it ought to be, freshly laundered and neatly folded. The phantom is also held responsible for the strange noises that emanate from the inn's famous skittle alley, even when it is locked, but although his appearances are largely limited to poltergeist activity, 'Charlie' does appear to have an actual ghostly presence, for a monk in a white, flowing robe has, on rare occasions, been seen in one of the bedrooms. Every subsequent landlord now knows that if anything goes missing at the inn, then 'Charlie' has appropriated it and it is likely to mysteriously reappear weeks – or even years – later, as though dropped out of some kind of vortex.

There is another well-known haunted hostelry at Chard. Here (at the highest town in Somerset), the Elizabethan interior of the old, gabled Choughs Hotel has been jealously preserved, including its old woodwork and a tombstone in the fireplace that bears an inscription: '*Winifred*'. There is held to be multiple low-key ghostly phenomena here, but the most famous legend about this inn is that it is impossible to take a photograph of the tombstone using a flash – a circumstance that is laid by popular supposition at the door of the mysterious 'Winifred'. The hotel's name, incidentally, is on account of the mortal remains of a chough – or crow-like bird – being kept in a metal box that was passed from one landlord to another. Of the chough, we learn from *Hotel Monthly* (1931), 'The chough [the landlord said], is an extinct bird. There is a picture of it on the sign, but no living creature to compare it with.'

Many pubs now actively promote themselves as having a 'ghost' and the stories are good ones, even if the public has little appetite to discover if the ghosts are real, or just yarns inspired by the consumption of other 'spirits'. On Glastonbury's High Street can be found the ancient George and Pilgrims Hotel, its frontage consisting of mullioned windows, octagonal turrets and niches, and dating back to at least 1489. In June 2010 an administrator at Glastonbury Abbey told me that the inn 'is reported as being haunted.' Formerly known as the George, or Pilgrim's Inn, it has a tradition of a phantom monk, fat and jovial in the traditional Friar Tuck mode, and an elegant lady who, it is suggested, appears to follow him about. One of the curiosities of this place is that it houses a subterranean chamber, reached by a steep flight of steps, in which there is a recess housing a stone seat. In this chamber, it was popularly said that penitents and wayward monks were thrown, to be confined in the dark and up to their knees in water, often for some considerable time. There was also a legend (recorded in Warner's 1826 history of the town) that spoke of a secret tunnel that linked the George to the abbey. This tunnel was so small that it had to be navigated on knees and elbows, emerging into a cellar and then a passage before 'a flight of steps which conducted privately to the abbot's chamber, wherein was a large handsome bedstead, on which King Henry VIII once lay.' Perhaps these two ghosts are linked to some sexual misdemeanour in Tudor times related to this vault, but I understand that there is another ghost here, more modern-looking: a smiling man wearing a blue sports jacket who glows with an ethereal light.

In 1974 the then-landlord of the Fleur de Lys Inn at Norton St Philip was reported to have heard the clanking of iron chains in the ice-cold passage, whereas his wife had seen a shadowy figure walking along a corridor at the historic pub. There is a story that the dog of a previous landlord was left alone in the place, and upon its owner returning the animal was so crazed with terror that it shot out of the door and into the road, only to be killed by a vehicle. Traditionally, they say that the ghost here is of an innocent drinker who was hustled in with a group of Monmouth rebels who were being led through the bar and into an orchard behind the inn, where he was strung up and hanged with the rest of them.

The Wells Journal reported in 1978 that the mediaeval pub called The King Charles Parlour that stood off High Street, Wells, was found by two successive owners to have a ghostly cavalier within. The cellar man had rather matter-of-factly told one owner, 'Oh yes, he's always on the stairs!' At the Ilchester Arms Hotel and Restaurant on Church Street, Ilchester, it was reported in the Yeovil Weekly News of 7 February 1996 that the place had been plagued by mysterious events over the past few months. These included strange rumbling noises like heavy beer barrels being rolled over a flagstone floor, clattering noises like someone at a typewriter, arbitrary disappearances of beer glasses and, most unnervingly, a bed in a closed and empty room that appeared to bear the depressions of having been slept in. And then there was the Wagon and Horses on Bath Road, Peasedown St John, that ghost hunter Andrew Green learned was haunted by a strange man in a black hat, who was apparently forward enough to appear at a woman's bedside, standing and looking directly at her.

I was told by a resident of Goathurst that the George Inn in Middlezoy, dated c.1624, is haunted by the ghost of a murdered former landlady, who was killed 'by a deserter or prisoner of war.' This might be a reference to Emily Bowers, who was strangled there in 1947, and I was informed that a subsequent landlady was born in the house opposite on the night of the killing and subsequently came to believe that the pub toilets were haunted by the dead woman's ghost; she 'was totally convinced' of the phenomenon.

In fact, haunted pubs are now more likely to crop up in local newspapers as the residence of ghosts than churches or castles, and are often reported in the local media as hotspots for paranormal investigators or ghostly sleepovers for charity. On 11 November 2008 it was reported that a paranormal investigation was taking place at the Bell Inn, Buckland Dinham. Here, the landlord told the Western Gazette, 'Something happens most days of the week. There are often unidentified bangs and crashes, a bolted door which opens itself and something that, rather worryingly, lights candles in the middle of the night. It is something I don't feel comfortable with, and have resorted to sleeping in a caravan in the garden on some occasions.' The newspaper was also told that there were three ghosts here, 'including a 15-year-old girl called Emily, who paces the restaurant searching for her dead baby who was buried in the nearby barn. [She is said to have died during childbirth in 1756 aged just 15]. Other visitations include a man sitting at table 10 supping whisky, and a little boy who has been seen many times by diners at table 12.' (Some people have told me that the 'haunted table' is, in fact, number 13.) The Standard and Guardian also reported on these ghosts in 2003, adding the detail that the man at table 10 is elderly and that the cleaners sometimes could not get past him and had to wait for him to leave by which I suppose 'dematerialise' is meant.

Next, it was the turn of the ancient Slab House Inn at West Horrington, near Wells. On 25 August 2009 it was reported that the owners had called in an exorcist, as staff and customers had seen, among other strange phenomena, a little old lady wearing a bonnet, shawl and long, black dress sitting in a wing-backed chair, and also a ghost that appears to have lost its legs; a dark figure in a cape had been glimpsed, although he faded away below the waist, but on another occasion a pair of ghostly legs in black riding boots were seen walking across the kitchen floor, cut off at the knee.

During the research for this book, I visited and contacted literally scores of public houses and inns across Somerset and was told numerous anecdotes. At the 500-year-old Ship and Castle in Congresbury, for instance, one of the directors made a tongue-in-cheek reference to having had 'many conversations

This church carving at Monksilver seems to show a landlord forcing cider down a drunkard's neck.

with my friends that go bump in the night!' But despite the potential business that a resident spook might generate, it seems that some take the phenomenon with a pinch of salt. At the Monkton Inn, West Monkton, the owners told me, 'I'm sorry, there is nothing that we know of at the Monkton that would interest you. You may see a ghost if you have one too many pints of Butcombe, however!'

CAUGHT ON FILM…

In July 2009 a lady from Cheshire contacted the *Yeovil Express* with a strange tale. She and her sister had been staying with friends recently in East Coker, and the paper reported that on the Friday evening the group had been strolling down Longlands Lane. The lane was a narrow, mediaeval affair with high sides and overhanging tree branches, and in this claustrophobic atmosphere the person at the back (they were walking single file) began to feel depressed and hemmed in, convinced that in the gloom something, or someone, was following them.

After turning several times but seeing no one, this woman began to walk backwards, holding up her mobile phone and videoing her route. After the holiday, the sisters viewed the video and, to their astonishment, the footage depicted a 'very tall man wearing a long, hooded cloak!'

HUNTSTILE'S 'WEEPING WOMAN'

Huntstile is a working organic farm between North Petherton and Goathurst, licensed by the Soil Association and producing cereals and herbs for south-west England, and also functioning as a wedding venue and a B&B. Parts of the farmhouse, set in the beautiful, rolling foothills of the Quantocks, date back to 1430, and Lizzie Myers told me a curious tale about the ghost who haunts her family home – that of a young woman who has been nicknamed 'Susannah'.

It seems that Susannah has been around for at least 100 years, but she is not a happy ghost. Several people who have stayed at Huntstile told their astonished hosts that they had been disturbed by the sounds of a girl crying, and the ghost earned the name 'the weeping woman'. Her likely identity, however, was discovered quite recently and in a strange way.

Susannah is, in life, thought to have been Susanna Bruford, who was burnt at Cure Green near Wells on 3 September 1753 for poisoning her husband John, a farmer, at West Monkton. She was but 19 years old, and the pair had only married in March that year before she killed him two months later. Susanna came from 'Huntstile in Chilton', the farmhouse being in the parish of Chilton Trinity at the time.

Lizzie herself moved into Huntstile in 2004, being fascinated by a story that had passed down through generations of the resident Ridout family that 'the last witch to be burned at the stake in England' lived there. Lizzie quickly disproved this myth through research, but some time later, while perusing an article from the *Oxford Journal Of Notes And Queries* (1922) in an attempt to trace her family history, quite unexpectedly she came across a reference to Susanna Bruford and her crime.

Piece by piece, the jigsaw was being put together, but Lizzie was astonished when some years ago a psychic lady stayed at Huntstile and informed her that Susanna was Lizzie's sister from a past life and she had wanted to make contact with her, which was why her ghost had led Lizzie to the journal that told her story. Lizzie told me, 'She [the psychic] also said that Susanna was a beauty and wore a grey silk dress. She said that Susanna had really enjoyed all the parties we had been holding and was much more at peace now her "sister" had returned. The psychic returned a few years later [2008] and told me that Susanna was no longer here; she had finally "found peace and moved on".'

Susannah's weeping has most often been heard from the Panelled Room. According to the contemporary *Scots Magazine*, at the time of her execution, 'She died penitently; mentioning, as the beginning of her misfortunes, her having been seduced by an attorney's clerk when she had been to see some fireworks at Taunton.' This may be a clue to the motive for her crime, but as Lizzie Myers says, 'Susanna Bruford was just 19 years old and had only been married for a month before her husband died. So we like to think that his death could have been either an unfortunate accident, or he must have really been asking for it!'

WOODLANDS CASTLE'S ANGRY WOMAN

Between Taunton and Ruishton can be found Woodlands Castle, a beautifully decorated Georgian villa situated in 12 acres of its own land, commanding stunning views of the Cothelstone Hills. Dating to 1810, but remodified *c*.1833, this private residence also functions as a popular conference, wedding and party venue, and despite its modernity appears to have attracted a ghost.

Gemma Halliwell, the Events and General Manager at Woodlands, told me that around August 2008 she and a colleague, Chris Kolodziejczak, were locking up after a wedding, when from inside the marquee on the lawn they both heard, very clearly, a woman's voice say, 'Please leave!' The voice sounded very urgent, and Gemma's dog, Harvey, also with them, 'went crazy'. This was late at night and the last wedding guests had left two hours previously.

Gemma and her colleague searched the grounds, but without finding anyone at all. Two days later it appeared that this angry phantom lady still lingered, for in the morning the accountant arrived, turned off the alarm to the place and, while in the office, from out in the corridor heard a woman's voice say, 'Get out!' At first he thought that it was Gemma playing a trick, then remembered that he was alone in Woodlands Castle, having been the first to arrive.

The mystery was compounded when a psychic was called, who explained that she 'could feel different things going on, mainly a woman who hangs around in the upstairs rooms and on the veranda.' When the house was remodelled in 1833, it was for a Mrs Lock, which may be a partial explanation for the strange voice; but, as Gemma says, 'Since these incidents we've heard nothing, so maybe she likes us now!'

A SHORT CONCLUSION

And so it goes on. The following final selection of well-attested hauntings in Somerset serves to illustrate, if such were needed, just how far-reaching the phenomenon of belief in ghosts is in the county.

The spirit of a pioneering mental health doctor, John Westover, is repeated to have been glimpsed in the doorway of his former home in West End, Wedmore, despite the good doctor having died in 1706. Brockley Hall is believed to be haunted by the rapier-wielding ghost of John Piggott, who died in 1727, and whose monument can be found in the Piggott aisle of the local church. Wookey Hole Caves, the tourist attraction that was the site of one of the first cave dives in Britain, are haunted by the ghost of a drowned potholer, or else one of several who have lost their lives in the act of diving. On 9 April 1949 Gordon Marriot, a guest of the Cave Diving Group, lost his life in a siphon. Hammering noises are also held to echo through these caverns, and the great excavator of Wookey Hole, Herbert Balch, heard strange gurglings, as of a man struggling and shouting somewhere in the recesses of one of the 25 caverns.

Of phantom ladies, the White Lady of Compton Martin is thought to be the ghost of Alice, wife of Ralph Wake, whose family owned not only land here, but also at other places in Somerset and Dorset. During the reign of Edward III, Wake met his death by the 'unnatural connivance' of his wife, and Alice was subsequently burned to death for her crime. At Crowcombe, Ruth Tongue tells us that it was a Blue Lady who haunted the Elizabethan part of the Rectory, 'She appears at very rare intervals, and then only to children. The last time she was seen was in 1929...'

Phantom echoes of the gibbet creaking on Shute Shelve Hill, north of Axbridge, and where the felon Humphrey Hawkins dangled in 1609, are long said to have been heard, although these stories may have begun with smuggling gangs wanting to keep people away from their hideouts and routes. A phantom smuggler also haunts the neighbourhood of Crewkerne, sometimes to be heard exchanging pistol fire with revenue men in the vicinity of Windwhistle. Galloping hooves were also heard, echoes (according to G.F. Munford's *Ghosts And Legends Of South Somerset* in 1922) of a life-or-death struggle between a smuggler and member of the coastguard during a heavy snowstorm in the days of King George II. The woodland near Frome, where, at one time, a lawless banditti and also a gang of coiners operated from, but which by 1844 had been partially cleared and a number of small farms established by 1844, has attracted similar stories.

Along the A39 there has been a recent observation of a phantom highwayman, according to the *Wells Journal* of Halloween 2002. This road has long been considered haunted by the ghost of a highwayman named Pocock, who appears lopsidedly slumped on the saddle of his horse as though mortally wounded. Not much is known about Pocock, although in 1954 Sedgemoor historian Desmond Hawkins related what little information there was from the early ballads: that he was probably active c.1720, that his horse had its horseshoes on a pivot to confuse his pursuers, and that he operated from a cave somewhere in the region of Chilton Priory. Pocock is supposed to have died in this cave after being fatally wounded in a skirmish with the law, and sometime after a grotto called Pocock's Cell was built in his memory 'at the end of a long and deep gully, through which ran the stream that supplied Ford Mill.' At Duddlestone, near Corfe, a ghostly horse gallops silently on winter nights, spurred on by a headless horseman, according to Ruth Tongue in 1965.

Some ghosts appear to be pure folklore. The skies north of Bath resonate with the noise of phantom battle, in a psychic echo of the disputed Battle of Lansdown on 5 July 1643, where the brave and honourable Bevil Grenville met his death. A monument dated 1720 marks the spot where he fell on the battlefield of Lansdown Hill, but as to the truth of phantom replays of the encounter, I am highly dubious; this type of allegation is attached to almost every major Civil War battlefield. Wells Cathedral, like all cathedrals, is believed to be haunted by the shades of phantom monks, and some declare that the upper landing of the Chapter House is haunted by the ghosts of those afflicted with the Black Death who were locked away in isolation.

I was also told by a resident of Carhampton, 'Many years ago they killed the vicar at Old Cleeve and some say they ate him afterwards. I've heard he stands at the side of the railway tracks covered in blood.' This must be a reference to the murder of a curate of Old Cleeve called Trat, who a 1624 pamphlet tells us was brutally murdered near here as part of a village conspiracy and subsequently dismembered, 'his quarters and bowels afterwards being perboyled and salted up, in a most strange and fearful manner'. The plot, in its own primitive way, was almost Byzantine in its complexity and efforts to avoid detection, but, ultimately, four – including 'young Peter Smethwicke' – were hanged at Taunton on 24 July. I can only suppose that anyone hearing this macabre tale for the first time, and then repeating it half-correctly to someone else, might have added the ghostly element as a sort of punchline. Still, who knows? Maybe the poor curate does wander the area between Old Cleeve and Blue Anchor in bloodied, zombie-like ethereal form.

In some instances we can see modern ghost stories actually being created. On 11 April 2008 *The Sun* published a too-good-to-be-true photograph taken five years earlier at Evercreech, by someone using a disposable camera to take a shot of a random field. Behind the gate there can clearly be seen the transparent figure of a little boy aged about 10, wearing the peasant clothing of a bygone era. The photograph caused quite a lot of excitement at the time, but it is a strange paradox of this type of image that the more defined the 'ghost' is in the photo, the less likely it is to be a bona fide phantom; it is more likely to be some sort of double exposure. Such was the publicity at the time, however, that it would not be surprising if in future years some kind of historical 'back story' was unearthed to account for this eerie – but not convincing – photograph.

A more convincing photograph was taken inside Oare church in the Doone Valley in 1959 by a visitor, and was kept secret until it was loaned to a Torbay paranormal concern in 2004. It was also later submitted to *Fortean Times*, and displays nothing so much as a group of four blurry heads, all looking upwards towards the Carver Window. Their bodies fade away beneath their necks, but it is clear that they are people. How could this have happened? The photographer was adamant that there were no other people in the church at the time. And writer Joseph Braddock declares in *Haunted Houses* (1956), 'I possess a beautiful colour print of two ghostly figures on the steps going up to the Chapter House in Wells Cathedral, Somerset. There are two figures: a small child and a much taller, perhaps maternal figure, in white, standing framed in the archway at the entrance to the covered archway leading over the road to Vicars Close.' The photograph had been taken by a friend on Easter Monday in 1954.

Some ghosts are certainly more substantive than others. The writer Paul Gater was told first-hand of an incident in the mid-1960s when a witness clearly saw three men and a boy in out-of-place clothing on the shingle of Porlock Bay, who appeared to dematerialise in Marsh Field, where, according to tradition, in the 1700s there had been buried four such victims of a sea tragedy who had been washed up on the beach.

And in 2001 and 2002 there were claims among the readership of *Fortean Times* that Ashton Court, a mansion house on the Ashton Court Estate, west of Bristol, was haunted in the mid-1960s. This was during a period when the mansion, the core of which dates back to 1545, was derelict, and both a former security guard and a former pupil at the nearby school testified that the mansion's Long Corridor was undoubtedly haunted. The rumour was that electricians in a room off the corridor had heard a furious whirlwind noise and discovered that all their cables and wires had been neatly rolled into balls. Doors leading off the corridor were also found to have opened themselves simultaneously and later to have all closed themselves. the most famous ghost here concerns a phantom headless horseman.

Places like HMP Shepton Mallet, which dates back to 1625 and has seen innumerable executions – including those of 18 US servicemen convicted of murder or rape – are naturally said to be haunted. What we have seen is but a mere fraction of some of the more commonly-known ghost stories in Somerset, and in theory this chapter could continue indefinitely. But what does the sincere persistence of belief in ghosts tell us about Somerset folk? After all, a perceived sighting of a ghost is only 'real' to the person who sees it, not the world at large, although when one's own friends, relatives and witnesses with not much to gain – often the opposite – look you in the eye and tell you of their own supernatural encounters, it becomes somewhat difficult to disbelieve them. Presumably, they would not see ghosts unless there were ghosts to see.

Currently attracting the attention of ghost hunters and the curious alike is the buffet at Yeovil Junction railway station, where the area around the old counter is reported to be haunted by the mischievous spirit of a former employee who died in the 1960s. Known as 'Molly the Tea Lady', her poltergeist-like pranks are held to stop as soon as one says loudly, 'Good morning, Molly!' As to the eternal question of what 'ghosts' are, we learn of the Somerset expression 'spunkies'; these were the souls of the un-baptised, doomed to wander the countryside until Judgement Day. Perhaps the simplest explanation is the correct one...

CHAPTER 7:

ANIMAL ENIGMAS

INTRODUCTION

The stag hunts of Exmoor were at one time a major event in the cultural calendar, and John L.W. Page's *An Exploration Of Exmoor* (1890) devotes much space to this pastime. The chase was frantic and Page observed that remarkable events often accompanied the hunt; stags would charge into the Bristol Channel, and such was the bloodlust of the hounds that at least one had drowned swimming out to sea after an escaping hind. At Glenthorne on the Devon/Somerset border a stag had, in its panic, leapt off a cliff in 1884 and plummeted to its death, followed by the baying pack of hounds; one was killed instantly, two had to be destroyed, a fourth was made lame, but, curiously, one lucky dog managed to escape entirely uninjured from the fall. Perhaps the most remarkable event occurred in 1903, when *Punch's Almanac* tells us that a warrantable stag made it into Minehead, charging through the town and along the new pier, where it flung itself off the side and into an excursion steamer that happened to be leaving at that point, thus evading its pursuers.

Page's work devotes a lot of space to the tradition of 'the chase': 'Stag-hunting is a science.' There were sad echoes of these times in February 1993 when Snowy, the famous pure-white Quantock deer, was killed illegally near West Bagborough. Snowy had, in her 19 years, achieved a kind of legendary, almost supernatural, status, those glimpsing her in the bracken often believing themselves extremely fortunate. White deer have a good deal of folklore attached to them – King Henry VIII is said to have spared one in the New Forest because it enchanted him so – and it would not be surprising if in the coming years they claimed that Snowy herself haunted the land outside the village.

As needless as the stag chase was, it is clear that many humans, conversely, suffered death and serious injury in days gone by due to accidents with horses or large domestic livestock like cattle. Death by charging bulls and from kicks by horses – or, more commonly, startled horses throwing their occupants out of traps – were phenomenally common. Sometimes exotic animals from travelling menageries fatally mauled poor unfortunates, and one instance was reported in the *Bristol Mercury*: in February 1827 a caravan of wild animals was being kept at the Star Inn, Bedminster, Bristol, and a Dorset man employed as a keeper negligently entered the cage of a normally docile and placid lion called Nero, in order to impress some gentlemen who wanted to see the beast. Nero woke up and instantly attacked the keeper – one Joseph Kiddle, aged 25 – mauling him so violently that the inquest could barely bring itself to speak of the horror of the details. The lion was not put down, its worth outweighing the danger it posed, and there the matter rested, but it is a story that seems to belong to the jungles of Africa, not suburban Bristol.

Curious animal stories always intrigue us, and there is a never-ending source of such tales from Somerset. Who would not be curious, for example, about the story of a Wyandotte hen at Saltford that was reported in April 2006 to have spontaneously changed sex? Apparently, this was not entirely unheard of, although an extremely rare event. And for pure ridiculous fancy, consider the 'wonderful news' from Bristol in 1676 of a hen that had 'brought into the world a kitling, or young cat'!

For my part, the most interesting animal stories concern the occasional unearthing of prehistoric remains belonging to beasts that no longer inhabit these islands, and in some cases no longer exist anywhere on the planet. In the caves of the Mendip Hills in 1859 were found the bones and teeth of such animals as woolly rhinoceros, hyena, reindeer, cavebear and lion, among relics of more familiar animals such as stag, wolf, fox and horse. Flint tools and arrowheads evidenced that Somerset's earliest inhabitants lived and

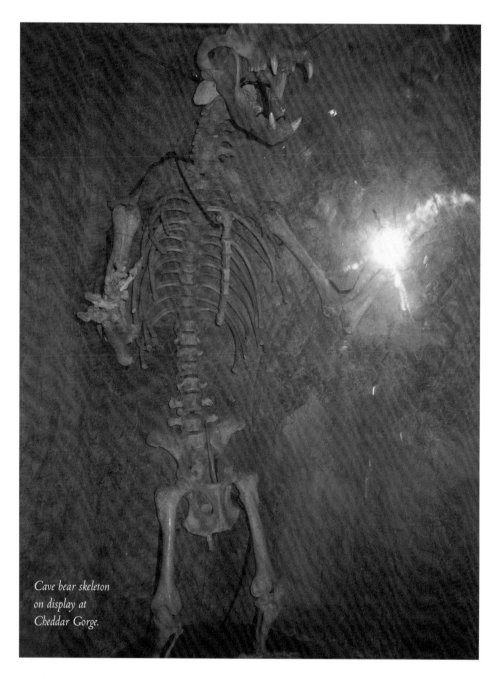

Cave bear skeleton on display at Cheddar Gorge.

hunted among this menagerie, *Memorials Of Old Somerset* (1906) remarking of this, 'How such a number of animals lived in so limited an area as the Mendip Hills is explained by the supposition that the great moor now extending from Wells to the sea was a rich valley at a higher level than present, joining the westward plains now submerged under the Bristol Channel.' In 1770 the skeleton of an elephant was found 'four fathoms deep' among loose rubble during excavations at Sandford Hill. In the later 1800s the enormous tusks and teeth of the mammoth *elephas primigenius* was discovered in the foreshore off the mouth of the Doniford Stream at Watchet. This enormous animal – a contemporary of the early Somerset inhabitants and now long extinct – was presumed to have been part of a herd that inhabited a now-submerged forest. In January 1821 excavations in High Street, Bristol, revealed the upper jawbone of an alligator. Such finds, while not being particularly 'mysterious', do remind us that Somerset was at one time home to some fantastic and awesome animals; at any rate, it reminds us that no way of life stays the same forever.

This chapter is concerned not so much with historical enigmas, however, but with the curious lore and folk belief surrounding animals in the county: the tales of their curious and humorous behaviour, their out-of-place appearance and instances where there may even be a supernatural or paranormal explanation for their very being.

TOM FAGGUS' ENCHANTED STRAWBERRY MARE

John L.W. Page observed in 1890 that there was at Simonsbath 'an old house – older than it looks – the occasional residence of the Lord of Exmoor, Sir Frederick Knight', that in the late 1600s had been the scene of a remarkable escape by the fabled outlaw, Tom Faggus. The building at the time had been a tavern, and Tom was captured, 'but, with that wonderful luck that attended him, contrived to make his escape.' Faggus or, more likely, Fergus, owed much of his luck to an 'enchanted strawberry horse', according to *Murray's Handbook For Cornwall And Devon* (1865). This marvellous animal was said to have actually fought with hooves and teeth on behalf of its master and to have been the instrumental factor in his escape, the horse's devotion to Tom Faggus forcing the would-be captors to flee in terror. On another occasion, Faggus was surround by an armed mob in Porlock, but once again escaped by charging his fearless horse and scattering the mob. The horse is even believed to have jumped 40ft from a bridge in Barnstaple, Devon, with Tom Faggus on her back – until one day she was shot in her stable by men planning to ambush and arrest Faggus. The bandit whistled his horse as he had so many times before, but the animal lay dead, and on this occasion Faggus was taken and eventually hanged at Taunton.

Faggus plays a part in the rich intertwining of real places, romance and folklore that is R.D. Blackmore's *Lorna Doone*, where he is introduced as a merry gentleman highwayman; his horse is a young mare named Winnie. Like the Doones themselves, there is likely to be more than fiction to the stories of this daredevil highwayman, and he was certainly not an invention of Blackmore's, although precisely when he was active and the nature of his demise are unclear. The riddle of who the historical Tom Faggus was aside, however, his legend reminds us that there will always be a fascination with curious animal stories, and there is no shortage of these in Somerset.

MYSTERIOUS APPEARANCE OF HORSES' HOOVES

In January 2010 I was informed by a former resident of the village of Colerne, on the North East Somerset and Wiltshire border, that there was a tall cross in the grounds of St John the Baptist's Church that, if one were to walk round it seven times and then look at the stonemasonry, spontaneously displayed the images of horses' hooves that appeared to the beholder to 'walk' up the cross before their eyes. My informant was told this in the 1960s by an elderly resident who would sit and watch the ritual. Afterwards, he would laugh out loud and say, 'Can yew see 'em yet? Everyone falls for that one!' The supposition is that the effect that was observed in the stonework was an existing pattern, but one that 'morphed' due to dizziness and suggestiveness on the part of the beholder; nonetheless some 40 years ago the story of the 'invisible horse' making its way up the stone cross was being cited orally as a real phenomenon.

BELIEFS ABOUT ANIMALS

In West Somerset it was still believed as late as 1890 that if you went into the cattle shed, you could see the oxen bow their knees in worship of the infant Saviour. This happened on Christmas Eve.

There are many beliefs about animals in Somerset, most ascribing them some kind of portentous attribute. For instance, dogs howling at the bedside of the sick were a sure indicator that the ill person would die. Similarly, dogs were believed sensible enough to howl dismally upon the sudden death of their master. It was also thought that a hare crossing the path of a man undertaking some journey was as plain an evil omen as could be imagined.

Curiously, it was believed, even into the 20th century, that anyone who rode a horse in Somerset on Twelfth Day would meet with an accident, as this was a day designated by the horse itself as its own special 'holiday'.

But in some cases animals affected a cure to help the sick. To cure an ill child it was the practice to carry the child into the sheepfold and allow the sheep to breathe in the child's face, before laying him down in a spot from where a sheep had just risen. This had to be carried out seven mornings in succession and the child would be cured. Folklorist Edwin Radford noted at least three instances in the county since 1940 when the 'cure' had been performed.

Some animals were also considered a bridge to the spirit world, particularly so the white fox, two of which writer T.F. Dale reported in 1906 as having been recently killed in Somerset, with one of them being preserved in Cothelstone Hall. Thomas, or 'Tom', Poole, the famous tanner, land agent and farmer from Nether Stowey, observed that the gibbeted corpse of the murderer John Walford was guarded by two white foxes after darkness fell on Shervage Wood.

THE CANINE POTHOLER

The Somersetshire Archaeological and Natural History Society recorded in their *Proceedings Vol. 12-13* a story, possibly fictitious, concerning a remarkable journey by a dog. At Goatchurch Cavern, the largest cavern in the Mendips, it was said that this dog had been put in there and was eventually found after many days at Wookey Hole, having navigated the great distance and also having lost all its hair from scrambling through the narrow rock gullies and channels. At Cheddar Gorge they told the same story of the same dog, while at Wookey Hole they said that the dog had travelled all the way to Cheddar. The story speaks to a locally-held belief that all these landmarks were connected by way of subterranean tears, fissures and caverns, but it is unclear whether the eponymous dog – the hero of the story – ever existed, or was simply an invention.

THE COW JUMPED OFF THE TOWER

Page's *An Exploration Of Exmoor* (1890) mentions how the writer was told that 'at a farm with which I am very familiar' in West Somerset the labourers were forced to gently and awkwardly remove a calf that had somehow been found on the barn roof. It was a mystery how it had gotten there, but whispered rumours spoke of a recently dismissed employee who was reckoned to be a wizard.

There are other tales of animals that have turned up in bizarre places and in bizarre circumstances. At the 140ft high Burton Pynsent Monument, west of Curry Rivel, there is a story that the tower, built in 1757, was closed down because of an unusual incident. An inquisitive Jersey cow is alleged to have three times awkwardly clambered the spiral staircase to the viewing platform, on the first two occasions somehow managing to come back down to ground level backwards. On the third occasion, however, its curiosity got the better of it and it fell to its death from the top. At this, a decision was made to close the entrance.

Although many now consider this to be modern folklore, it is at least possible. There have been other instances of animals displaying similarly unexpected behaviour: in November 1979 an escaped heavily pregnant ewe apparently attacked its own reflection in the window of a house at North Wootton, crashing into the living room in a shower of glass and causing £1000 worth of damage in the lounge. In December 2009 a photograph was taken and published in a number of newspapers showing a cow standing on the roof of a house at Blagdon, having somehow managed to scale 6ft of wall to get there. *The Sun* ran the story with the title 'Cow the Hell did it get up there?', but puns aside, it certainly makes the Burton Pynsent Monument legend more believable.

Incidentally, I have also been told that people have, in the past, been put to flight on the Somerset Levels by the ghostly sounds of cows bellowing nearby, although no such animal could be seen anywhere. My informant suggested that, rather than the sounds being caused by 'ghost cows', the noises came from living animals that were too far away to be seen – their bellowing being 'carried', in the correct conditions, across the flatness of the wetlands at night and merely giving the impression that the animal was somewhere nearby, yet invisible.

SNAKES ALIVE!

Snakes, too, have their place in the lore of Somerset. County belief held that a sure-fire cure for an adder bite was to tie a circlet of ash twigs around the neck of the afflicted.

We have already seen that there are legends of fatal adder attacks at Brown's Folly, Bathford, and Clifton. In the 1820s at Weare, near Axbridge, there was a strange kind of urban legend circulating, to the effect that six people – a gentleman, four labourers and their master – all died in terrible agony in that village after partaking of cider from a barrel. When the barrel was prised open a dead adder was found floating inside, together with the decaying bodies of its offspring, and this had fatally contaminated the cider.

The *Bristol Evening Post* reported in August 1991 that a 10ft-long python was found in the car park at St Nicholas School, Lawford's Gate, Bristol. Presumably an escapee or a released pet, it appeared sluggish and starved, indicating that it was not used to looking after itself 'in the wild', but those with a congenital fear of snakes might not wish to reflect on the shock that the unexpected sight of a huge serpent like this might cause!

THE FLYING CAT

In November 1899 *The Strand* magazine published a photograph of a remarkable phenomenon: a 'winged cat' called Bessie owned by a lady in Wiveliscombe, who had been given the curiosity as a kitten. In 1927 the publication *Cat Gossip* carried a piece on this strange animal, its wing-like appendages being an actual, documented wonder, but the subject of no small debate among zoologists. There was even a bizarre suggestion that cats like Bessie represented a leap in evolution, being the first examples of a 'flying cat' that would some day be able to catch birds in the air.

The 'wings grew from the cat's back and were about six or eight inches long and placed in exactly the position assumed by the wings of a bird in the act of taking flight.' The kitten was not born with them, the wings in fact beginning to grow some weeks after its birth. The photograph in *The Strand* does indeed show the wings very clearly on the tortoiseshell tabby, and they appear to actually be 'lifted' from the cat's back, rather than laid across it, almost giving the impression that it is trying to take off! No doubt the village wags of the time had a great laugh with this, perhaps joking that Mrs so-and-so owned a 'flying cat', but, sadly for the animal, it died when an attempt was made to cut the appendages off. But the bi-monthly newspaper, the *Wiveliscombe Messenger*, has Bessie as its logo, and also a section called 'The Flying Pussy' in her memory.

A FELINE FIRE ALARM

The Weekly World News for 3 February 1981 reported on an amazing Persian cat called Zoe Blue. The cat had a habit of waking its owner, Christine Fackrell, at half past five in the morning, in time for work, and it was a habit that Christine encouraged, stating, 'Zoe Blue is like a four-legged alarm clock.'

The cat had recently charged up the stairs of the family home in Bristol and leapt on the bed, licking Christine's face to wake her, but two hours earlier than normal, however. When she awoke, she realised why: the house was on fire, smoke was filling the rooms, and the cat – amazingly – had woken its mistress up, rather than bolting out of the cat flap. Christine, her husband and their two sons managed to evacuate the house and, with the heroic cat under Christine's arm, they stood in the street as the fire brigade arrived to quell the flames.

THE INSECT WORLD

The humble insect has earned a place in Somerset folklore, most famously at the Theatre Royal, Bath, where in winter 1948 a dead tortoiseshell butterfly was found upon the stage. The stage was due to be the scene of a pantomime that included a large butterfly set centrepiece and chorus girls colourfully dressed up for a ballet performance with tortoiseshell butterfly wings. The dead insect was apparently found during rehearsal, and shortly afterwards the manager of the production died. The show went on, however, but with the butterfly ballet hastily dropped; strangely, rehearsals from then on were dogged by misfortune. The show seemed doomed to close before it had opened...until a curious thing happened. During one rehearsal another black, white and orange tortoiseshell flittered onto the stage and about the performers. Upon this, the butterfly ballet routine was reintroduced into the show, and from then on the mood of the performers and the fortunes of the pantomime began to improve.

From that day onwards there has been a well-known tradition that at panto-time a dead tortoiseshell butterfly heralds a disastrous performance, or even a fatality, while the appearance of a live one heralds a great show. The butterfly set piece has been retained in the theatre, and is generally not moved: to do so is considered portentous. I am told that over the years actors, the audience, members of the press and even royalty have observed this little fluttering omen. I have attempted to contact the Theatre Royal about this mystery, but at the time of writing have received no reply and perhaps I never will. After all, the stage is rife with rituals and omens; maybe to idly or flippantly speculate about the butterfly to non-thespians is in itself considered a jinxing factor! The theatrical anecdotes of the late stage director Ned Sherrin do indicate how seriously the phenomenon was taken though: 'Another dead butterfly heralded the suicide by hanging of a conjuror during the run of the 1952 pantomime. More recently, a stagehand bet a large sum on a seven-horse accumulator at Bath Races. First, he asked the butterfly's blessing. Six horses came up, and then he lost all on the seventh. Back at the theatre, he cursed the butterfly. When the stage crew moved out the heavy set, a massive moulding broke his neck...'

Other insects feature in the folk belief of the county. It was thought that as a spider trapped in a box gradually died, then whoever owned the box would start to recover from any ague they suffered. But most insect folklore concerned bees. Bees were considered exceptionally sensitive and had to be told when there was a death in the hive owner's family, or else they too would begin to die off. F.J. Snell's *A Book Of Exmoor* (1903) tells how he was acquainted with a Dulverton man whose son had died recently, who instructed his brother to 'tell the bees.' This the brother did, but rather half-heartedly, and consequently all the bees died in the winter. Some believed that bees became embarrassed and angry when they were observed to drink, while other 'West Country dames' professed a special rapport with the swarms of bees; they would stand there with hundreds of them buzzing about them, and even put their hands in the hive for minutes at a time without being stung. Snell was told by one such lady, 'Why, when I have got my hand in the hive, it do "zim" all the while as if I was touching velvet, pretty little dears, their wings be so soft-like.' I wonder what Snell would have made of a remarkable photograph, taken in 2008 and published in the *Daily Mail*, that showed a swarm of bees that had massed outside Wells Cathedral. Hundreds of the insects had settled on a boundary post in the grass by the path and then spread out horizontally along the interlinking chains – the whole giving the impression of the bees somehow having created a 'cross' in veneration of the cathedral.

STORIES OF THE AVIAN WORLD

A barely believable story from Victorian Weston-super-Mare concerns a farmer who fired a shotgun at a pheasant while he was in his field. Having no shot, he fired a plum stone at the bird, but only winged it. Some weeks later he fired at the same bird but this time killed it, and upon going to recover his prize he was amazed to see that a small plum tree actually grew from the bird's plumage where it had been hit the first time! Of factual stories concerning birds, a strange tale was related in *The European Magazine* in 1809. It concerned the recent death of one Mrs Jones, wife of the rector of St Peter's, Bristol and Kilve, at St James' Parade in Bath. She was aged 88 and her lifelong pet was a cockatoo alleged to be an astonishing 102 years old! What is even more remarkable is that within a few hours of his mistress's death the bird itself died.

The antics of birds are curiously prominent in Somerset lore. In June 2010 I was told of a little treasure that resided in the village of Corfe. A parish councillor informed me of a tree in the village called the 'Notable Tree', 'The notable tree is a fine old oak and [a] little owl has lived there for several seasons and raised some young. There is also evidence of little owls in the large barn when you first come into the village travelling south. Regrettably, that old farm and ancillary buildings are slated for new development, but I think the developers will have to take their habitat into consideration.' Later in the year I visited this tree, near the Village Hall, where the 'little owl' hides in a hollow in an upper branch, and remarkably was told of the owls in the barn by a villager, 'I hope they stay because they keep watch over the village.' I suppose this meant that the residents were a little proud of their seasonal visitors, but it reminds me nonetheless of the ancient belief that certain birds were considered lucky.

Ruth Tongue was told in 1917 an intriguing story about a chirruping bird that indicates a link with the divine in Somerset. A stonemason was finishing a church in the county, but this attracted the attention of the Devil, who sent two imps in the guise of his granddaughters to abduct the stonemason. The stonemason was led out of the church by the sight of the little girls, but on the threshold he halted, his attention drawn to a saintly-looking man who himself was gazing at a 'colley bird up in a tree singing to praise God so sweet and tuneable as any angel.' The stonemason, whose name was Old Jacob, shook his head at the momentary distraction and returned to his 'granddaughters' – but they had gone, so had the Devil, and the part-completed church now stood fully functioning and full of parishioners. Old Jacob did not understand what was happening, but then the saintly man told him that 300 years had passed and he was to be awarded a rare honour: a shaft of heavenly light fell at his feet and this was his ascension to Paradise. Old Jacob climbed the ladder with the saint, disappearing as they did so before the humbled parishioners. When they had vanished fully the colley bird stopped its singing. I wonder if this story has any link to the 274 steps gouged into the face of Cheddar Gorge, known as Jacob's Ladder.

In Crewkerne in April 2010 I was told the story of a man who lived in Somerset who saw, while he lay in bed at sunrise, a yellow-breasted bird looking in at his bedroom window. Fascinated, the man quietly bade the bird to fly across town to the house of his sweetheart and tell her that he loved her. At this the little bird flew off.

When the man met his girlfriend later that day she told him something remarkable: that as she lay in bed that morning a little bird with a yellow breast had alighted on her windowsill and chirruped noisily at her through the glass before flittering off. Both the man and the woman were amazed when they put their two halves of the story together. Far from being a contemporary story, I suspect that this is an old one indeed, although it does not seem to have been written of before.

THE FOLKLORE OF BIRDS

There is greater evidence that certain birds in Somerset were considered unlucky and treated with superstitious caution, however. People would tip their hats to ravens, it being believed that a baby was destined to die if eggs were ever poached from a raven's nest. To even see a magpie was judged unlucky, the ritualistic carrying of an onion for some reason fending off the ill luck that such a sighting could bring. And it used to be said across the county, 'If a bittern flies over your head, make your will.'

Snell's *A Book Of Exmoor* (1903) notes numerous superstitions like this. Hearing a cuckoo after 'Old Midsummer Day' meant that you would die within a year. When a cockerel walked up to the door of a farm and crowed, it meant that a stranger was on their way to the premises. But if a 'hen forgets herself' and crowed, then it meant ill luck that could only be remedied by the farmer's strangulation of the unfortunate bird. A cock crowing in the dead of night was regarded as an infallible sign of impending death. If any bird tapped the window with its beak, this also meant a fatality, as did a bird entering the room.

A strange story of birds and windows was told at Bardon House near Washford, concerning a milk-white dove that flew against the window of the attic and with eerie persistency broke it as often as it was mended. This dove vanished, never to appear again, upon William Leigh's discovery of important papers in the attic in 1834. Bardon is a 15th-century house of one storey only and built of cob, with picturesque roofs and gables, much in the shape of the letter 'E'. The papers that were discovered by such a mysterious accident concerned the imprisonment and trial of Mary, Queen of Scots, at the hands of Queen Elizabeth I. Mr Leigh (who died in 1844) found it doubly unaccountable that such important historical documents should be found so far away from the site of Mary's final days in Northamptonshire.

This reminds me of a story carried in the *Bristol Evening Post* of 1 September 1986. A four-year old girl living at Southfield Farm, Backwell, south of Nailsea, had opened the curtains one morning to find the perfect imprint of a barn owl on the window, made of a substance like dust. It was assumed that an owl had collided with the window, but no one had heard a crash and no body had been found at the foot of the windowsill, despite the bird presumably hitting the pane forcefully enough to provide such a fine imprint...

The appearance of a single jackdaw was greatly feared by the workmen employed in the quarries of the Avon Gorge, Clifton, 'at the time when the river was simply spanned by a single chain', according to *Notes And Queries*. More than once, the men had noticed the portentous jackdaw perched by itself upon the centre of the chain prior to some disastrous fatality or other accident among their number.

Robins were greatly venerated in Somerset. They tapped on windows three times to announce a fatality, and woe betide anyone who struck one dead, for they would also perish. There was a belief that the supernatural aura of the robin could be attributed to the story that robins originally had white breasts, but one flew into Christ on the cross and ever after they had red breasts and were thus deemed holy. Wrens were regarded in a similar light, and in Somerset they sang of this belief:

> The robin and the wren
> Are God Almighty's cock and hen.

One family, who J.L.W. Page was acquainted with in Exmoor, actually considered a robin's appearance as a family banshee, heralding the 'approaching dissolution of a son or daughter of the house.' He even cites an instance of a farmer riding home from Taunton Market who noticed a white rook among the other birds larking over a field. When he got home, his cattle were highly agitated and the family dog howled all night; in the morning the farmer was found dead.

THE PHANTOM BLACK DOG OF SOMERSET

Quite apart from being a ghostly animal, the phantom black dog of Somerset was sometimes thought to embody the spirit of a human being. Great excitement was occasioned in Bath in December 1733 when rumour spread throughout the town that a house in St John's Court, owned by a wealthy Quaker, was haunted. The reason, they said, was that in the near past a sea captain's servant had been murdered under the roof, as well as being robbed. His body had been subsequently anatomised and 'on which account his distracted soul was returned to Earth to take vengeance of those that had deprived him of his life and fortune, cut and mangled his corpse, and boiled his flesh and bones.' For some reason, the spirit haunted the house in the guise of a great mastiff dog, although 'his teeth, his eyes, his ears, his tail and his claws were remarkably different from those of any living mastiff. Vigils were undertaken at the property with little success, although a few nights into the scare Bath was hit by what would appear to have been a tempest so violent that the oldest residents in the town could not remember the like. Slates were ripped from rooftops, and lamps and windows shattered to atoms. The noises that had originally terrified the household in St John's Court were eventually rationalised into nothing so much as a loose window shutter, but it is interesting to note that the restless 'spirit' was supposed to have taken a canine form.

There is another instance of a human spirit taking a canine form noted in W.H. Thornton's *Reminiscences And Reflections Of An Old West-Country Clergyman* (1899). In his younger days Thornton had interviewed one Mary Stenner, who had been terrified by an apparition that materialized before her on Budleigh (Buddle) Hill near Selworthy. The thing, which had four legs, was as black as the night and had great, blazing eyes, chased her as far as the point where the stream crossed the road. For some supernatural reason, however, it could not cross the water, and Mrs Stenner watched it disappear upwards in a flash of fire. Later, Thornton learned from the sexton that exactly 25 years earlier there had been a funeral procession along Budleigh Hill which had encountered a mishap: the coffin handle near the head had broken loose, so the sexton, John Hobbs, had bashed it back in with a stone. He supposed that the nail had penetrated the dead man's brain and set his spirit free to haunt the lane.

The black dog was commonly believed by the superstitious to guard tumuli and cairns, protecting the treasure that was buried beneath. One such creature lurked at the Wambarrows on Winsford Hill, where, towards the close of the 19th century one Arthur Locke, the secretary of the Devon and Somerset staghounds, had 'seed something' supernatural hiding thereabouts.

Sometimes, this loping canine phantom was referred to as the Gurt Dog. In Langport the inhabitants sang a traditional rhyme, *The Gurt Dog of Langport*, whose image they professed to see in certain features in the countryside. Part of the song mentions 'the gurt dog of Langport have a-burned off his tail', and the ditty was a wassailing (good health) song. Only visible from the air, the Gurt, or Girt, Dog is sculptured into the land, his outlines made up of rhynes, roads and the River Parrett, and he is some 10 miles from nose to tail, according to true believers.

The phantom dog of Somerset has taken many guises, and so his variants cannot really be considered the same phenomenon. According to folklorists, in Somerset black dogs were sometimes buried on the north side of new churchyards to protect the building, a kind of spiritual guard dog that was called the Church Grim. This phantasm could be glimpsed at funerals by knowing parsons, who could tell where the deceased was heading in the afterlife by the dog's behaviour.

Ruth Tongue's *Somerset Folklore* (1965) explains that there were numerous places in Somerset where the phantom hound was judged to be an omen of death. For example, she wrote, 'A large dog, "bigger than a hound dog", which has eyes "so big round as saucers", is sometimes seen in the lane near Stapley. It is always an omen of death. Some people say it is white and others grey, but all agree on its glowing saucer eyes.' She also recorded as late as 1960 that children referred to a straight track on the northern Somerset coast as 'Death Mile'. Two people – a man and a young girl – had lately died within a year after seeing the hound there, although on the occasion that the young girl saw it, her companion did not and was unaffected. This track was between St Audries Bay and Perry Farm on the coast near West Quantoxhead.

Some have it that the spectral 'black dog' is a member of the pack of Yeth Hounds, or the Wild Hunt, and we shall look at this later.

OTHER PHANTOM ANIMALS

Animals other than dogs also sometimes haunt a particular place. A ghostly white horse is said to clip-clop its way through the village of Wrington, and in the 19th century a ghost in the form of a white donkey would sometimes accompany travellers for the two miles between the halfway house on the Yeovil road to Gallows Five Acres. I have also been told that a ghostly cat pads around Halswell House, a 14th-century manorial seat rebuilt around 1689, between Goathurst and woodland called The Thickets. And at the Halfway Inn on Westonzoyland Road, Dunwear, they tell me that another phantom cat brushes up against the legs of drinkers. The owner explained, 'The ghost cat…is definitely supposed to be here. I say supposed as I myself have never seen it, although I have on occasion felt as though hairs were brushing against my leg and it has made me look, but see nothing. Two years ago a small group of clairvoyants were in the restaurant having a meal and it was them who asked about [the] cat who had passed over.' It was subsequently established from an elderly village resident that 'this local remembered an elderly relative who would always sit in a rocking chair, sewing, in front of the open fire in the centre-bar area. She always dressed in a long, black skirt and was remembered as quite a stern person. She had this very loyal cat that followed her around and particularly liked to sit with her in front of the fire. They were always remembered as "together", and as far as I could establish it was assumed that the cat died at the pub, as apparently did the elderly relative, although I have never tried to confirm this. The centre-bar area is quite a dark area, with little natural light, and the fire is still there, but closed off with boarding.'

It would seem that the cat was so loyal that it could not bring itself to leave the pub. The Halfway Inn became famous a few years ago when the *Mercury* reported the story of 'Socks the disappearing cat', a missing black-and-white moggy that turned up, and was identified beyond doubt, at the Halfway Inn, having apparently run away from home and made the inn her new pad. Socks became quite a local celebrity, a grand old dame who enjoyed the pub life until (at the time of writing) she was rehomed. A pub with a phantom cat seems an ideal place for Socks to have sought out.

But perhaps the most unnerving encounter with an animal phantasm occurred near Yeovil around 1624. Richard Bovet's *Pandemonium* (1684) tells the story of Mr Edmund Ansty of South Petherton, who was returning home from Woodbury Hill Fair when, at a place called Outhedge, his horse began acting up, snorting, trembling and forcing itself over to the hedge that lined the lane. At length the hedges crackled with a dismal noise and Mr Ansty saw, to his horror, an awful phantasm up ahead: 'A large circle of duskish light, about the bigness of a large wheel, and in it he perfectly saw the proportion of a huge bear, as clearly as if it had been by daylight!' This monstrosity passed by the petrified Ansty and his horse, and looked fully at him with two great blazing eyes. As soon as it was gone, Ansty's horse took to the road and bolted all the way home, and it was as much as Mr Ansty could do to stay in the saddle. Bovet observed that the man concerned had recently died, and he had been telling this story as a truism for the past 60 years to neighbours of good repute, who had believed it all.

THE WILD HUNT

Perhaps the most frightening manifestation of phantom black dogs came in the form of the Wild Hunt – the very hounds of Hell, whose vicious, manic barking led the demonic huntsman, Satan himself, on wild, insane chases over the heathland of the Quantocks, or crashing through the woodland of Exmoor. Often pursuing a terrified victim or on their way to claim some poor unfortunate's soul, it invariably meant bad luck to glimpse the Wild Hunt, even from afar.

This phantom pack also went by the name of the Yeth Hounds, with an 1875 book on the West Somerset dialect explaining that they were 'A phantom pack of hounds, believed to hunt in the night, and whom some superstitious people declare they have heard. The legend is not very common, but is steadfastly believed in out-of-the-way places.' Over the border in Devon it was speculated that the Yeth Hounds were not demonic, but 'dogs without heads, the spirits of unbaptized children, which ramble among the woods at night, making wailing noises.' This was written in 1868. Some referred to them as the Wish or Wisht Hounds. Some even believed that the Bronze-Age Triscombe Stone in the Quantocks was a stopping-off point for these hounds of Hell.

Occasionally, the demon pack were given an origin other than Hell or distressed children: a county-wide story involved a 'certain field' where there could be seen the phantasm of a woman accompanied by a pack of baying spectral hounds. In life, hundreds of years ago, she had been a rich lady addicted to hunting, who could not give up her pastime in the afterlife.

But more often the phenomenon was labelled demonic or a harbinger of death. The Somerset folklorist Poole wrote in 1870, 'I may remark that in this county, many years ago, I once heard of a man dying, Hell Hounds were said to have rushed to his chamber to carry his soul to Hell…' *The Quantock Hills* (1904) wrote that even at the start of the 20th century the paths that led to the ancient fort south of Combwich were avoided after dark, because 'there the wild hunt was constantly seen.'

It was written that locally a man was supposed to have encountered the Wild Hunt, which consisted of a pack of demonic hounds, huge and black in colour with fiery tongues. A 'terrible rider who rode a headless horse' accompanied them in the lane. On another occasion, it was the phantom huntsman himself who was headless. The manifestation was silent as it charged along.

But for one man here, making for home, the demon huntsman actually halted and asked of the terrified traveller, 'How does your steed amble?', perhaps meaning to entice the man into a race. The man invoked the Holy Name and replied, 'Her ambles well enow', and the huntsman vanished in 'vlash of vire.' The Devil's own steed in this case was not a horse, but a monstrous hog that also vanished along with its master.

In 1955 Ruth Tongue was told that the drive to Norton Fitzwarren Manor was haunted by the ghost of a hunting squire, who rode from Langford Budville and only appeared on specific nights, New Year's Eve being the most commonly cited date. But the story appeared much older, and very well known. The local tradition was that the squire galloped in wild-eyed terror, for in life he had been pursued to his death 'over the Common from Carter's Gate to the French Nut Tree' by the demonic hunt – an ironic instance of the huntsman becoming the hunted. He never made it to his home, Norton Manor, but was killed by the Hell Hounds even as he lost his steed and scrambled through the underbrush in an attempt to escape. His ordeal had added torment in that he was doomed ever after to haunt the scene of his death, his last frantic moments replayed spectrally over and over.

The Wild Hunt is often linked to stories of the Norse god Odin, who led a host of slain warriors across the sky accompanied by a pack of barking dogs, and the story has its variants in the mythology of all parts of north-west Europe. It was also called the Gabriel Ratchet. But for those who think it is a relic of a more superstitious past, Ms Tongue also recorded the Wild Hunt as being heard thundering via Stogumber as recently as 1960, a phenomenon that caused the locals to lock their doors and shut their windows in fear.

In parts of Somerset, when the rain lashes and the countryside becomes almost impenetrably dark, I suspect that the Wild Hunt is still to this day caught on the ear or heard from afar – for, if it be true, then this is the place where it would materialize.

The Wild Hunt appears to form the background to a truly bizarre sky-borne apparition observed in May 1580, when 'divers hounds' were seen in the air. The spectacle was accompanied by visions (on two occasions at short intervals) of violent clashes between two factions consisting of some 60 or so men robed in black, who attacked each other on 'Brodwels Down' about a furlong from the 'worthy gentlemen' who witnessed the action. A third spectral encounter shortly after consisted of several dozen men dressed in bright armour battling each other; on each occasion the combatants faded away before the view of the observers. Perhaps the Wild Hunt had encountered an equally supernatural Wild Hunt Protest. Whatever it was all about, the chronicler Holinshed wrote of these events in 'Summersetshire' that four honest men swore they saw this and were examined by Sir George Norton.

THE BIG CATS THAT PROWL SOMERSET

There can be few today that are not at least aware that the county is supposedly the stalking ground for a large, feline-like animal, variously named the 'Beast of Exmoor', or Banwell, Sedgemoor, Brassknocker, Blagdon, or the 'Mendips Monster', etc: the fabled 'black panther' that, legend has it, hides in Somerset's darkest corners. It might be more appropriate to use the plural 'animals', however, since there are surely more than one of these beasts, given that it appears to have been on the prowl for decades now, as well as in Somerset's neighbouring counties.

The emergence of the Beast of Exmoor in early 1983 created a national furore. When reports spread that a creature described as a large black panther with a smooth coat, yellow eyes, small ears, muscular haunches, a powerful chest and long hind legs and tail was being spotted along the Devon/Somerset border, there was something akin to a manhunt. This was largely due to farmers reporting the discovery of decimated livestock in their fields simultaneously. The events were largely confined to South Molton, Drewstone, Lynton and Longstone Wells in North Devon, although the creature apparently made forays into Somerset: in the autumn of that year a huge paw print displaying features unique to a big cat was found by a sheep herder at Simonsbath. For a time the region was almost in a state of siege, with gangs of armed farmers, civilian watching posts, the police and big-game hunters all tracking the Beast of Exmoor; even the Royal Marines were drafted in at one point, following their quarry briefly over the border into Somerset towards the end of May 1983. The Marines were kitted out with high-powered sniper rifles, but they fired no shots, despite some of those deployed believing that they had caught a fleeting glimpse of the animal. It is said that after the Marines were recalled, the rate of attacks on livestock increased, and although such kills have continued sporadically, to all intents and purposes the beast has vanished back into the shadows, to become a phantom or an urban legend, although still a very real mysterious terror to the farmers, who in some cases lost great quantities of livestock to the creature's vicious attacks.

The publicity surrounding the affair brought to light the observation that such creatures might have been around a lot longer than was being currently reported, and Somerset now finds itself with a county-wide mystery, as the Beast (or creatures like it) has been spotted elsewhere. It would perhaps be somewhat self-defeating to note every report of a big cat over the last 25 years or so, and the variety of names ascribed to the creature are testament to the fact that it cannot be pinned down to one locale. But some reports do stand out as bearing standard aspects or containing interesting details.

This animal – or another one like it – resurfaced in 1991, when the *Bridgwater Mercury* reported that a family on the Polden Hills saw a black panther-like animal, and even managed to capture footage of it using a handheld camera that was at the time being used to film a fox and some cubs. The *Mercury* was told, 'We could see it was a cat of some sort and about the size of a Labrador with a big tail. It began circling around the vixen with its lashing tail and looked ready to attack.' Apparently, the video footage degraded during the transfer to VHS. But if this was the Beast of Exmoor, then it had entirely relocated and, given the lifespan of such animals, it is far more likely that this huge feline was an entirely separate creature. In fact, if the steady incline in sightings through the 1990s and into the 2000s is anything to go by, then it is entirely likely that there is not a single, or even a handful, of these creatures prowling the Somerset wilderness at any one time, rather small colonies of them existing almost as part of the natural flora and fauna. This is backed up by a story I was told that *c.*2000 many people were seeing a female panther by the roadside somewhere in the Blackdown Hills, which appeared to be accompanied by a small litter of cubs. Then, by the middle of 2003, armed farmers and the police were being forced to set up night patrols in this sparsely-populated Area of Outstanding Natural Beauty south of Wellington because of a spate of fatal attacks on livestock. But this would only appear to concern one 'pocket' of these animals, for it is no understatement to say that between 2003 and 2006 they were spotted in almost every part of Somerset and in places too diverse for it to be the same animal 'on the prowl'.

Perhaps the atypical sighting is the one covered by the national media in 2003, when the 'Beast of Sedgemoor' was spotted and photographed. At around 9 o'clock in the morning on Sunday 16 March a woman contacted the police to say that she had seen a large, black feline animal the size of a Labrador and resembling a panther in a field near Puriton, north of Bridgwater. The animal was actually photographed by the woman, and in response a police spokesperson stated, for the benefit of the media, 'Police are aware and are increasing patrols in the area. If we get a lot more sightings in the same area then it would be something we would actively investigate further.' I cannot seem to find out what happened to this 'photograph' – perhaps, like so many images of this creature, it was not judged sufficiently impressive upon evaluation.

In January 2004 the carcasses of a number of ewes and a calf were found mutilated and eaten in pastureland at Stoke St Michael, displaying vicious rents on their necks as though brought down in a similar fashion to the way that a lion brings down a gazelle. Amazingly, the savage creature that decimated this livestock returned to this land in the Mendips – or never left it in the first place – and began killing the Chislett family's prize sheep again five years later. The national media picked up on this new spate of attacks, and the *Daily Mail* of 21 November 2008 reported the owners as saying, 'This is no dog. They [the sheep] have slashes across them, deep rips in their sides, their guts have been pulled out and their ears ripped off. Two have had their throats ripped out. We have no insurance to cover this sort of thing and it is heartbreaking to see our prize stock being decimated.' A week later the *Wells Journal* reported that one of the family and his fiancee had actually seen the culprits while out patrolling during the night and discovering yet another ravaged carcass: 'I shone the lamps on my truck on them for several minutes and they just stood there looking back at us. Unfortunately, I didn't have my camera or my gun on me. If I had had my gun on me, I would have definitely shot them. We saw them for several minutes and then they just went. I am sure it was a male and a female, as one was bigger than the other.'

The clearest account of one of these creatures appeared in the *Somerset Guardian* of 12 August 2004, when a woman walking her dog in a field between Holcombe and Coleford momentarily became distracted. Her pet disappeared briefly and returned with the hind leg of a deer in its mouth. As the dog trotted on, it suddenly stopped, pricking its ears up in an inquisitive fashion. The witness very descriptively told the *Guardian*: 'When I went over I saw a large, healthy, shiny cat with big hips turn away from the carcass of a dead deer and run up a tree. It had an elongated body about 5ft-long, not including the tail, was jet black in colour and stalking, like a puma or large wildcat.

I stood back in shock and, for a moment, thought it was going to pounce, but it just sat there, still and silent. My dog then wandered off, as she was a bit wary, and I then walked back home. I am absolutely positive it was large cat, and I know several other people from the village who have spotted a similar beast in the last few months.'

There is no ambiguity here, if the lady concerned did indeed see what she claimed, then these animals exist beyond doubt.

THE FOLKLORE OF THE BIG CATS

And so it goes on, and one cannot help but make some fascinating observations at this juncture. The case of the Somerset alien big cats (or ABCs) presents no coherent structure: masses of evidence and yet no absolute proof, and genuine uncertainty as to the number, location and even the species of the elusive beasts. The traditional picture painted of the animal is that it is large ('as big as an Alsatian' is often the standard quote, together with, 'It definitely wasn't a large domestic cat'), with short, shiny black hair and a small panther-like head. It moves stealthily on its muscular haunches through a field and its thick, powerful tail usually catches the attention of the witness.

But this description is not always a truism, which further confuses this entire picture. In 1982, prior to the Beast of Exmoor scare, there had already been rumours that a colony of wild animals that made screeching noises in the night haunted Claverton Down, east of Bath, earning the animal(s) the nickname the 'Beast of Brassknocker' (making it difficult to differentiate from another, apparently separate 'Beast of Brassknocker', see below). Some thought that the creature was a polecat. In the mid-1980s there were rumours that an aggressive, hissing lynx-like creature was at loose in the Mendips, and it was reported in 1987 that a large cat the size of a Labrador, but beige or tan in colour with a white patch on its chest, had been spotted through binoculars apparently sunning itself on a hillside near Timberscombe. These creatures appear distinct from the black panther-type animal of lore so beloved by the local media, which adds another dimension to an already confusing mystery. The latest big cat is a 'marmalade-coloured animal the size of a Labrador' (that quote again) that I am told has been seen in the vicinity of Watchet as recently as 2009. Such an animal again appears to be distinct from the black panther-type animal.

'Explanations' for the sightings, such as they are, are consistently trotted out, yet the phenomenon remains a mystery that is tantalizingly out of reach. Some link the big cats to UFOs, claiming that the beasts are displaced animals that have been 'abducted' from their natural habitat, only to be mistakenly returned to the wrong country. Or else they were released by their owners. Or they escaped from circuses or private collections. Some believe that they are a resurgent population of the native British wildcat, although where they have been hiding for two centuries is unclear; the last native wildcat is believed to have been shot in 1853 in Northumberland.

It appears that the riddle of the big cats concerns several overlapping mysteries, and animals like this continue to split opinion in Somerset. The police and wildlife experts have, on occasion, speculated that it is at least possible for such an animal to exist in the British wilderness, but fundamental objections exist. There would seem to be more than one species, but even if one were to take a single species, such as the traditional black panther, then there must be more than one animal, perhaps small colonies of them. Any less and there would not seem to be a viable breeding population; any more, and one would assume they would be seen more frequently and their existence proved beyond reasonable doubt.

At the moment, however, we are in a kind of limbo in our knowledge of this phenomenon. The 'Beast' will never be caught or conclusively photographed or filmed, although we will be tempted to imagine that it might just be true by a few almost-convincing seconds of blurred footage or a fuzzy, indistinct black-and-white photo. A few footprints may be found, although these will be contentious. There will, however, be much reliable witness testimony. The legend will also be dubiously fed by stories that appear to be outright urban legends: people will tell you that 'a friend of a friend' says that one of these animals meandered calmly into the house of the aunt of someone they know. Or that they know for a fact that decimated livestock has been found hanging from a sturdy tree branch somewhere, blood dropping onto someone passing by underneath alerting them to the ravaged carcass hanging over their head.

And after the furore has died away in a particular part of Somerset, the big cat will vanish into history, only to appear somewhere else in the county some years later, and it cannot help but be noticed that, in this respect, these animals are phantoms not too dissimilar to the 'black dog' himself. There was, even during its earliest appearances in 1983, already a suggestion that the Beast of Exmoor displayed a kind of 'human-like' intelligence that allowed it to stay one step ahead of the Royal Marines and even, according to folklore, raid a field and make a livestock kill under the noses of those very soldiers during the night: a story which is probably based on an actual incident. It is also curious that sometimes it is only a single paw print that is observed, rather than the true walking pattern of tracks that would very quickly identify the beast beyond reasonable doubt. It is almost as if some supernatural creature has left some tantalizing, accidental evidence of its incorporeal existence.

This is modern folklore in the making. One thing can be tentatively regarded as 'definite', however: unless every single witness is mistaken, exaggerating or lying then we have a real, true mystery on our hands. Photos, footprints and alleged carcasses aside, quite often it is the simple sincerity of the witness that is the most convincing evidence for the Beast of Exmoor and his ilk. It is often the very banality of the witness reports that appear to convince, the lack of sensationalism somehow creating a weird paradox that makes the testimony more credible. The witness is inevitably naturally nonplussed and frequently unnerved, but the big cat does not ever seem to growl, pounce or give chase. The sincere bemusement is best illustrated by a resident of Banwell, who told me in August 2010, 'There are reports of large black cats around Cheddar and Axbridge and along the Strawberry Line [a cycle route on an old railway line]. My Mum and I have seen "something" so I can vouch for this! I say "something" as it was a long way in the distance and in fairness could have been a dog, but there was a large black creature with a longish tail that ran across the path. That was all we saw and our dog got a bit spooked, but other people have said they have seen something similar. My mum is certain it was a big cat...'

While driving through Exmoor I have seen a sign which is of the triangular warning design that displays a black cat, its back arched, which I can think of no reason to be there, other than to serve as a cautionary warning to motorists that 'big cats' lurk in the area. One is certainly left with the feeling that out of all the phenomena jotted down in this book, this is the one that the average person is most likely to experience. Who knows, maybe you will be driving along a poorly lit road somewhere away from a large town and your car headlights will simply fall on the shiny, black coat, muscular haunches and yellow eyes of one of these creatures looking right back at you as if it were the most natural thing in the world.

A MENAGERIE OF MYSTERIES

Joseph Strutt's *The Sports and Pastimes Of The People Of England* (1801) reflects on the sad demise of the pine marten in Somerset, 'That beautiful animal, the marten, once so common in England's forests, is now rapidly disappearing. It is supposed to still linger in the Somersetshire and Devonshire confines of Exmoor.' But later testimony by J. Charles Cox provided brief evidence that this lithe, shy little mammal with its distinctive 'bib' marking on its throat had, in fact, survived well beyond this, when he wrote, 'I several times saw specimens in the 1850s and 60s...that had been shot by the keepers of Sir Thomas Acland and Mr Knight on the Somersetshire side of Exmoor. I once saw one wild in the Horner Woods, below Cloutsham, I think in the year 1860...'

Although pine marten numbers have increased in other parts of Britain, after nearly becoming extinct, these animals appear to be gone entirely from Exmoor for now, until such time as they are re-introduced. But it does indicate that certain species linger a lot longer than reckoned; however, in the following instances the appearances of non-native wildlife are somewhat more perplexing.

An eagle was shot in Sir John Smyth's Park at Ashton, Bristol, in November 1694, it being a rare-enough event to excite much comment. Page's *An Exploration Of Exmoor* (1890) makes reference to some of the out-of-place wildlife that was sometimes found in Somerset: 'Polecats appear occasionally; the Montagu's harrier (*cireus cineraceus*) is sometimes seen. A snowy owl has been shot of recent years, and in 1884 a pelican was seen in the North Forest. As Mr Fortescue suggests, he had probably escaped from confinement. He adds that the moor folk attributed his presence to the firing at Tel-el-Kebir! The ring ousel (*turdus torquatus*) is also found, and an eagle was lately seen upon the Quantocks, where it swooped down upon, and for some distance carried, a little dog. And some years since, a golden eagle was shot by Mr Nicholas Snow's keeper and is now in his house at Oare.'

But even more exotic creatures may haunt our countryside. The 'original' Beast of Brassknocker Hill (a crossroads east of Monkton Combe) appeared to be some kind of escaped primate, although it was variously described as a spider monkey, a lemur, a baboon, a gibbon and even a young bear. Whatever it was, in July of 1979 it appeared to have been swinging beneath an oak tree, stripping the bark off it at a great height. The police officer who spotted it in the summer of 1980 thought that it resembled a chimpanzee. Its appearance, according to folklore 30 years on, seemed to have a tremendous effect on the natural wildlife of the area, it being observed that birds fell silent or deserted the woodland and livestock became extremely agitated. Where it came from, or indeed where it went to, are also unanswered questions, although the reports in the *Bath Evening Chronicle* at the time created a minor sensation. Some thought that it resembled a bear about four inches tall with rings of whitish fur around its eyes.

Near Minehead in early December 1985, tracks found at Brenda Cornish's farm were identified as belonging to a wolverine. Mrs Cornish had previously been unnerved by a horrific animal-like screaming noise emanating from nearby woodland. The wolverine is a stocky and ferocious carnivore about the size of a small dog, with a reputation as an insatiable glutton; more importantly, its natural habitat is Canada and Siberia and the Nordic countries of northern Europe, not the Somerset coast.

On 17 August 2001 a number of people witnessed what they swore was 'a lioness' climbing the hillside near the Rowberrow petrol station, south of Churchill. The newspapers dubbed the mysterious animal the 'Beast of Blagdon', and its proximity to the Dolebury Warren hill fort would appear to add to it a kind of 'supernatural' dimension, although it was (or was reported to be) an animal of flesh and blood. I am not aware that the mystery was ever solved. In June 2010 a surprised motorist was forced to halt because he encountered a wallaby, of all things, in the road at Fore Street, Winsham, near Chard. This was no tall tale: he actually managed to photograph the animal very clearly before it bounded into a garden and away. At the time of writing it is unclear where the wallaby came from.

I have even heard bizarre urban legends that there is a colony of bears residing in the impenetrable parts of woodland that make up the vastness of Exmoor National Park in West Somerset. And this would seem an appropriate juncture to join the next chapter and investigate the strange and fantastic creatures of folklore, legend and modern myth that at one time supposedly inhabited Somerset's more remote corners.

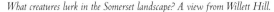

What creatures lurk in the Somerset landscape? A view from Willett Hill.

CHAPTER 8

CREATURES OF MYTH AND LEGEND

INTRODUCTION

On Saturday 3 November 2001 a carnival of the strangest kind occurred in Dinder, a small village between Shepton Mallet and Wells. The people of that place prepared a 'dragon' to slay, made out of willow withies, bamboo and strong masking tape, and carried it aloft before ceremonially 'killing' it to great cheers and applause. The act was in memory of an event that legend has it occurred *c*.1240, when Bishop Jocelinus Thoteman of Bath and Wells killed a dragon. The monster had been terrorizing Dinder, North Wootton and Dulcote, snatching children and ravaging crops, and Jocelinus supposedly venutred out and beheaded it single-handely. The bishop died in 1242 and is buried in the choir of Wells Cathedral. There is a mosaic of the event set in stone at the Bishop's Palace, made by local children, who will be grandparents themselves the next time this ceremony is performed. This will be in 2051, and the legend says that should the ceremony not take place every 50 years, then the dragon will be back – a circumstance that almost makes one wish that the ceremony is not carried out, just to see what might happen! According to tradition, the incident is also depicted in a corbel in the stairway of the Chapter House at Wells, which shows a monk-like figure pinning a serpent to the floor by means of a stick thrust in its mouth.

The spear still resides in Low Ham Church, but may in fact have been a gift to Ralph Stawel, created Baron Stawel in 1683, from a native North American.

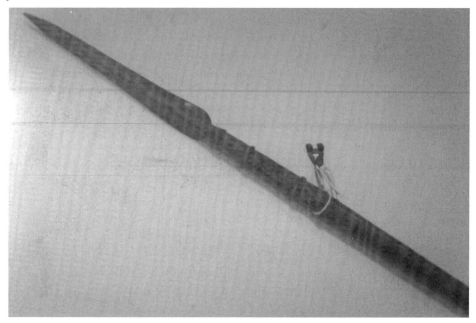

At one time it seems that Somerset was fertile ground for dragons, for they are held to have inhabited many other places. The Somerset Archaeological and Natural History Society's *Proceedings* for the years 1861-1862 recorded that there was a legend that a dragon lived on Aller Hill and devoured all the crops in the neighbourhood, to the great injury of the locals. Other retellings have it that the dragon lived at Curry Rivel and would periodically fly over the marshes, flapping its great, leathery wings and scorching the fields with bursts of fire from its mouth. Local people were also killed by it, until one day a man named John Aller attacked it on Aller Hill after it had alighted there. After a titanic struggle he managed to kill it, although the fiery blood that gushed from its severed neck set the land ablaze. During the conflict, John Aller had been scorched by the dragon's breath and so lost his life in the battle. It is said that nothing would ever after grow at the site of the dragon's death, and that John Aller was buried at St Andrew's Church. The spear that inflicted the fatal wound upon the monster is in the undedicated chapel at nearby Low Ham; it is 9ft-long with double feathering, but would appear to be too 'new' to be what tradition says it is. Nonetheless, the Village Hall in Aller has a modern mosaic of the dragon being slain by the spear-wielding John, and the dragon is Aller's mascot.

Another famous dragon lived in Shervage Wood near Holford, devastating the neighbourhood in the traditional fashion. A common woodman ventured into Shervage Wood when he thought the monster was away, and at dinnertime sat on its slumbering length, taking it for a fallen tree among the fern. When the log moved, however, the woodman cried, 'Her do be you, does her? Thee do movey, do 'ee? Well den!' And with that he stuck his axe in the moving creature and fled. The story appears to have first been written down in 1904 in *The Quantock Hills: Their Combes And Villages*, and it is interesting to note that in 1908 the story is recorded elsewhere as being used as a deterrent to children who might linger too long at the Dowsborough hillfort. The Somerset folklorist Ruth Tongue elaborated on the original story; in her 1965 collection of Somerset legends and anecdotes, often penned in the broad Somerset dialect, she calls the dragon the 'Gurt vurm' and has it that its two halves slithered off in different directions, one half to Bilbrook and the other to Kingston-St-Mary.

One of the bench ends in the church at Crowcombe depicts two naked men sticking spears into a monstrous dragon that appears to have a second head in its belly. Another dragon carving at the church in Bishops Lydeard depicts a dragon that was killed by a champion of the Fitzwarren family, nearer Taunton at Norton Fitzwarren. This enormous serpent supposedly had its lair at the old earthwork known as Norton Camp. Ruth Tongue was informed in 1911 that a 'bold veller' had climbed Ivyton Lane, near Kingston St Mary, and rolled a stone down and into the dragon's gullet, killing it as it attempted to belch flames at him. She was shown the place where the rock had been collected and was told that the 'bold veller' was one 'Filk Fitz Warine.'

The partial and oft-repeated explanation for stories of dragons is that the legends were generated wherever the Danes had made inroads into England: the Saxons referred to the Danes as 'dragons'. At Kilve we see another partial explanation for these legends. Blue Ben the dragon lived in a tunnel at Putsham, to the south of the Kilve crossroads, but his official job was to pull the Devil's chariot around Hell. One day, this gigantic, fire-breathing lizard slipped from a causeway and into the mud of Putsham Hill and was sucked in until he suffocated to death. The Somerset Archaeological and Natural History Society's *Proceedings* tells us that numerous deposits of fossilzed Ichthyosauri remains were discovered in the 19th century in the region: 'The eyes of the first Ichthyosaurus we discovered had tumbled out of their sockets and were lying seperated from it in the clay, and were at first mistaken for ammonites.' The remains of one of these gigantic, long-beaked Jurassic fish is now in possession of Taunton County Museum, it being said that they belong to Blue Ben himself. It can be no coincidence that there is a headland nearby called Blue Ben, and the legend of him being a dragon would appear to be a modern intertwining of natural history and storytelling. The folklorist Poole observed of these tales, 'It is very difficult to account for this universal legend, unless we travel back to a time when great lizard monsters occupied the earth with man…' This was written in *c*.1876.

There are numerous other stories with similar themes in Somerset. Dragons are the most familiar creatures that, according to legend, once inhabited the land, but there are many other fantastic creatures from the world of mythology and cryptozoology; if it can be imagined, then it has been seen, or there is at least a legend concerning it. Generations have grown up with local stories of giants, fairies, pixies, otherworldly beings, wild men, sea creatures and strange visitors from outer space. One might wonder under what circumstances these tales came to exist, unless – somehow – they had a genesis in factual events.

FAIRIES AND PIXIES

As many children know, fairies at one time inhabited many parts of Somerset. *The West Somerset Word Book* (1886) clearly indicates that there was a blurring of the lines when it came to definitions of the little people, however. They were generally called a 'pixy', but what is interesting is that they were, apparently, still believed in at the time: 'A belief in these little creatures is still prevalent, although there is great confusion of idea between them and witches, bogies, goblins, hags and other uncanny things. The green rings so often seen in pastures are pixy-rings, round which they dance on moonlight nights. Toadstools are always pixy-stools. Rusty horseshoes are nailed over stable doors to prevent pixies from "terrifyin" the horses.' It was widely thought that pixies got into the stable to ride the horses round in circles, and there was barely a stable that did not have a horseshoe attached to the inside lintel to ward the pixies off, although quite why this worked is not clear. Their pixy-rings also possessed a supernatural power; anyone guilty of a crime who stepped into one would never escape the gallows, it was said. (Perhaps this has something to do with the story that a type of pixy ring could be observed in the 1800s near Stone Gallows, Taunton. In 1801 nine men were hanged there for stealing bread during rioting, and were taken to the site sat in their own coffins on the back of a wagon.) From folklorist Katherine Briggs we learn that 'In a Somerset description of fairies…seen in the twinkling of an eye, they were smaller, about the size of partridges, and of a reddish-brown colour.' The Reader's Digest *Folklore, Myths And Legends Of Britain* (1977), however, repeats the oft-told story that the fairies and pixies were in actual fact two distinct races, who had clashed in an almighty battle near Buckland St Mary, with the pixies (with their distinctive red hair, pointed ears and green clothes) winning the day. The fairies, we learn, fled to Devon, Dorset and Ireland.

The 'little people', then, are enigmatic indeed. Perhaps the most famous story about the fairies, or pixies, is the one originally mentioned in Richard Bovet's *Pandemonium, Or The Devil's Cloister* (1684), and we are told that at one time they were seen frequently on the Black Down Hills on the Somerset/Devon border. People making their way to Pitminster described them as differentiating greatly from the traditional winged sprite: 'fairies' were more akin to elves, appearing like small men and women dressed in red, blue or green habits and with high-crowned hats. Sometime around 1634 a person on his way to Combe St Nicholas saw a great company of people on the side of the hill like country folks assembled at a fair. The man could not attribute the gathering of people, stalls, peddlers and all manner of food and drink to any local fair he knew of, so, remembering the story of the 'fairy fair', he opted to ride his horse in among them to see what it was all about. As he did so, at some point they became invisible, although the man could feel himself being jostled, as though stuck in a crowd he could not see. He passed through this and then, a little way on, turned – he could now see the fair once more! He found himself feeling increasingly unwell and made for home. By the time he reached Combe St Nicholas he was afflicted with a lameness that lasted all his life. Bovet recorded that for the next 20 years this person would explain his strange affliction with this story, which was related in turn to Bovet by a mutual acquaintance 'of known honour.'

The story implies that, if left alone, the pixies co-existed reasonably well with their human companions. There are other stories of misfortune encountered by those who interfered with this uneasy peace in some way, including one to the north at Minehead. *A Book Of Exmoor* (1903) notes that there were many legends about pixies here: of particular note is the one about a woman at market in Minehead who saw a relative of hers stealing meat from one of the stalls. She remonstrated with him, and he asked, 'Which eye did you see me with?' The woman told him, and at this the man blew on the woman's face: she became instantly blind in that one eye. It goes without saying that the relative 'had dealings with the pixies.' There were also stories of farmers and women who had encountered a bunch of 24 fairies at 'Great Gate' when returning from Minehead market. Those who did so were spellbound and led on a disorientating, pointless route over moors and through woodland until daybreak, when the pixies would depart and leave the luckless traveller lost and alone. One way to avoid this fate was to take your jacket off and turn it inside out.

In the parish of Selworthy, writer Fredrick Hancock recorded that the pixies lit fires and dressed their children in a particular meadow. They also sat on the cattle grid called Comer's Gate, at Comer's Cross on Winsford Hill, and as late as 1903 it was written that folk avoided the spot after dark. In Taunton, according to F.W. Matthews' *Tales Of The Blackdown Borderland* (1923), at one time a midwife had been struck blind after noticing some fairies stealing food from stalls at Taunton market. Her ability to espy them came from an earlier incident, when she had herself entered the fairy kingdom to assist in a birth and accidentally wiped some magic potion in her eyes while there. The story seems to be a variation on the one at Minehead.

Pixies also bedevilled Knighton Combe, to the west of Withypool. There is a story that on one occasion, when the bells of St Andrew's Church were being rung, an irate pixie stormed into the dwelling known as Knighton and demanded that the farmer provide him with a horse and trap, saying, 'I want to take my wife and family out of the noise of the ding-dongs!' Some said that this was the very King of the Pixies himself! At this same place, farmers would leave a floor full of corn overnight and in the morning find it had been thrashed, by the pixies, they supposed. One night they stayed awake and peered through the keyhole to see what was going on and saw a number of pixies with no clothes on gambolling in among the corn. Since it spared them some work, the family one evening left some little clothes out for the pixies, who, however, were offended by this charity and left, never to return.

But, sometimes, dealing with the pixies could be a mutually beneficial arrangement: in the district of Selworthy the pixies would enter cider cellars or dirty houses through the keyhole to complete the fermenting or to sweep up. For this they expected to be rewarded with a basin of milk and some bread that was left for them in the corner. *The Reader's Digest Folklore, Myths And Legends Of Britain* (1977) tells another story of this type. A ploughman found a tiny broken wooden peel – a flat, wooden shovel for delivering loaves of bread into old-fashioned ovens – at the Wick tumulus, on Wick Moor at Hinkley Point. Thinking it a child's toy, he took it home and mended it and left it where he had found it. He returned later and found a hot pixie cake in its place, fresh from the oven. The Reverend C.W. Whistler noted for the benefit of *Folklore* (Vol. 19, No. I) in a 1908 piece called 'Local Traditions Of The Quantocks' that people were supposed to have been 'pixy-led' near this (at the time) 11ft-high and 90ft-long mound, which was in itself held to move about Wick Moor of its own volition.

Folklorist Ruth Tongue observed that to stand beneath an elder tree on Midsummer Eve actually enabled one to see the fairies and be granted his or her heart's desire, but it came at a price: the person would pass away inside a year. This reflects the belief that interaction with fairies could promote wealth, or else that wealth could be obtained by treaty or by cunning from the fairies, although at great risk. At Dolebury Warren Camp, a relic of the ancient Britons outside Shipham, there was a long tradition that treasure lay buried thereabouts. The traveller and antiquarian Leland recorded a rhyme: 'If Dolebyri dyggyd ware; Of golde shuld be the share.' According to Ruth Tongue, who was told the story in 1907 by an informant at Axbridge, the gold was the property of a race of fairies called the Redshanks, who clothed themselves in red and smoked little clay pipes – this last being supposed from the frequent discovery by miners of such an article. With the departure of the Redshanks, the treasure had begun to sink and so would now never be recovered. Legend also had it that Cadbury Castle, South Cadbury, was the treasure house of the fairies, full of gold. In fact, robbing the little folk of their hoard even had a specific name: 'pixy-wordng'.

Many place names have associations with the little people, although often without attendant legend. In the Mendips between Stoke St Michael and Harridge Wood there is a cave complex, quarried since the 1920s, called Fairy Cave. East of Brushford we find woodland known as Pixy Copse in the vicinity of the remains of the old motte-and-bailey Bury Castle. East of Butcombe there can still be seen a long barrow called Fairy Toot, which *The Gentleman's Magazine* noted in 1789 was 'considered the haunt of ghosts, goblins and fairies.' This prehistoric burial chamber was enormous in its time, and was guessed to be the burial chamber belonging to 'the great temple at Stanton Drew', but by 1835 it had been largely destroyed. And, as befits Goblin Combe, a rocky eminence near Cleeve clothed with woods that terminates near Cleeve Toot, there is naturally a story. H.H. Wilson's *A Somerset Sketch-Book* (1912) notes the place had a sinister reputation: 'There are "sights seen" here, though their nature remains vague.' Ruth L. Tongue was told in 1945 that at some point long ago a little girl collecting primroses had got lost in the combe and had sat down against a rock. With the primroses touching the rock, the rock opened and there appeared the fairies, who comforted the little girl's tears, gave her a gold ball and led her home safely.

Some mariners in the Victorian era even returned to port boasting that they had weighed anchor at a mysterious island in the Bristol Channel, called the Green Meadows of Enchantment, that was inhabited by the fairies, but which could not be seen from land and did not feature on any map. If it was seen, it was only glimpsed through mist, and if the story has any basis in truth then it might have been a bizarre natural phenomenon or one of the actual islands in the channel approached by poor navigation. The legend of the Green Meadows of Enchantment was collected by Ms Tongue in her *Somerset Folklore* (1965) and based around fragmentary scraps of an old folk song she had recorded. There is a well-known story that some 19th-century sailors actually beached at this mysterious island and joined in a fairy revel; upon departing they observed the island to gradually fade away into the mist, never to be seen again.

GIANTS OF SOMERSET AND BRISTOL

In lore, Norton Malreward is named after Sir John Hauteville, who, upon receiving the manor of Norton by order of William the Conqueror, complained, 'Mal reward! An ill guerdon for my exploits!' This, according to the original compiler of Somerset lore, C.H. Poole, accounted for the parish's subsequent name of Norton Malreward. Poole thought this unlikely, but the 'exploit' at any rate concerned a remarkable feat: it was said that Sir John, from the height of Maes Knoll to the north, had lobbed the standing stone now called Hautville's Quoit. This stone landed just short of the River Chew near the stone circles of Stanton Drew. The legend reinforces the belief that Sir John was something of a 'giant', or at least possessed of prodigious strength. In fact, so powerful was he that he once carried three men up the tower of Holy Trinity Church, Norton Malreward, two under his armpits and one in his teeth! The two under his arms protested, and so were crushed to death; the third kept his mouth shut and so survived. *Somerset Notes And Queries* noted other details of the story in 1856. 'Vulgar tradition' held that Sir John Hautvil had carried out his exploit at Norton tower during the reign of Edward I (not the Conqueror) and that 'the church at Chew Magna contains a statue of Sir John Hautvil, in armour, cut out of one solid piece of Irish oak.' In fact, this may be an effigy of someone else, but the article is entitled 'A Giant Of The Olden Time' and I suppose the myth outweighed any factual elements considerably.

Although the legend indicates a man who was merely supposed to be the most powerful in the region, there are other stories that hint at actual giants of supernatural stature having lived in the county. Many of the long barrows and ancient tumuli that dot the Somerset landscape were referred to as 'giants' graves', and similar stories are attached to other landmarks. Robin Hood's Butts, for example, are supposed to have been caused by two giants flinging handfuls of mud at each other across the Blackdowns. Maes Knoll, the massive Celtic hillfort south of Whitchurch, Bristol, which commands stunning views of North Somerset, was rumoured to have developed from the scrapings of a giant's spade. According to another very old tale, there were two antagonistic giants – Vincent, Lord of Avon, and Gorm (or Goram) – who were always in competition with each other. John Chilcott's *New Guide To Bristol* (1826) stated that the 'remarkable cavern' in the cliff-face of the Avon Gorge at Clifton was at one time the retreat of the giant Vincent, and so had earned the name 'Giant's Hole'. The two entered into a competition to cut the chasm that is now the Avon Gorge, but Goram sat down to take a nap 'while Vincent, more watchful, completed the undertaking and obtained all the credit.' Some say that the competition was for the hand of a woman called Avona, which is why the gorge is called what it is. Others say that the gorge exists because the two giants lived on opposite sides of the river and continuously threw stones at each other. Goram himself resided 'at Westbury, on the side of the brook Trim, which runs to Sea Mills.'

The tradition is a little confusing; this part of the Avon Gorge was also called St Vincent's Rocks, on account of a small chapel dedicated to St Vincent of Valencia, of which the cave may have been a part for the purposes of seclusion. The cliff was also called Gyston Cliff, on account of the story that a Saracen giant of that name was believed responsible for erecting Roman entrenchments on the summit of the rock. It would seem plausible that the legend of Vincent the giant and Goram developed from these elements. Chilcott also wrote, 'There is a rock pointed out at Kingsweston as Goram's Chair' – this last a limestone outcrop in the grounds of the 650-acre Blaise Castle Estate, which is often scaled by professional climbers. A walk into the valley at this breathtakingly beautiful site also affords one a view of Goram's Soap Dish by the Henbury Trym and the Giant's Footprint in the limestone pavement. At any rate, the bickering

The Avon Gorge with St Vincent's Rock and the Hot Wells in 1779.

According to folklorist and storyteller Ruth Tongue, giants dwelt in Nether Stowey Castle hill, reaching out to snatch villagers passing by.

between Vincent and Goram came to an end when Goram fled and tripped over Maes Knoll. He crashed into the Bristol Channel and so died, and they do say that Flat Holm and Steep Holm are parts of his head and shoulder, with Brean Down, off Weston-super-Mare, also being part of his skeleton.

There is also a formation called the Giant's Chair on Grabbist Hill, west of Dunster. This is a cavity on the south side of the top of Grabbist Hill, and in it the giant used to sit and dip his toes in the River Avill. When linen was hanging out to dry at nearby Dunster Castle, he would reach over and swipe a towel to dry his feet!

The Glastonbury historian J. Armitage Robinson wrote in 1926 that some believed giants once inhabited Brent Knoll hill fort near Burnham-on-Sea, and it was at one time called the Mound of Frogs. Here, a protégé of King Arthur called Ider managed to kill the three giants that lived there, but also lost his own life in the battle.

WILD MEN

The excavation of Gough's Cave at Cheddar Gorge and the discovery of the 9,000-year-old skeleton of Cheddar Man in 1903 have provided a remarkable insight into the types of early human that existed in this region in approximately 7150 BC. In 1906 *Memorials Of Old Somerset* observed, 'Man appeared from time to time on the scene [in the Mendips], a miserable savage, armed with bow and spear, unacquainted with metals, but defended from the cold by coats of skin. Sometimes he took possession of the den and drove out the hyenas, for it is impossible for both to have lived in the same cave at the same time. He kindled his fires at the entrance to cook his food and to keep away the wild animals; then he went away, and the hyenas came to their old abode. While all this was taking place there were floods from time to time, until eventually the cave was completely blocked up with their deposits.' Of Cheddar Man himself, the book noted, 'In any case, the man found at Cheddar ranks for certainty among the oldest known inhabitants of Europe. He was [says the Dean of Wells, who saw some of the remains *in situ*] "a short, powerful, carnivorous savage, fleeing, perhaps, from a foe, with all his stock-in-trade, to a fissure in the rock, there to die of starvation. In his skull were found human finger bones. Were they his own?" What a field for speculation the question opens!'

There is a strange fascination with later examples of wild men, who lived a lawless and primitive existence in the style of Cheddar Man, despite the surrounding towns developing and modernizing, that captures the imagination. When the 200-tonne ship, *Anne* or *Ayde*, came into Bristol in 1577, returning from its voyage to find the north-west passage to the East Indies, it brought with it a family from the Kingdom of Cathay (supposedly northern China). Captain Martin Frobisher presented these tribesmen to the sponsors, who were more interested in the huge hoard of 'gold ore' that the *Anne* had brought back, which turned out to be near-worthless.

The three tribal people were apparently left to their own devices in Bristol. They consisted of a man called Cally Chough and a woman called Ignorth, who suckled an unnamed infant, 'casting her breasts over her shoulders.' All three were clad in stag skins and tried to live their traditionally primitive way of life in one of Europe's busiest ports. Thus, Cally Chough could be found that October rowing a boat made of animal skins (which he had brought with him) up and down the river at the Back, it being at full sea. The boat was about 14ft-long, sharp at both ends and like a canoe, with a central hole that he sat in, killing ducks with a dart. When he left the water at the Marsh, he carried the boat on his back. All three could

Cheddar Man in Gough's Cave.

eat nothing but raw flesh, and after a month they all died, having been brought back as a curiosity by those who then lost interest in them and let them starve to death.

John L.W. Page wrote in 1890 that 'within living memory' there was a cave dweller who lived in a hole beneath the rock in the hillside at Cothelstone Hill, north of Cothelstone itself. This wild man was called Blackietops, or Blackatops, and he lived an almost savage existence among the remarkable 9ft-tall thistles. In Page's time the hole had been filled in with earth, leaving us to wonder who this person was – a vagrant, a shipwrecked foreign national, an outlaw? No doubt at the time people wondered if he was a relic of prehistoric man, a throwback to the Neanderthal age.

THE 'ACARUS CROSSII'

Could it be that a 19th-century scientist created life in a laboratory? At his estate, Fyne Court, in the parish of Broomfield in the Quantocks, a country gentleman named Andrew Crosse may have done just that.

Crosse conducted electrical experiments on a great scale. Utilising two enormous Leyden jars, charged by means of wires that snaked for miles through woodland, he would subject various matters held in solution to electrical action simply to see if the matter mineralised itself, or what the other results might be.

In 1837 he performed an experiment mixing two ounces of powdered flint with six ounces of carbonate of potassa, fusing the lot together in an intense heat, before reducing the mass to powder and dissolving it in water. From this, he obtained a silicate of potassa, a portion of which he diluted in boiling water, slowly adding hydrochloric acid to supersaturation. This fluid he subjected to a long, continued electric action through the intervention of a porous stone, in order to form, if possible, crystals of silica. Two weeks into his experiment Crosse observed through a microscope a number of small, whitish developments projecting from the middle of the electrified stone. Four days later these white things had grown, and by the 26th day they had assumed the shape of what were clearly insects of some type, which stood erect on bristly tails. Two days later they had developed spindly, delicate legs and were detaching themselves from the electrified stone to move about by themselves. A week later 100 of these creatures were moving around, the smaller ones with six legs and the larger ones with eight legs, possibly an indication that they were either male and female or two separate species. They hid themselves whenever they were presented with a shelter, and the cold appeared to be fatal to them.

Crosse originally considered that these insects must have already been present as ova in the water he had used, but he repeated the experiment and produced exactly the same results. The scientific community became interested and flocked to Fyne Court, where others repeated the experiment under even more rigorous scientific conditions and yet achieved the same result. The insects were called *Acarus Crossii* in veneration of Crosse, but their discovery split – and still does spilt – the scientific community right down the middle, with some believing that such a circumstance was simply not possible and must have been brought about by scientific oversights combined with unsanitary conditions in Crosse's laboratory.

Had Crosse created a new life form? As astonishing as the story is, this is no urban legend, but a true tale. *The Living Age* magazine of 1858 published a lengthy autobiography of Crosse upon his death three years previously, observing of the 'life' he had apparently created, 'Loathsome things they certainly were, for they apparently belonged to the genus *acarus*, which is famous for its ugliness and numbers some of the most nauseous parasites in its ranks…'

Andrew Crosse died at Fyne Court on 6 July 1855, having lived his entire life at the place and spending his time there literally bottling lightning and performing other tricks that would have earned him a reputation as a wizard two or three generations earlier. Sadly, Fyne Court suffered a disastrous fire in 1898, but is now managed by the National Trust; one of Crosse's laboratory tables is in St Mary and All Saints Church, Broomfield.

THE LIVING DARKNESS

One of the most puzzling of Somerset superstitions was that the pitch-black darkness of night had a 'life' of its own. In the hill country of Brendon, the writer Frederick Hancock observed in 1897, 'A man going to an outhouse in bright moonlight saw an indefinable black object in the clear light, which, as he looked, grew larger and larger, until it shut out the moonlight altogether. He struck into the darkness with a stick he held in his hand, and the darkness passed away.' On another clear, starlit night a farmer driving his wife in a trap saw this phenomenon: 'It was small and undefinable at first, and then expanded into a huge, black, uncouth appearance which occupied the whole road.' The thing spooked the horse, causing it to turn and run down the hill, and when it had been brought to a halt the farmer looked back up the hill to see the road empty.

I, for one, can testify how phenomenally dark some of the lanes in rural Somerset can become, and although there is a suggestion that this mysterious darkness was thought supernatural, perhaps it was something natural, but inexplicable. The general impression given is that the darkness had an actual, living presence and could manifest itself almost physically.

THE 'MONSTER COW' RIB

One of the most famous of English mythological animals is the Dun Cow, a creature that features in the Anglo-Norman romances of the legendary warrior hero Guy of Warwick. Guy is first mentioned in the 13th century as Gui de Warewic, and scholars have tentatively placed the 'historical' context of his adventures as taking place during the reign of King Athelstan of England (d. AD 939) in the Warwickshire/Oxfordshire region of the Midlands. According to legend, Guy, in an attempt to win the hand of a lady of higher social standing than himself, endured all manner of trials and feats in order to prove his worth. He travelled widely and battled all kinds of dragons and giants, while nearer to

Another whalebone, this time at Glastonbury.

home he killed the animal known as the Dun Cow on Dunsmore Heath, between Coventry and Rugby. The Dun Cow is said to have been a real, monstrous bovine animal that produced an inexhaustible supply of milk.

It is with this in mind that 'proof' of the clash with the Dun Cow crops up in Bristol. In a bizarre realm, where myth met what was allegedly visible proof of reality, there supposedly existed numerous relics of the clash on Dunsmore Heath, or else with other Dun Cows elsewhere. Around 1823 a traveller named Twiss wrote, 'In Bristol I was entertained with the sight of a rib of a famous Dun Cow, killed by Sir William Penn. This knight and his rib are both deposited in the church of St Mary Redcliff.' The church folklorist George S. Tyack wrote that this relic supposedly came from a 'monster cow' that once upon a time supplied the whole city of Bristol with milk. The reason the creature had to be killed was that it had, according to folklore, gone berserk during a prolonged drought and rampaged through Bristol.

The implication is that in the minds of the people the 4ft-long relic at St Mary Redcliff belonged to a distinctly separate animal to the one that was killed at Dunsmore Heath by Guy of Warwick, although Sir William Penn might have been amused by the suggestion that he was regarded as the champion who slew the beast; he died in 1670, by which time the bone had been in Bristol for over 170 years.

It is likely that the observations relate to a whalebone, which is said to have been presented to the church by John Cabot in 1497. Nonetheless, despite the unlikeliness of the myth that surrounds the rib, it is tempting to idly speculate that the Dun Cow was more than a mere mythological creature; perhaps she was even a remnant of some gigantic beast from prehistory that had survived until the Anglo-Saxon era and beyond in small pockets in parts of England. Or perhaps Cabot brought back some kind of unfamiliar animal that escaped and had to be trapped and killed?

The relic is still to be found at the entrance to St John the Baptist's Chapel.

STORIES TO FRIGHTEN CHILDREN...?

Some of the horrible monsters that lurked in Somerset fell into the fairy-tale realm, and – I suppose – existed only to pacify misbehaving children. Certainly this was the case with 'Bloodybones', a nondescript bogy or goblin, whom Victorian parents in West Somerset used to threaten their children with: 'If you are not a good girl, I will put you in a dark hole with the Bloodybones...' This malignant creature was generally considered to be a bloodied bogle with mutated, scarred and twisted flesh that hid in the grime under sink pipes, waiting to drag naughty children to a grisly fate down the drains and through the sewage system. This monstrosity also went by the dual name of Rawhead.

Possibly the most sinister and unnerving creature that haunted Somerset, however, was the Barrow-wight briefly described by Ruth Tongue in *Somerset Folklore* (1965): 'A crouching form like a rock, with matted hair all over it, and pale, flat eyes.' This thing was seen in 1908 by E. Dauncey Tongue (presumably a relative), near the Hangley Cleave tumuli, who described it as 'the most terrifying thing he had ever seen.' This witness in 1928 became an East-African District Commissioner with a reputation for coolness when big-game hunting, yet the creature – which he considered some kind of barrow guardian – had been the one thing that had genuinely unnerved him. Hangley Cleave rises near Kinsford Water, south of Simonsbath and deep in the Exmoor National Park – a true place of mystery and just the sort of place for these 'bogles' to hide.

MONSTERS OF THE DEEP

On 10 April 1607 a weird fish was caught in King's Road, Bristol, and 'brought to the Back in a Cardiff boat.' Its description is curious: 'It was 5ft-long and 3ft-broad, having two hands and two feet [fins?] and a very wide, gristly mouth. The fish was hauled upon a dray to Mr Mayor's house.' Another strange fish was taken in King's Road in 1763, something dark brown, 4ft 9in in length and entirely without scales; in fact, something that resembled part sea lion and part fish, with three rows of sharp small teeth, a foot-wide mouth with no tongue, horns, fins and 'two short paws somewhat like the fore half of a human foot, with five toes joined together, having the appearance of nails.' It had a tail, and a wide, square mouth; a depiction of it in *Philosophical Transactions* (1764) displays a monstrosity that resembles no known fish at all. Its carcass was being displayed 'at the Hot Wells', having been killed with great difficulty while struggling in the fishermen's net. There are, of course, numerous stories of strange marine creatures that lurk in the waters off the Somerset coast. The folklorist Ruth Tongue was told a seaman's yarn in 1961, by a member of the Brean Women's Institute, about a truly gigantic fish off 'Barrow Sands' that had, according to seafaring legend, eaten all the other fish and even sailors, scooping them up in its gigantic maw. The conger eels would bark when this fish was hungry, and in the end a brave fisherman sailed out in a little boat and dropped an anchor down the fish's gullet, killing it.

The conger eels themselves seem to have been regarded warily off the Somerset coast. Katherine Briggs' *The Fairies In English Tradition And Literature* (1967) mentions a vague story of 'a kind of syren' who lured fishermen into the water off Somerset so as to give the conger eels something to feed on. The stony beaches of the coast often saw the practice of 'glatting', or hunting conger eels using dogs up until the First World War. There is even a bizarre legend of an eel of prodigious size that swam up the Severn Estuary and began to deplete the fish population with its voracious appetite. So the local fishermen, using their boats to form strategic blockades, forced the eel towards Brean Down and along the River Axe, and eventually into Wookey Hole. This monstrosity is said to have been some 30ft-long, and is now, according to legend, stuck in the caves somewhere, submerged, although goodness knows what it is supposed to live off.

The Graphic newspaper of 20 October 1883 briefly reported that a 'sea serpent' had been spotted in the Bristol Channel heading out towards the Atlantic at a speed of 25 miles an hour: 'The monster was about half a mile long, and left a greasy trail behind him.' But surely the tallest tale appeared in the *Daily Chronicle* of 30 April 1907. Under the headline 'Fight with a "Sea Serpent"', it reported the allegation of a Scottish tourist called McNaughten, who had visited Clevedon and had been rowing in a little skiff about a mile off Clevedon Pier. A massive snake-like creature that he described as 'like a huge mummy, with large, sunken eyes enveloped in a sort of hairy flap' suddenly began harassing the boat from about 20 yards away. Leaping and diving, it approached the boat and it was all Mr McNaughten could do to keep it at bay by hitting out with an oar. All at once, the 'flabby monster' leapt out of the water as though attacking the boat, and Mr McNaughten dimly recollected lashing out with the oar and perhaps hitting it, before being flung into the water. Having clambered back into the boat, he found that the creature had submerged, and he made his way to Portishead in a state of shock – although the thing never reappeared. Apparently, this bizarre incident happened in front of 'many spectators', although perhaps by this it is meant the people who helped him out of the boat when he made dry land.

Maybe the monster was the same one seen by the Chief Officer of the *Campania*, off County Cork, who, about the same time, saw a great, serpentine head rearing some 8ft out of the water. It had protuberances where eyes might have been in its great head, but the officer saw none; it had a neck some 14ft long, with the suggestion of a very great bulk beneath the waterline. It dived very near the propellers, and the officer was able to make two very good sketches of it. The connection is made because, according to the *Daily Mail* of 23 October 1933, when the captain visited Liverpool shortly after, he heard of a 'man who had been found drifting in a rowing boat in the Bristol Channel' who claimed to have lost both oars and his boat hook during a battle with a sea serpent. So perhaps the story is, Heaven forbid, true...

VISITORS FROM PLACES UNKNOWN

Perhaps one of the strangest stories ever marketed as 'fact' appeared in Gervase of Tilbury's *Otia Imperialia* (*c*.1214), which places the event in an unnamed village in the region of Bristol. The villagers were leaving the parish church (implying a mediaeval church; there is no suggestion that this was ancient history) on a Feast Day, when in the fog of a cloudy day they all saw a ship's anchor caught on a heap of stones, with its cable reaching up and into the dark clouds of the sky. The cable strained and then slackened, as though someone far up above were trying to free it, and then those assembled heard voices from above their heads, apparently in clamorous debate. Then 'a sailor' came climbing down the cable! As the townsfolk crowded around him, he died, suffocating as though 'our damp, thick atmosphere' had drowned him somehow. After an hour the cable fell loose and the anchor clattered on the ground; the airborne ship's crew had apparently cut it through and sailed off. The anchor they had left behind was made into fastenings and ornaments for the church door. Geoffrey noted that the story was 'widely known' and the ironwork was still on the church door as evidence that there was, in fact, a sea in the sky. This region, some thought, was called Magonia.

Presumably terrestrial, but still unexplained, were the mysterious airships piloted by unknown navigators that menaced parts of England in the years before the First World War. They appeared to be the advance guard of some great invasion force, or else sinister, airborne agents of a foreign power identifying targets in preparation for a full-scale attack; yet always they sailed away into the clouds, no government ever admitted responsibility, and there is something of the later UFO about these strange 'phantom dirigibles.' London newspapers reported that on 4 January 1913 an unknown airship had been seen above Dover, from the direction of the sea, for instance; but around the same time, on the other side of England, the lights of one of these mysterious airships were seen sailing through the sky over the Bristol Channel.

MODERN FAIRY STORIES

Some think that the traditional stories of pixies and fairies, in Exmoor at least, might have been started by the parties of armed banditti and smugglers that haunted the caves and woodland. *A Book Of Exmoor* (1903) lamented that, 'owing to an alarming spread of enlightenment', belief in fairies and pixies was by that time so difficult to uncover that 'very soon the schoolchildren will stand in need of a definition.' But this might not be quite true just yet. At Weston-super-Mare, near Birnbeck Pier, can be found another ancient British camp, Worlebury, where (according to Lillian E. Meyer's 1938 booklet *West Mendip Fragments*) a fairy or pixie had been glimpsed earlier that decade in a coppice on the camp's northern embankment facing towards Bathing Cove.

In May 1977 *FATE Magazine* published correspondence from a Cynthia Monteflore of Bath, which – if true – indicates that the little people are very much still with us. The incident appears to have occurred in her childhood, when she was in the garden pruning rose bushes at her mother's house, Highgate on Wells Road (specifically where this place was is not said). Both Cynthia and her mother saw 'a little figure about six inches high, in the perfect shape of a woman and with brilliant diaphanous wings resembling those of a dragonfly. The figure held a little wand and was pointing at the heart of a rose. At the tip of the wand there was a little light, like a star. The figure's limbs were very pale pink and visible through her clothes. She hovered near the rose for at least two minutes, her wings vibrating rapidly like those of a hummingbird, and then she disappeared.' This is a description of the 'literary' type of fairy that all children are familiar with, but which does not, in reality, tally with most folkloric descriptions of 'fairies'. But Cynthia also saw in the same garden, at a different time, a figure like a 'gnome' that conforms more to the type of 'pixie' that is supposed to have existed at one time in Somerset. This figure was about 18 inches tall, sturdy in frame and wearing a brown one-piece suit, and she glimpsed the figure running across a path and lawn to disappear under a fir tree. A search of the fir tree revealed nothing there. Some time later a family friend also saw this strange figure while digging vegetables in the same garden.

There are persistent stories that when the Hinkley Point nuclear power station was being built between Wick Moor and the coastline of the Bristol Channel, an excessive number of accidents bedevilled the project. It is true that during test runs problems were encountered with excessive noise, unexplained drops in mass flow rate, fatigue, and structural and mechanical damage; by the time the station began generating electricity proper in 1965, it had gone considerably over budget and was two years behind schedule. Wick tumulus was not actually built upon, but some people claimed to remember that when the tumulus had been excavated in 1907, there had been instances of illness and bad luck that had befallen the labourers and organizers. In fact, according to folklore, no less a personage than King Edward VII himself ordered work on the mound to stop.

The barrow is actually designated Pixies' Mound Tumulus on OS maps. It seemed that the vengeful pixie folk were displaying their anger supernaturally at the desecration of their centuries-old habitat by the situation of a huge, ugly atomic power station there.

The building of the reactor had occasioned several serious accidents, including a number of fatalities. The recent history of the controversial atomic plant indicates that, to the believer, there is still something of a 'curse' hanging over the place. The power station was decommissioned in 2000, but misfortune has still clung to it. Part of Hinkley Point B was closed in May 2003 after radioactive dust was reported to have leaked out into the atmosphere, and there have been numerous anti-nuclear demonstrations there. When the go-ahead was given for its demolition in July 2003 it was also announced that some low-level nuclear waste would continue to be stored there, meaning that the reactors would have to remain for the next 100 years before they can be dismantled – a circumstance that will, no doubt, ensure that this curious modern-day urban legend regarding the 'little people' survives for quite some time.

MODERN MONSTERS

In the early 1900s a freak of nature – or a true monster – was exhibited at the (now closed) Birnbeck Pier, Weston-super-Mare. Laid on his back, wearing a loincloth and holding a club, and with a snake on his chest, visitors paid to see the famous Kap Dwa – the 'Two-Headed Patagonian Giant'. This monstrosity was allegedly the stuffed and preserved body of a 12ft-tall, two-headed giant, who died in 1673 when he was run though with a pike during a fight with Spanish sailors who were attempting to capture him in Argentina or Paraguay. Kap Dwa was exhibited for some 35 years, and John Fothergill's *An Inn Keeper's Diary* (1931) tells us that the body was studied by two doctors and a radiologist, who found 'no perceptual evidence of its being fake.' Laurie Lee's *Cider With Rosie* (1959) writes that as a child he marvelled at 'the two-headed Indian', and today North Somerset Museum, Weston-super-Mare, displays a publicity image of this monster, which at the time excited speculation that it represented one of the last specimens of a dying race of two-headed giant humans. Many still remember the horror and curiosity they first experienced when they saw this creature. I will leave the last word on this to the museum curator, who told me, 'Personally, I think that it owes more to Victorian showmanship than anything else…'

Although Kap Dwa was not native to Somerset, some of the native monsters we seem to have produced here are almost as strange. Cryptozoologist Nick Redfern's *Three Men Seeking Monsters* (2004) mentions two: a 7ft-tall ape-like man covered in brown hair seen on Smitham Hill, near East Harptree, in November 1993; and some kind of horrific, other-worldly, gargoyle-like demon with huge, leathery wings, that apparently guards the entrance to another dimension around Glastonbury. To these, I might add that there is also a persistent urban legend among the students at Shapwick School, Shapwick, that two former pupils a few years before had seen two upright, hairy, very tall and long-snouted creatures that looked like animals walking on their hind legs and sniffing at the air. Pupils will repeat that the two boys 'are supposed to have seen werewolves' in the vicinity of Loxley Wood, and run away from them. For those that think such creatures as are mentioned in this chapter are nothing more than tales to frighten children, it should be stated that there is a school of thought that considers them to be very real, possibly inter-dimensional, creatures.

WHERE DO THEY COME FROM AND WHAT DO THEY WANT?

To the true believer, Somerset and Bristol have been visited by a mind-boggling array of Unidentified Flying Objects (or, to be more up-to-date, Unidentified Aerial Phenomena) from other planets, other galaxies, other universes, even other realms. To the traditionalist, these aerial visitors represent evidence that the fairies we once shared our environs with retreated into the upper atmosphere. To the sceptic, the witness statements represent, alternatively, hallucinations, publicity-seeking falsehoods or complete misidentification of something cosmically natural, perhaps something that we do not yet have an explanation for.

It is really the first of these that concerns us here: instances where 'something' seen in the sky would appear to be either of mysterious terrestrial origins or even extraterrestrial, a visitor to the skies over Somerset that we have no explanation for. The range of strange things seen in the skies is really quite phenomenal, and it seems that the local media never has long to wait before there is another sighting of a mysterious, multicoloured bright light, or a lazily sailing orange globe, or a sinister black triangle. But sometimes the entities that inhabit these 'craft', as many of the observations are supposed to concern, are occasionally encountered by ordinary folk, who later swear that they have experienced a true close encounter or 'alien abduction'.

In 1973 there occurred an incident that has, over the years, entered regional UFO folklore. I was assured while visiting the Wellington Memorial some years ago that, 'There was a woman that got abducted by a robot, well I read that somewhere. Quite a lot of people knew her, I think.' From this flimsy (and highly improbable) throwaway observation (which caught me off guard, since I was asking about Sir John Popham's ghost), I have traced the story back to Thomas E. Bullard's *UFO Abductions: The Measure Of A Mystery* (1987). The story is a terrifying one, concerning a woman who, in the late evening of 16 October 1973, found her car failing as she drove in the darkness along the B3187 past the little road to Langford Budville. The automobile failure had coincided with the appearance of a bright light approaching from fields off the road. As the woman stood outside in the lane wondering what to do, her attention was drawn to a growing humming noise, following which a heavy hand pushed down on her shoulder. Before she blacked out she found herself looking at a tall, dark-coloured, metallic robot-like humanoid. When she briefly came to she found herself in the field, the robot-like figure next to her and her view filled by a giant, brightly glowing, metallic domed object that rested on legs, which had been making the humming noise. When she subsequently awoke in a freezing, circular room she saw that the robot had been 'deactivated' and leant against a wall, while she herself lay on a table with a console full of dials and buttons next to her head. Three men of average height now stood before her, all dressed identically in light-blue tunics, long aprons and gloves that rode up to the elbows. They wore skullcaps and masks, and all that was visible of their faces were round, blank eyes that never blinked or registered emotion. None of these three beings appeared to breathe, or even communicate, although they nodded at each other and seemed to be telepathic. There were bumps under the skullcaps that indicated hair, and all three moved with the deliberate, precise motions of surgeons.

After undergoing a torturous examination and an ordeal of such distress that it need not be dwelt upon, the woman simply found herself standing, fully clothed as though none of it had happened, in the road next to her car. She arrived home in a state of extreme distress and confusion in Taunton, having lost some two hours of time during her ordeal.

Pressed for more information, the person who prompted me to look into this tale suggested that it might have been reported in the newspapers locally, although possibly as a violent attack, and pointed me towards the *Wellington Weekly News*. But, as incredible as it sounds, the story has been treated credibly by a number of researchers, such as the world-authority on UFOs, Jenny Randles, in her alien harassment piece *Abduction* (1988), and two UFO investigators, Barry King and Andy Collins of UFO Information Network (UFOIN).

These types of paranormal encounters have supplanted legends of pixies and the like, and are modern folklore in the making. Whether they concern true extraterrestrial visitors or not, the answer remains unclear as to just what did happen and where the 'abductors' came from.

The September 1993 issue of *Northern UFO News* # 162 repeats another story that has entered Somerset's UFO folklore. In May 1988 a man taking photographs at North Petherton in the Quantock Hills found the sun blocked out by an enormous flying structure the shape of two saucers with stacked decks, wings and an incredibly technical-looking exterior. Amazingly, some kind of humanoid entity was seen standing on the rim of this object, and the witness used his camera to take a number of photographs as this immense flying craft passed overhead making a low noise. A wave of accompanying heat obliterated the negatives, however, and the subsequent effects of being caught in this heated force led to a later illness; eventually he contacted the MoD and the UFO organization BUFORA for an explanation.

Allegations of alien activity are part of the UFO mythology. The Avon and Somerset Police website declares, in response to an enquiry from a member of the public, 'Avon and Somerset Constabulary do occasionally come into contact with persons who state that they are in communication with "extraterrestrial beings".'

It is also clear that UFOs are a very definite form of modern folklore. There was excitement in Yatton in late January 2009 when children at Yatton Junior School were told that the caretaker had been called out at quarter past 11 the previous night to investigate the alarms going off. This coincided, the children were told, with televisions exploding in the village, and they were next shown a cordoned-off area displaying three large circles burnt into the grass in a triangular pattern and globs of silver-coloured alien matter. After being shown a photograph of a UFO hovering above the school that directed a beam of light down towards the playing fields, the 10-and-11 year olds went home and told their parents, and the allegation swept through the village like wildfire. Of course, the story was an invention – part of an imaginative class literacy project that involved props and even a guest speaker, but some of the teachers forgot to tell their pupils at the day's end that it was a hoax, and many children sincerely believed the story, running home to tell their families. In true *War Of The Worlds* style, according to the *Bristol Evening Post*, the story spread. Some even said that at quarter past 11 in the evening all the clocks in the village had leapt forward an hour and television channels had changed simultaneously! I wonder how this story might be misremembered in 25 years time, when the children concerned are adults.

There are also rational explanations for some famous sightings of 'real' airborne phenomena. On the night of 30th August 1993 a wave of observations from many parts of the western British Isles concerning strange aerial lights included reports of something variously described as two bright lights flying parallel to each other, a large, bright flying catamaran, or two Concordes connected together. Reports came in from Taunton, Bridgwater, the Quantock Hills, Bristol Airport, Bishops Lydeard and Minehead. At East Harptree 'two very bright, star-like objects in an echelon military formation' were reported to the MoD, and it looked like a classic UFO case...until it was put forward that the cause was Russian space debris burning up. Similarly, *The Telegraph* reported on 11 February 2009 that holidaymakers at Brean had, the previous year, filmed a remarkable black, metallic and cylindrical object moving erratically against the clear blue sky of a July day. It was clearly not a doctored piece of footage, and it was very puzzling, until it was suggested by investigators that it was a solar weather balloon, an object that came in all shapes and sizes and could be anything up to 50ft long.

The mystery was not solved to everyone's satisfaction, however, and *The Times* noted another minor enigma from Brean as an addendum: 'Last June, local coastguards were called out to search Somerset's coastline after sightings of a mystery parachute and canister, which were never found.' Of unidentified aerial phenomena in general, it is certainly true to say that some of the things witnessed are singularly puzzling. In fact, a quick look at the recently released MoD archives reveals what a fabulous wealth of strange things have been witnessed in the skies over Somerset. In 1994 a 'twirling set of moving lights attached to what must have been a circular object' glided silently out of the sky, flashing red, yellow and green, and appeared over the jazz tent at the Glastonbury music festival for the benefit of two 'sober' witnesses stood in a nearby field, although apparently not for the benefit of the other revellers. Nonetheless, the witnesses drew an intriguing sketch of the craft which, until August 2009, stayed hidden in the MoD archives.

A simple look on the Internet can reveal an amazing range of weird and wonderful UFO stories concerning Somerset and Bristol, including the famous 'prank' UFO story of 4 September 1967, when a metre-wide 'scout craft' was found near some gorse bushes in Clevedon by a 10-year-old paperboy. It contained a transmitter and produced a high-pitched whining sound when turned over. The discovery was one of six around the country, and had the local media scratching its head, the assumption being that the 'thing' was a cleverly constructed battery-powered experimental student prank. But it is the recently released Ministry of Defence archive information that is becoming an invaluable source of data for the UFO researcher, and one wonders what marvels are hidden away in the archive's depths, waiting to be unearthed at a future date. In fact, it may seem to some that UFO reports crop up on 'slow news days', but this is not the case: there is a remarkable repository of information concerning Unidentified Aerial Phenomena that simply was not reported in the newspapers at the time, but was taken seriously enough to be logged by the MoD and which is now made available under 2005's Freedom of Information Act. On 10 August 1997, for instance, at half past two in the morning a bright-yellow, streetlight-type object was seen from Taunton to rise upwards 'until it disappeared into a black hole in the sky.' On the night of 16th August 1998 'many white, small beams that were flickering' were seen from Frome and Bristol. Perhaps most impressively of all, at 9 o'clock in the evening on 12 January 2001 an RAF pilot some 25 miles over Bath saw a triangular object, stationary and solid-looking at this high altitude. Between half past nine and 10 o'clock many people from various parts of Somerset saw an amazing flash of bluish-green light shooting across the sky, that left a white tail and looked as though it was disintegrating.

Surely this could not have been an alien craft breaking up upon entering our atmosphere? It has to be something natural…or does it? Maybe the 'low-flying cloud' seen flying a mere 100ft above ground level from Bath in the very early morning of 09 September 2007 was some kind of attempt at disguise by an alien invader? Whatever it was, the thing had a light that flashed on it. In 2008 the MoD even received a vague report – time and date unknown – that alleged that a 'big alien craft' had landed on top of a witness's house in Bristol, before flying off over the city. On 18 July 2009 a multicoloured 'metallic aircraft shaped like a missile', without wings, was spotted circling from Weston-super-Mare. It made a noise like a motorbike. On 22 October that year someone reported a metallic ball in the sky above Yeovil that was pursued by a fast jet and then a helicopter from the direction of Yeovilton.

Recently making the national headlines was a bizarre story published in the *Sun* newspaper (among others) concerning a Royal Navy aircraft engineer, who spotted one night in June 2008 an airborne hovering disc above Junction 21 on the M5, near Weston-super-Mare. The disc was 'hundreds of feet up', glowed brightly and had antenna protruding from its back. After three minutes it shot off at an amazing speed.

Surely other drivers must have seen this strange sight? Whatever the meaning behind it all is, it does indicate that there is either a phenomenal variety of alien craft scouting earth, or else there is a great deal of inexplicable natural phenomena that we do not as yet understand; that is, assuming all the witnesses to be reliable. And all this aerial weirdness leads us very nicely into our final chapter.

CHAPTER 9:

INEXPLICABLE INCIDENTS, BIZARRE BEHAVIOUR & PECULIAR PLACES

INTRODUCTION

Following on from the previous chapter, there have been seen spectacles in the heavens that are undoubtedly natural cosmic oddities, but which are no less amazing for it. Wherever one lives and in whatever era, there has, and always will be, a fascination with aerial phenomena. Although much of what we can observe in the heavens is now explainable to us, as compared to the terror it must have caused our ancestors, cosmic displays can, nonetheless, still be exceptionally impressive. In 1752, for instance, *The Gentleman's Magazine* reported on a 'great ball of fire [that] was seen to issue from the clouds' above Bristol on 16 December. It 'shot with great swiftness to the northward.' And *The Illustrated London News* of 21 August 1852 carried correspondence concerning a remarkable meteor seen from Yeovil earlier that month. At about 20 minutes past nine in the evening, people's attention was drawn to a flash of 'lightning' in the darkened night sky, which appeared to be the meteor shooting through the heavens, before defining itself into a stationary mass of light that hung in the sky for 10 minutes. As it faded, 'it resolved into two or more distinct bodies nearly of the apparent magnitude of the planet Saturn', which themselves faded from view after another 10 minutes. Another correspondent, from Bristol, made the claim that the meteor had shot out of a 'dense black cloud in the north', before disintegrating into three portions. Furthermore, 'The light from this meteor was so great that the smallest objects could be discerned as clearly as in full daylight.'

Clearly, in whatever era, an exploding meteor turning night into day would be a remarkable phenomenon. There is even a report of a 'hot stone' having fallen to earth near Glastonbury in 1816, which, if true, is most likely to have been a meteorite. The weather could play strange tricks, too. *The Gentleman's Magazine* records in July 1808 that a ferocious storm broke over the South West, with cattle and livestock being struck dead in the fields and two people also being struck by lightning at Keynsham and Rope Walk, Backwell. Thousands of windows across the region were smashed by hailstones, although the description of these indicates that they were of a type not usually seen; they were more akin to shards of glass between three and nine inches across, which scythed through the sky as though some great window had shattered in the heavens. At Kingweston the ground was littered with the corpses of rooks that had been caught up in the onslaught, but, most remarkably, the thunder was heard to roll continuously for an hour and a half, accompanied by near-continuous lightning flashes. On 2 November 1821 a tremendous electrical storm was experienced over Bristol. More than a dozen sheep were killed at Stanton Drew. The number of dead and the incident happening so near the stone circles no doubt prompted knowing comments from village elders about the Devil. A bolt of lightening struck the tower of St Mary Redcliff Church, Bristol, entering the bell loft window of the upper tower and then shattering the beam that held the bell, before passing down the bell wire and 'escaping' out of the south side of the tower, leaving blasted stonework and rolled-up lead in its wake.

One wonders what kind of storm whipped up and then deposited the following strange rain. On 13 March 1977 Mr Alfred Osborne and his wife were caught in an unusual deluge as they walked along a Bristol street: the pavement about them clicked as a shower of hazelnuts struck it. Literally hundreds of them fell from a clear sky, and Mr Osborne bit into one, finding it sweet and fresh; he commented (as reported on the TV show *Arthur C. Clarke's Mysterious World* in 1980), 'I have thought a vortex sucked them up, but I don't know where you suck up hazelnuts in March!'

There was similar bemusement in Coxley on the afternoon of 7 March 2010 when dozens of starlings simply fell out of the sky. An area some 12ft across was covered with about 100 small carcasses; all but six of the starlings died, the others being killed on impact or lingering feebly before expiring or being put down. They were observed to have bloodied beaks, physical injuries like smashed wings and curled-up feet. Quite what caused this curious incident is at present unknown: the birds did not hit a power line, nor did they appear to have all collided in mid-air. I have heard it speculated that some of the birds in this flock were dead before they hit the ground, having been frightened to death while in flight by something airborne that terrified them into a collective, evasive dive, but what the basis is for this assumption I am not sure, and the incident currently (at the time of writing) remains largely unexplained.

These last make it clear that there is much in Somerset and Bristol that does not make sense in any rational kind of way, and it is with this that our last chapter is concerned: everything from the general realm of documented weirdness, much of which we have no adequate explanation for just yet. After miracles, witchcraft, ghosts, prowling panthers and dragon-slaying, this chapter is concerned with all the rest: all the miscellaneous jokes that some cosmic comedian appears to have played on us to keep us on our toes — everything from curious natural wonders to human curiosities and bizarre phenomena. In short, everything that does not fit the perceived order of things in Somerset and Bristol.

INTO THE VORTEX

Gervase of Tilbury's expansive *Otia Imperialia* notes a mysterious incident that occurred in mediaeval Bristol. A man of that port sailed for Ireland, leaving behind his wife and family. While at sea (the vessel had been blown well off course on its voyage), it happened that he accidentally dropped his knife overboard while cleaning it after dinner. At that very moment, the sailor's knife fell through the open skylight of his home in Bristol and, landing with a 'thud', stuck upright in the dinner table in front of his wife, who recognised it immediately as her husband's. When he eventually returned home the sailor and his wife compared notes, discovering with amazement that the knife had been lost at sea and yet reappeared in the house at exactly the same time. 'Who then', exclaimed Gervase, 'after such evidence of this will doubt the existence of a sea above this earth of ours, situated in the air, or over it?'

There are more things in heaven and earth, as they say: perhaps Bristol is the place for vortexes. On 10th December 1873 the *Bristol Daily Post* carried a piece on the bizarre allegations of an elderly couple from Virginia Road, Leeds, who had been staying at the Victoria Hotel, Bristol. The pair, Thomas B. Cumpston and his wife, Annie Martha, 'occupied a very good position in Leeds', but during the previous night in their room both were repeatedly troubled by loud sounds, a circumstance that caused them to complain to the landlady. At about 3 o'clock strange noises were heard yet again and the married couple swung their legs off the bed, only to feel the floor moving and giving way beneath them. A huge hole appeared to be growing in the floor and, worse, it was sucking poor Mr Cumpston into it; strange cries were heard from within, which might have been echoes of their own terrified shrieks. Mrs Cumpston managed to manhandle her husband out of the yawning hole and both leapt for the window, Mr Cumpston discharging his pistol into the ceiling as they escaped over the sash. Outside, and in their nightclothes, Cumpston fired his pistol a second time before they ran for the railway station. The Cumpstons were arrested on the platform, Cumpston running behind his wife and holding a still-smoking pistol. It appeared at first that he was attempting to shoot his wife dead, but it was also observed that both of them kept looking behind them as though they were being chased. Cumpston was highly agitated when arrested for disorderly conduct, and could give no clear account of his experience, it falling largely to his wife to explain what had happened. The landlady confirmed that 'sounds' had been heard that strange night, but she could not clearly define them, and an officer who went to the hotel found no evidence of any holes or subsidence in the room they had occupied. There was no evidence of intoxication in either of them. Eventually, they were discharged into the care of somebody from Gloucester, their experience classed tentatively as 'mass hallucination'.

At the Crown Inn, Wells, however, the apports that mysteriously appeared on multiple occasions and in several rooms here seem to have been deposited *from* a vortex, rather the disappearing into it. At this 15th-century inn in the Market Place, the staff were puzzled by the inexplicable appearance of black barley seeds in the late 1990s. The inn is reputedly haunted, and I remember hearing of a seemingly unrelated mystery whereby a strange man was caught on a security camera in the bar, prompting the staff to look for him, only to find no one present. So are such vortexes linked to the supernatural world, or the physical? The mystery is an intangible one indeed.

ATMOSPHERIC ANOMALIES

There have been thought-provoking instances in the past where one natural phenomenon apparently preceded – or even acted as the catalyst for – another. There have been many documented instances of strange observations being made in the heavens prior to some cataclysm on land. For example, on 15 October 1484 there was a great flood in Bristol that claimed some 200 lives, with merchants' cellars being devastated and several ships being lost in King's Road. Strange to relate that during this disaster the moon was eclipsed for between two and three hours. Similarly, the *Chudleigh Weekly Express* of 13 January 1869 reported that three nights earlier a meteor had been seen between 9 and 10 o'clock by persons in Weston-super-Mare; five hours later three earth tremors were felt.

Equally mystifying are the worrying 'sky booms' that have on occasion been heard. Just after 3 o'clock in the afternoon on 18 November 1905 three enormous detonations were heard from the sky above Somerset, which – according to the report in the *English Mechanic* – were 'as loud as thunder, but not exactly like thunder.' There are other reports of such sky-borne 'booms': *Fortean Times* magazine, the publication that takes its name from Charles Fort, the Albany-born compiler and uncritical analyser of all things out of place, reported in its summer 1980 edition that residents of Bridgwater had been troubled since 1977 by unaccountable sounds in the area. Correspondents from the town wrote, 'Sometimes they sound like explosions, sometimes like the rumbling of thunder. On some occasions the vibrations have been felt in the house...' Some along the northern Exmoor coast even claimed that they been hearing them with a frightening frequency – almost every evening at 9 o'clock – since the 1950s. Many theories were put forward, including Concorde passing by, quarry blasting in the Quantock Hills and 'something to do with the army or government.' But the nature of the explosions was too random to be pinned down to any one specific cause. The *Bristol Evening Post* reported on 5 July 1991 that a tremendous bang was heard at Radstock the day before, with vibrations felt as far away as Stratton-on-the-Fosse.

Perhaps the most famous mystery of this type is the so-called 'Bristol Hum', a widely publicised buzzing phenomenon in the late 1970s, that for many years hundreds claimed they could detect, and which had caused a variety of health problems in those that could hear it: nausea, nosebleeds, insomnia or migraines. It seemed as though some kind of human 'dog whistle' drove some to the edge of madness, with the phenomenon continuing into the 1990s – one sufferer was even reported to have committed suicide in 1996. Others remained unimpressed, blaming the 'hum' on radio transmissions, gas pipes, mobile phone masts, wind farming, or simply factory noise and/or traffic. Even today it is a mystery that splits opinion, with some believing it little more than an urban legend – while in some Bristol families, one member will claim to be able to detect it, at the dismissal of his relatives and siblings who simply cannot. Some claim that detection of the hum depends on where you actually live in Bristol. The 'hum' still occasionally makes headlines today, with the *Bristol Evening Post* of 20 May 2009 carrying an interview with the head of audiology at Addenbrooke's Hospital, Cambridge, who believed that the answer to the hum lay with those who heard it and their 'internal volume control' in times of threat, alertness or anxiety. This is little by way of an explanation to conspiracy theorists, however, some of whom believe the hum to be anything from microwave transmissions or messages broadcast from 'secret research stations' to low-frequency communication with submarines. Some even claim it to be some kind of social experiment.

One of the Bristol's most amazing and mystifying legends, discussed in great depth in Charles Fort's seminal work on anomalies, *New Lands* (1923), was to the effect that every year between 21 June and 10 July a phantom city was visible in the clouds over a glacier in Alaska. Every year for generations the mirage had been known to the Alaskan Indians, who wondered what the vision might represent. But it took expeditions by settlers, prospectors and European pioneers making inroads into Alaska to identify the vision, which, according to a member of the Duc d'Abruzzi's expedition in 1897, 'required no effort of the imagination to liken it to a city, but was so distinct that it required, instead, faith to believe that it was not in reality a city.' The 'city' was identified as Bristol in England, and numerous attempts were made by a famous prospector called Willoughby to photograph it in the late 1880s. One photograph of this mirage appeared in Miner Bruce's *Alaska*, and was also featured in a later work, Bedlam's *Wonders Of Alaska*. But Fort was justifiably sceptical of this image: 'So definite, or so un-mirage-like, is this reproduction, trees and many buildings shown in detail, that one supposes that the original was a photograph of a good-sized terrestrial city, perhaps Bristol, England.' The subject has caused much contention, with 'hoax' being labelled at not only the photographic representations of the mirage, but also the whole thing. Or maybe the city in the sky was entirely misrepresented as Bristol. An account in the *New York Times* in 1889 by a witness who had seen the mirage near Mt Fairweather posited, 'We could see plainly houses, well-defined streets, and trees. Here and there rose tall spires over huge buildings, which appeared to be ancient mosques or cathedrals...It did not look like a modern city – more like an ancient European City.'

I can only wonder if it is still seen.

DRAKE'S CANNONBALL

One of the most famous curiosities in the whole county is Drake's Cannonball, a large, polished, iron-looking ball, a 1ft in diameter and weighing 120 pounds, that is kept at Combe Sydenham House, an ancient Elizabethan mansion close to the road near Monksilver, deep in the woodland of Combe Sydenham Country Park.

The story behind this is that Sir Francis Drake and Mistress Elizabeth Sydenham pledged undying love, and upon Drake leaving for sea he warned her to be faithful in his absence – threatening that, if she was not, he would use his conjurer's skills to send her a token of vengeance, wherever he might be on the high seas.

Drake was away for years, and so it came to pass that Mistress Sydenham became betrothed to another beau. But upon the day of the wedding, an immense thunderstorm grew overhead, and at length a whistling in the sky announced the arrival of a glowing ball. This was red-hot, and landed between Elizabeth and her new lover, smashing the pavement. The terrified woman screamed before all those assembled, 'It is the token from Drake! He lives, and has sent this fearful thing to reprove me for my inconstancy: I will not go into the church!' On the next tide Sir Francis arrived back at Britain's shores and married Elizabeth in 1585. The rejected suitor may have been Elizabeth's second husband after Sir Francis, William Courtenay of Powderham.

It was naturally said that the ball was a cannonball, fired by the great circumnavigator from the Antipodes, and has ever since gone by the name of Drake's Cannonball. Page's *An Exploration Of Exmoor*

Combe Sydenham House.

(1890) declares that it is, without doubt, a meteorite, but nonetheless one wonders where it was collected. Perhaps it really did hurtle out of the skies and disrupt a Tudor wedding in Combe Sydenham. Whatever its origins, Page wrote, 'At the spot in Combe Sydenham Hall where the mysterious ball stopped, there it still remains, and there, according to vulgar tradition, will it ever be, utterly refusing all efforts to roll it elsewhere.' *Notes And Queries* commented on this legend, 'It has been, on several occasions, conveyed away, and once even thrown into a distant horsepond, but all to no purpose. After a very short interval there it was again, with ardour undamped, and obstinacy undrowned.' The cannonball, I have been told, is also said to 'roll up and down' in times of national trouble, with a throwaway comment added that the last time it did this 'was no doubt in 1979 when Thatcher was elected!'

MORE STRANGE RAIN

On 18 September 1992 many places in the South West were coated with a light sprinkling of red dust, thought to be light Saharan sand carried on warm air currents. But imagine the surprise of the pensioner enjoying lunch with his wife in his garden near Bristol who heard an overhead whistling noise and was suddenly struck on the thigh by a grapefruit-sized chunk of ice that came hurtling out of the sky. This was reported in June 2009 and, as unlikely as it sounds, it is true: the family home was in Stoke Bishop, a suburb in north-west Bristol, a place directly under the flight path of Bristol International Airport, it being guessed that the ice fell from an aeroplane.

As odd as this is, it is practically ordinary compared to some of the things the Somerset skies have thrown at those on land. On 7 June 1753 Bridgwater was lashed by a storm that began at 6 o'clock in the evening; enormous hailstones pounded the town and smashed windows, making holes in the ground like cannonballs. Some of these hailstones were upwards of nine inches across. Several people were struck by them and injured.

In August 1821 snails were said to have fallen upon a three-acre field in Bristol in such quantities that they could be shovelled up. To compound the mystery, the sun was observed to have had a bizarre azure-blue appearance at the time. Be that as it may, even this was little as compared to the mystery discussed at great depth in the *Entomologist (Vol. 5)* in 1871, concerning the 'shower of insects' that had fallen on Bath during a tremendous thunderstorm. The insects, apparently in their larval stage, were deposited near the Midland Railway Station, pattering on the coat of a young boy, who raised the alarm. Larval jelly covered the station platform, which upon microscopic examination revealed 'animal-formed bodies, the motion of the viscera in which is perfectly visible, with locust-shaped heads bearing long antennae, and with pectoral and caudal fins like feet.' All were approximately one and a half inches long. The Reverend L. Jenyns wrote for the benefit of the *Meteorological Magazine*, '…a person who keeps a small inn [near the station], on my requesting to see them, showed me some of the organisms still alive, which he had kept in a tumbler of water since the time of their falling.' There must be something about Bath, for in September 1894 *Notes And Queries* maintained that August had seen thousands of jellyfish, about the size of a shilling, land on the town.

CURIOUS EFFECTS OF LIGHTNING

Lightning, on occasion, can play strange tricks and almost act as though it is somehow 'alive'. *The Edinburgh New Philosophical Journal* (1861) relates that in 1812 six sheep in a meadow at Combe Hay were killed by lightning, and 'when the skins were taken from the animals, a facsimilie of a portion of the surrounding scenery was visible on the inner surface of each skin.' In short, the lightning had somehow 'photographed' the meadow and its surrounds, burning the image under the skins of the dead sheep. A Mr Shaw observed, 'The small field and its surrounding wood were so familiar to me and my schoolfellows, that when the skins were shown to us we at once identified the local scenery so wonderfully represented.' The *Bath Express* of 8 June 1861 quoted a local landowner named Wiltshire as correcting some of these details, however: the incident had happened on his land at Twinhoe during turnip-sowing time, when three rams had sought shelter beneath a tree. When the skins reached the fellmongers, on the inside of each was found a very accurate representation of the tree under which the rams had sheltered.

Presumably, the two events concern a misreporting of the same incident, but that does not really lessen the strangeness of the episode. In May 1827 it was guessed that lightning killed William Webber, a 21-year-old labourer at Ridler's Farm, close to the Devon border and south-west of Dulverton. A group working in the field burning the sward one afternoon saw that the day had become very gloomy, and as a few raindrops began to fall a huge shockwave blasted one man, Robert Hill, off his feet and forced the others to flee for the farm. When Hill recovered and got to his feet, he saw that Webber lay nearby, fully naked and quite dead. Webber's death had been remarkable: from wounds in his head and his feet, it was assumed he had been literally blasted by a bolt of lightning that had gone through his body and fired the nails from his hobnailed boots into the earth, as well as destroying his pocket watch. Furthermore, his clothes were found in tattered pieces in a radius of 2ft about his body, accounting for his nakedness. The clothes had been forced into the earth, much scorched, and nearby a horse had been lifted off its feet, being so badly injured that it had to be put down. No one, however, had actually seen the tragedy happen, the story being pieced together from the remarkable evidence.

More recently, we find that the phenomenon of ball lightning still continues to puzzle us. Broadly speaking, ball lightning falls under the umbrella term of 'earth lights', typically manifesting itself as a globe of light that can perform mesmerising aerobic manoeuvres and not, it would seem, actually requiring an electrical storm to manifest itself. The question of just what exactly ball lightning might be has yet to be properly answered, with some scientists even questioning its existence; but it would, apparently, explain the strange ball of light that danced on the bonnet of a driver's car on the A39 near Minehead at about 6 o'clock on the evening of 4 November 1997. Even stranger, this caused the car's electrics to cut out for a short time.

WONDERS OF THE NATURAL LANDSCAPE

We have already seen that the landscape of Somerset boasts a great many wells that were, in their time, noteworthy for their healing properties. There have also been other curious natural discoveries, such as the finding in 1804 of 30 maiden oak trees 12ft beneath the ground. The discovery was made while excavating the ground near the mansion of the Dowager Lady Smyth in Bristol for the new course of the Avon, and the amazed labourers observed that the trees, which were hazel, lay parallel with their roots pointing towards Ashton and their branches towards Clifton, Some of the trunks were 70ft long.

Trees growing beneath the ground? It appears that they were an example of phenomenal natural preservation, as hazelnuts were also found, together with the teeth of a beaver and a wild hog, and a preserved brilliant-green beetle.

There is a healthy veneration of nature across Somerset in general. The folklorist Christina Hole noted in 1950 the practice in Cannington of blessing the fields during Rogation Week. The clergy and children visited all the fields, allotments, crops, animals and labourers, armed with 'wands' of flower-adorned staffs, banners, hymns and prayers.

It was widely believed that a good apple crop could be ensured by placing a piece of toast in the fork of the biggest tree in the orchard. This was part of the practice called 'wassailing the apples', observed for many years now at Carhampton. It was recorded as being practiced prior to the Second World War, and probably dates back about 100 years before that, when men of the village formed 'wassail parties', proceeding to the orchard where they were joined by the farmer and his labourers. Standing round the trees, they sang the old wassail song, the last part of which went:

> Old apple tree, old apple tree;
> We've come to wassail thee;
> To bear and bow apples enow;
> Hats full, caps full, three bushel bags full;
> Barn floors full, and a little heap under the stairs.

The ceremony generally takes place on Old Twelfth Day, 17 January, and the toast is soaked in cider. Cider is also poured around the roots of the Old Apple Tree, which is then given three cheers, and shotguns are ritually fired through its branches. The crowd then retires to the Butcher's Arms (the orchard is situated behind this), where musicians play and people sing, dance and drink cider. Carhampton is the oldest-surviving apple tree wassailing ceremony, but there are others: at Nether Stowey, for example, on 16 January.

Fires were also lit on Midsummer Eve to bless the crop. The apple tree wassail is, in essence, a survival of a very ancient practice of sacrificing to the spirit of the harvest. Perhaps it is no surprise that some even believed that certain trees were possessed with a spirit that enabled them to act almost human-like. Ruth Tongue was told a version of the now-famous story of the Apple Tree Man in 1920, concerning two brothers in Pitminster who received very unequal portions of their late father's estate when the will was read out. When the younger brother was willed virtually everything, he gave his sibling an old donkey, an even older ox and an ancient, overgrown orchard. The older brother, in the face of this insult, mulled some cider and wassailed the oldest of the apple trees in his newly acquired orchard; this so pleased the spirit of the orchard, the Apple Tree Man, that his voice called to the brother, 'Yew take a look under this gurt diddiky root of ours!' He did so, and found the box full of gold that had long been rumoured to be hidden somewhere on the property. Ms Tongue wrote an interesting aside to this well-known tale, saying that in her childhood at Pitminster she was 'gravely and proudly conducted by a farm child to a very old apple tree in their orchard, and told mysteriously that it was "the Apple Tree Man."' Ruth Tongue also noted a guardian spirit of the orchard called Lazy Lawrence, who 'appears to take a pony form at times, like the colt pixy who attacked the boys who took the griggling apples.' This spirit apparently gives apple thieves a hand cramp. There was a similar belief in Oak Men, which were tree spirits. Angry Oak Men haunted any coppice growing from felled oaks, and it is thought wise by local country folk to avoid such a coppice after sunset. I have also heard many allusions to the belief that certain trees are supposed to be able to walk, thanks to these spirits; and, according to Tongue, the barrow at Tyning, near Radstock, called Round Hill, at one time supported an elm with an 'uncanny reputation': if it was cut with a knife, it bled.

I have myself seen on numerous occasions that the tree next to the Wells marker stone at the foot of Glastonbury Tor has been colourfully bedecked with ribbons and streamers. Such practices go hand in hand with some rather interesting Somerset folklore concerning the natural landscape. *The Reader's Digest Folklore, Myths And Legends Of Britain* (1973) asserts that the Primrose Peerless – the two-flowered daffodil – was brought to Somerset by a crusading knight in the Middle Ages from the Holy Land as a gift for his sweetheart in Churchill. Unfortunately, she had died in his absence, so he threw the rare bulbs on the ground by her grave and committed suicide; here they took root and still grew within living memory, supposedly. At the ancient hill fortress called Mounsey Castle, by the River Barle near Dulverton, John L.W. Page recorded the belief that the ground beneath was hollow, and as a consequence people were afraid to dig there. Horner Water, between Luccombe and Hawkcombe, was believed to owe its name to the Anglo-Saxon word 'hwrner', or snorer, because of the sound it made, although Page wrote, 'I have never been able to discover in its tones anything more sonorous than that possessed by the voice of other mountain streams', leaving the riddle of its nickname open to debate.

Some even professed an ability to 'connect' with nature. C.H. Poole remarks on the great number of men who practised 'rhabdomancy', or water divination, using a rod or magic wand of willow, shaped like a small pair of tongs with which they used the undivided end to lead them to water. Charles Hardwick's 1872 *Traditions, Superstitions And Folklore* remarks on a typical example concerning a dowser named Mapstone, who was employed by a Wedmore farmer to find a supply of water on his farm. Mapstone used a hazel rod that became agitated at a certain spot, which he declared confidently would bear water if a well could be dug to a depth of 15 or 20ft. Digging therefore commenced, and water was indeed found at a depth of 19ft.

A MYSTERIOUS SKULL

Few churches in the west of England are placed in a situation more commanding than St Michael's at Minehead. From here, there is a fantastic view of the coastline, and one cannot help but be reminded of the old tradition that it was originally meant to be sited near the shore, but a supernatural agency twice moved the stones up the hill during the night, and so it was decided to build it there.

Within the church is a table monument displaying a recumbent figure in priestly robes (said to be Henry de Bracton), and during the 19th century this tomb was opened – and within there was found a skull displaying two rows of upper teeth. Bracton was a lawyer, but it is possible that the skull was not his, it being improbable that a man of such importance could live his life without this shark-like formation having been recorded anywhere. John L.W. Page wrote of this, 'A well-known Somersetshire antiquary, with whom I visited the monument, thought this malformation an excellent reason for assuming that the skeleton *was* that of the judge, remarking dryly that, "Lawyers being sharks, the peculiarity was natural enough!"'

LONG-DORMANT INFECTION

The Terrific Register (1825) remarks on the phenomenal longevity of a smallpox virus that had claimed the life of a resident of Chelwood around 1721. A gravedigger at St Leonard's Church, 30 years later, put the tip of his spade through the stout oak coffin that the deceased had been buried in. So stout had the coffin been, in fact, that the long-dormant smallpox virus had apparently survived, and – along with a foul stench – it was released through the crack in the oak. The grave was being dug for a respected villager who had lately passed on, and many people attended his funeral; it appears that the virus clung to the site, for very soon some 14 people were displaying the symptoms of smallpox, which within a week had stricken every soul in the village – some 30 people – and claimed two lives. Not only this, but it was transmitted to many surrounding villages, inflicting similar torment as attendants at the funeral returned home, only to fall sick and pass the virus on.

AN INCREDIBLE SURVIVAL STORY

The following incident is remarkable in that it is the kind of survival story usually associated with the Australian outback, the Brazilian jungle or the Arctic tundra, not the countryside of South Somerset.

During the severe winter of 1708-09 a 'poor woman', having been to Chard to sell her yarn, was returning to Yeovil when she fell ill by the wayside and was forced to knock on the door of a small house and request heat from the fire. Evening was setting in and it was beginning to snow, but the occupants of the house refused to admit the woman and she was forced to lay down under a hedge, her sickness preventing her from doing anything more constructive.

It snowed very hard, and soon she was almost covered. Presently, a neighbour passed by and recognised the poor woman. He lifted her to her feet and made a half-hearted effort to walk her on, but it snowed so heavily that he soon left her behind in the blizzard, and she retreated back to the hedge, where she wormed herself underneath it. Very soon she was covered in snow, the landscape losing all its landmarks in a blanket of white.

Many of her neighbours made enquiries as to what had become of her, and presently a woman came forward claiming to have 'dreamed' the exact location of the missing woman. More likely, the man who had left her began to suffer a guilty conscience and, perhaps worrying that he would be hanged, he persuaded a close acquaintance to pretend that she had dreamed such a thing.

It might have been expected that a week would have been too late. But a party set out with sticks and as they poked in the snow they heard a feeble groan, and then a cry of, 'Oh for God's sake, don't kill me!' The woman had lain under the hedge at least seven days, and it appeared that her metabolism had slowed down to such a rate that she had entered a state of suspended animation, or hibernation. She claimed to have lain very warm, and slept most of the time, although to have been forced by her situation to begin eating her upper garments. The one part of her leg that had lain in the open had become almost mortified by frostbite, but other than that she was well and in good spirits. Very soon she was walking about, her leg beginning to heal itself.

Although the story was recorded 'on the most unquestionable authority' in a letter addressed to Mr Charry of Shottesbrooke, the lack of a name when so much else is recorded in detail may suggest an urban legend. But there are other incidents of this sort occurring in Cambridgeshire and Warwickshire, so perhaps it does contain a grain of truth. The story also reminds me of what some might consider an even worse fate: interment while still alive. The *Bridgwater Times* reported just such a nightmarish scenario in September 1884, when George Chilcott 'died' at Wembdon, being laid out in a coffin at St George's Church. Although his relatives wished for him to be interred without delay, the parson –

a scandalous character called Reverend Newman – nonetheless thought the 'corpse' too warm to be dead, and so kept the body hidden from the relatives. After three days the body stirred: Chilcott had not been dead after all.

PRODIGIOUS PEOPLE OF SOMERSET AND BRISTOL

There are truly astonishing reports of numerous people from the region whose prodigious strength, endurance, stature, age or ability has marked them out in local folklore. For example, there was still living in Ditcheat in 1804 a farmer called William Kington who was born without arms and performed all his tasks using his feet as though hands. He entered village lore when he engaged in a boxing match on 15 September 1789 with a local blacksmith who was a noted pugilist; but Kington won the day, using his heels and his head to beat down his opponent in half an hour of pitched violence that left the blacksmith with two broken ribs, and so severely battered that he had to be carried from the field of conflict. In 1784 there was born another prodigy at Quantoxhead: Sarah Biffin, who was born without arms and legs, and yet mastered the art of embroidery and painting by holding the needle or brush in her mouth. The merit of her work as a miniature-painter was recognized by the Society of Artists, who awarded her a medal in 1821.

There have been a number of people who have reached a phenomenally old age. *Notes And Queries For Somerset And Dorset* (1895) remarks on the longevity of a number of Pitminster residents in the mid-1800s, including Elizabeth Oaten of Feltham, who died in 1855 aged 108. Periodicals reported in 1793 the death at Bristol of 'Richard Brent, commonly called Tom Thumb, from his selling the history of that little hero', aged 110 years. He was born in the 'parish of St Cuthbert, Wells.' Harry Patch, the last surviving soldier to have fought in the trenches during the First World War, was a Somerset native who attained the venerable age of 111 years and 38 days. He was born at Combe Down, and his funeral at Wells Cathedral on 6 August 2009 made national headlines. But even Harry Patch was a mere youth compared to some: Catherine, the Countess of Desmond, for example, who resided in Bristol. In 1614 it was written that she came to London 'in ye 140th yeare of her age.' Here, she presented herself at the court of King James I to plead poverty. During her long life she had 'renewed her teeth twice', and may have actually lived some years beyond even this age. In 1771 there was amazement in Brislington when churchwardens at St Luke's, in clearing away the churchyard, found a tombstone inscribed '*1542. Thomas Newman, aged 153.*' They repaired and cleaned the tombstone, and added, '*This stone was new-faced in the year 1771, to perpetuate the great age of the deceased*' – only later suspecting that they might have been duped by some arch wag who had skilfully chiselled an extra 'I' onto the man's age. The tomb can be seen by the curious to this day, allowing people to make their own mind up.

Perhaps all of them have a long way to go to beat the curate H.J. Prince of Charlesworth, who was genuinely believed to be immortal by his followers. He notoriously founded the Agapemone of the Abode of Love at Spaxton. He in actual fact died in 1899, aged 88, however, his questionable legacy described to me by a resident of Goathurst, thus, 'I'm sure you have probably heard of the vicar at the Agapemone – or the "temple of love" as it was described – he seduced the young virgins of Spaxton.' The lack of any funeral plans whatsoever for someone who was expected to live forever meant that the curate was unceremoniously buried in his front garden in the middle of the night.

LIVING DEATH

A number of Victorian periodicals recounted the story of one Colonel Townsend, a resident of Bristol. The case was originally written of by a Dr Cheyne, and takes place some time before 1734, although the exact year is not clear. Nonetheless, the story is so remarkable that it almost forces one to question everything we think we know about death.

Colonel Townsend was a man of honour and integrity, but suffered from a chronic complaint that caused him to vomit regularly, and lately he had been brought to the Bell Inn at Bath. It being feared he was about to die, he was attended twice a day by two doctors, Cheyne himself and Dr Baynard, and an apothecary, Mr Skrine. As they attempted to diagnose his complaint, and surrounded by visitors and nurses, the colonel made a revelation: he had lately found that he could, quite literally, by sheer concentration of effort, fully 'die' and then will himself back to life again! He was naturally pressed to prove this, it being observed that he was in no way delirious, and so the doctors found his pulse, felt his heartbeat and his breath, and asked him to show them what he meant.

Baynard placed his hand on the colonel's heart and felt the beats become steadily weaker until they ceased entirely, and Cheyne simultaneously felt the patient's pulse die away. A clean glass was placed over his mouth, which was seen to remain unclouded: Colonel Townsend had literally stopped breathing, and there was not the least sign of life. Very soon they came to the conclusion that he had actually died during the experiment, and half an hour later the group began to sadly break up, when 'they observed some motion about his body, and upon examination, they found his pulse and the motion of his heart gradually returning; and he began to breathe gently and speak softly.'

All present were utterly astonished at this and unable to find any explanation. Shortly after, Colonel Townsend called his attorney, changed his will, settled legacies on his servants, received the sacrament and died at 5 o'clock the following morning – this time for real – leaving the doctors guessing as to whether he had actually willed himself into permanent death in order to end his sufferings.

A STATUE THAT MOVES AND COMES TO LIFE

In the 1800s children in Wincanton were told that, when it heard the clock strike midnight, the statue atop Ireson's Monument climbed down in order to partake of water, before climbing back up again. The monument is in veneration of Nathaniel Ireson (d.1769), who was responsible for rebuilding much of Wincanton following a devastating town fire in 1707, and can be found in St Peter and St Paul's churchyard. I was told, 'Well, they say that he rummages in the bushes looking for his head, since the skull at his feet is not his.' This is supposed to happen 'in the summer.' Perhaps he should look in the church itself; the administrator here told me, 'Poor Nathaniel lost his head some years ago. We do have it put away for safekeeping!'

There are other rumours of inanimate objects that are said to be possessed of life. The-then Princess Victoria, along with the Duchess of Kent, attended an auspicious opening of Bath Park on 23 October 1830, designating it 'The Royal Victoria Park' in front of the Mayor of Bath, the Lord Bishop of the Diocese and a crowd numbering in thousands. In 1833 there was donated to the park by Mr Geary, of Prior Park Buildings, a noble pair of bronzed lions to be placed over the Queen's Gate or City entrance, near Queen's Parade. These lions stand atop plinths, and quite naturally children are told that when the clock 'strikes 13' (I am unsure what this means), the lions begin to roll the balls at their paws about on top of the plinth in the manner of domestic cats.

The Ireson Monument.

SIMULACRA

Some natural patterns that appear in the most astonishing manner are so phenomenal that one almost comes to believe that there is a greater force at work. In 1789 it was reported that Mr Edward Yard, a joiner of Martock, had sawed into an oak plank and discovered in the veins of the wood the exact likeness of an 18th-century female in modern dress. The 'lady's' hair was fashionably frizzled on the sides and fastened back, her eyes, nose and mouth were as distinct as a picture and she wore a bonnet: 'the gown represents a dark-coloured sattin pink'd. There is no handkerchief, but the tucker is very visible.' A great many people came to see the curiosity.

In 1824 a 'Sherborne paper' reported that at Mudford, a little place north of Yeovil, a woman named Gardiner had given birth to a baby boy. Mrs Gardiner's husband earned a trade as a conjurer, or stage magician, but had recently absconded. The infant was born with deformed hands, the right 'resembling a magic lantern, the left hand a conjuring stick.' On his right cheek 'is a likeness of what is termed a peep show.'

Fort's *Wild Talents* (1933) pondered the strange number of images that were appearing spontaneously upon the pillars and walls of churches in the 1920s, including mysterious images that were observed in Uphill and Bristol. In Bath Abbey – 'where earth and heaven meet', according to its website – the simulacrum of a soldier with a pack was easily visible in a discolouration on a pillar near the monument to the Somerset Regiment. The incident was reported the *Bath Weekly Chronicle* in 1926.

MELANCHOLY COINCIDENCES

A melancholy accident occurred on 3 September 1819, when the two eldest sons of C.A. Elton, Abraham and Charles (13 and 14 years old respectively) became trapped by the tide on the causeway that separated Birnbeck Island from Weston-super-Mare during a family outing. Both were drowned and their bodies lost to the water, despite much effort. In fact, the Somerset magistrate and lieutenant-colonel of the Mendip Legion, Colonel Rogers, exerted so much effort during a 10-hour search in an open boat for the boys' bodies that he developed a fever and died himself on 6 October. The boys' bodies remained lost, until, as though guided there by remarkable providence, they were gently deposited on the shore of the Elton family estate at Clevedon, where they were interred beside their grandfather. This sad story becomes stranger the more one thinks about it: although Clevedon is geographically not that far from Weston on the Somerset coast, their bodies could have, hypothetically, ended up anywhere in the mouth of the River Severn or simply never have been seen again. For both boys to be delivered back home in this fashion almost looks like a miracle.

Of course, the event belongs to the realm of remarkable coincidence, and there are similar strange stories of deaths attended by such bizarre circumstances. Surely one of the most singular deaths ever recorded in Somerset happened at Luxborough. William Edwards, aged 71, had recently returned to the village in the employ of Sir Hugh Smith. On 2 March 1825 he met his brother in the grounds of St Mary's Church, and as the pair (who had not spoken for 12 years) strode round the church grounds, Edwards suddenly asked his brother whereabouts their aunt and uncle lay buried. The brother showed Edwards the spot, at which point Edwards simply collapsed and died without a sound at the plot where his relatives lay.

Perhaps the oddest instance, however, was the sad deaths of twins John and Arthur Mowforth, aged 66, who died at the same time on the same evening of 22 May 1975 from the same chest complaint in Windsor and Bristol respectively.

A STRANGE VEHICLE FROM THE FUTURE?

Sometimes, strange vehicles sighted fall into neither the realm of a phantom apparition or a UFO, but something even more inexplicable. On the night of 8 December 1965 motorist Ian Hann, from Montacute, was overtaken on the A36 between Warminster and Bath, at a speed of about 60 miles per hour, by a mysterious vehicle that was completely unidentifiable. It reminded him of a large built-in Land Rover with a solid roof, and when Mr Hann switched on his headlamps he was astonished to see that the strange object now zooming in front of him possessed no rear lights, no red reflectors, no number plate, and did not even appear to possess any wheels! Two green lights flashed on the roof, however.

Mr Hann was annoyed by these poor road manners, whatever the vehicle might be, and he pursued it for some two miles. Suddenly the vehicle emitted a sharply pitched whining noise of such an ear-splitting nature that Mr Hann was forced to stick his fingers in his ears and try to steer with his elbows. The noise stopped abruptly, and in a moment the vehicle ahead of Mr Hann was enveloped in a cloud of yellow smoke. With that, it was gone, and Mr Hann found himself slewing his car to a halt and stepping out on the roadside to look in both directions, and even in the fields that bordered the road, in frantic confusion. He was totally alone – the vehicle had vanished in the darkness, and even the yellow smoke had evaporated.

Two days later this bizarre story appeared in the local newspapers, and in 1967 Arthur Shuttlewood, a journalist with the *Warminster Journal*, linked the experience to the unprecedented UFO concern surrounding the Warminster 'Thing'. His book, *The Warminster Mystery*, discussed in depth the phenomenon that gripped neighbouring Wiltshire in the mid-1960s. But some have speculated that the bizarre vehicle was something else entirely – some type of human vehicle from the future, which Mr Hann was fortunate to observe as it flashed back into its own time following a joyride on the road to Bath. Perhaps it was lost in some kind of time wormhole and destroyed between dimensions, never making it back home.

A SMALL CONCLUSION

There has been so much that we have been forced to leave unexplored. Somerset's image as a land of mythology, mystery and enchantment is perhaps the reason why some legends seem almost feasible, or to put it another way, it is easy to see why some stories are attached, often proudly, to certain places. Some stories contain a fantasy element; it is even thought that some places are linked to certain fairy tales or nursery rhymes. In Kilmersdon can be found Jack and Jill Hill, leading to the famous well adjacent to the primary school. This is supposed to be where:

> Jack and Jill went up the hill;
> To fetch a pail of water;
> Jack fell down and broke his crown;
> And Jill came tumbling after.

Rather than being children, Jack and Jill are thought to have been unmarried lovers who used the hill as a rendezvous during Henry VIII's time, until Jack died in an accident at Balstone Quarry and Jill died during childbirth. The story appears to have coincided with a campaign to restore the well in the late 1990s, however, although I suppose that the well's proximity to the primary school means that this version of the origin of the nursery rhyme will probably never die out.

At Mells, we learn the origins of the nursery rhyme 'Little Jack Horner', who:

> Sat in the corner, easting a Christmas pie;
> He put in his thumb, and pulled out a plum;
> And said 'What a good boy am I!'

According to a tradition recorded as early as 1808 in *The Ladies Repository*, the 'plum' was in fact the title deeds to Mells Abbey and land, hidden in a pasty and intended to be conveyed to London by a young lad named Jack Horner, the son of poor parents who lived near the Grange. This was during the Dissolution of the Monasteries, and the intention was to present the deeds to the commissioners to avoid the King's wrath. During his mission, however, the boy became hungry and opened the pie, pocketing the deeds (he could not read them; he had not even been told that they were in there), and many years later they were found in the possession of Jack Horner's descendents. King Henry VIII was furious at the deeds being lost at the time, and ordered Abbot Selwood of Mells to be executed for hiding them from him.

Some curious stories concern that strange world of folklore, where real life and people blend with the world of storytelling: an old tale from Wookey Hole tells how the water flowed from the cave to a lake near Glastonbury that was always full of fish, no matter how completely it had been emptied during the previous year. This was until the greedy Bishop Thomas Beckington claimed the lake as his own, whereupon the fish deserted the lake for a full two years — only returning when the bishop granted the lake back to the common people.

Some tales concern real, though bizarre and inexplicable, events. For instance, the *Sun* of 28 February 1972 reported on the mysterious 'face and eye burns' that afflicted 200 students involved in a rag stunt pedal car race at Whitchurch. The cause was unclear, and many attributed the incident to some kind of odd, communicative mass hysteria sweeping through the students. Even stranger, the *Sun* noted that something similar had afflicted 300 students at the same event in 1968, cause unknown.

Sometimes it is a specific person that is the focus for strangeness, however. At Timsbury, near Midsomer Norton, the *Terrific Register* titillated its readers with the ordeal of a labourer called Samuel Clinton, aged 25. Clinton was prone to the most phenomenal bouts of excessive sleeping, an 'awful somnolency' that almost bordered on an illness. On 13 May 1694 he slept for a full month, and in April 1696 he slept until 7 August. On 17 August 1697 he again fell asleep and slept until 19 November. Although he apparently sleep-ate and defecated, no one ever saw him do so, and suspicions of an imposture were allayed by apothecaries, who yelled in his ear, blocked his nostrils, took 14 ounces of blood from his arm, pinched his nose, blistered and scarred him — all without obtaining the least evidence of his being awake. In fact, the sleep was so deep it almost resembled a coma. His last deep sleep was from 19 November — when he briefly awoke and ate bread and cheese — until early February 1698, when he roused and, unaware he had slept so long, got out of bed and merely carried on life as normal!

Some bizarre human attributes cross the border into the paranormal. Consider Barbara Booley, who seemed to act as some kind of fire conductor: unexplained spontaneous fires followed her from job to job in the early 1970s, including fires in a dormitory at St Hilda's School, Bridgwater, and Bath High School for Girls. The blazes sometimes occurred when Ms Booley was in a state of high emotion or anger, yet there was never any suggestion of arson. Some odd human attributes even transcend earthly laws into the realm of the spiritual. Frederick Bligh Bond's remarkable *The Gate Of Remembrance* (1918) deals with little-known archaeological discoveries at Glastonbury Abbey found by means of clairvoyant techniques, and those with a fascination for the Glastonbury mythology could do worse than study this work — adding as it does another, spiritual, dimension to the already multilayered mystery of the Glastonbury legends.

And then there are the modern paranormal mysteries: Somerset's love affair with the UFO appears to have begun in 1954 (according to a famous 1969 book, *The Humanoids*, citing the *Sunday Dispatch* of 13 June),

Mysterious Somerset personified: these rock formations within Gough's Cave look like they belong to an alien planet.

with the bizarre experience of Nigel Frapple. At 2 o'clock in the morning of 20 May this young man was cycling home from a dance at Wincanton when he saw a brilliant light in a field at Redlynch crossroads. From behind a hedge he saw an enormous metallic object hovering some 20ft above the ground, 50ft across and with an orange light flaming from a central point. After a minute it shot off at an accelerating speed and climbed into the dark sky. The following day Frapple led a reporter to the site, where a huge circle of grass, 100ft in diameter, was found pushed flat. This is a mystery that continues to intrigue, even in the post *X-Files* era, as we have seen, with the *Sun* lately reporting on 21 June 2008 that 'airline pilots have spotted hundreds of UFOs over the nearby Bristol Channel this year' – one incident concerning a police helicopter that nearly collided with a 'mystery craft', before chasing it across the Bristol Channel as far as North Devon.

As far as the supernatural is concerned, Sedgemoor appears indelibly stamped into people's collective consciousness; a typical observation being told to me by one Bridgwater resident: 'This whole area is somewhat steeped in tales of odd things. There are always rumours of sightings of soldiers [presumably from the 1685 Battle of Sedgemoor]. Locals will tell you that it is a well-known area for sightings.' And this 325 years after the battle...

Some mysteries are perhaps better suited to open debate in newspaper columns, although they are none the less intriguing for it. In January 2011 an enquiry was received from a Californian family, requesting any information that might have turned up on one Elizabeth Farley, born in the late 1800s and who died in Trull in 1950. This lady apparently had some connection with the local pub in Corfe, but most fascinating was the information that this lady was a 'seer' who had great success, it is said, in finding lost persons and lost objects. Surely such a character would be remembered by *someone*, even 60 years later, and I would urge anyone who knows of her to contact the Corfe village website.

As we reach the end of our tour of mysterious Somerset and Bristol, I cannot help but be reminded of the words of Mrs Kerton of Higher Farm, Chilton Cantelo, and others, to the effect that Somerset is 'only somewhere people pass through on their way into Devon and Cornwall.' I wonder if, when Cornwall and Devon become over publicized and over exposed, Somerset will, one day, become the destination of choice for those heading to the South West. It perhaps ought to be – it, in my opinion, has so much to offer, largely unspoilt – although I cannot but wonder if this would be a good thing or a bad thing. As for Bristol, despite its historic link to Somerset, long may it reign independent as the most historically famous port in Great Britain, maintaining its own identity, but still and at the same time being unmistakably part of the West Country and Somerset's proud cosmopolitan neighbour. I would like to thank everyone who contributed to the research of this book, and it is encouraging to observe how many people found its subject matter fascinating and were eager to relate, in some broad form, many of the stories within, which I have subsequently attempted to trace to their origin. It is equally apparent, implied by the number of first-hand accounts received, that there are yet more – many more – mysterious anecdotes out there. Most of all, it is reassuring to know that there is still a place in modern Somerset and Bristol for the mythological, the supernatural and the downright inexplicable; hopefully, complete scepticism of such oddities will not overtake us too soon.

INDEX OF PLACE NAMES

Aller 156

Athelney 16–17, 37, 73

Axbridge 106, 123, 141, 152

Banwell 8, 30, 99

Barrow Gurney 105, 117

Barwick 26

Bath 12, 24, 44, 57, 73, 125–28, 142, 145, 179

Bathford 76, 119

Bawdrip 25

Bishops Lydeard 73, 98, 156

Blue Anchor 44, 91, 135

Brewham 67–68

Bridgwater 70, 150, 176–77, 179, 189

Brislington 50, 184

Bristol 11, 24, 27, 50, 59, 100, 119–25, 166, 175–77

Brockley Combe 84, 102

Broomfield 23, 163–64

Buckland Dinham 22, 56, 78, 131

Cannards Grave 100

Carhampton 35, 135, 181

Chard 75–76, 130

Cheddar Gorge 7–8, 138, 140, 162–63, 190

Chedzoy 94, 96, 98

Chew Magna 50, 160

Chilton Cantelo 85–87

Clifton 101–02, 110, 145, 160

Combe Sydenham 113, 178–79

Congresbury 35–36, 49, 131

Corfe 22–23, 128–29, 135, 143–44

Cranmore 109

Crewkerne 31–33, 70, 134

Curry Rivel 141, 156

Ditcheat 58, 184

Dulverton 77, 104, 180, 182

Dunster 111–13, 162

Frome 114–15, 118–19, 173

Glastonbury 17–21, 24, 29–34, 38–40

Haselbury Plucknett 40–42

Hawkridge 53

Hinton St George 113

Huish Episcopi 21

Ilminster 50, 104

Keynsham 34–35, 174

Kilve 156

Kingsbury Episcopi 21

Langport 97, 105, 146

Mells 188–89

Minehead 42–43, 90, 124, 153, 158, 180, 182

Monksilver 22, 68–69

Muchelney 106–07

Nailsea 115–16, 145

Nether Stowey 27, 108, 140, 161, 181

North Petherton 80, 108, 132–33, 171

Norton Fitzwarren 148, 156

Nunney 118–19

Oare 10–11, 135

Priddy 22, 29,55

Porlock 70–71, 87, 106, 124, 136, 139

Selworthy 71, 83, 119, 146

Shapwick 45–46, 170

Shepton Mallet 11, 57–59, 64–65, 109, 136

Simonsbath 104, 139, 149, 166

South Cadbury 13–14, 21, 114, 116, 159

Stanton Drew 52–53, 77, 160, 174

Street 15, 99

Stogumber 70, 148

Taunton 65, 73, 80, 83–84, 98–99, 112–13, 117, 133

Watchet 44, 46, 124, 134

Wedmore 134, 182

Wellington 42, 88–90

Wellow 84

Wells 24, 44–45, 80, 131, 135, 155, 184

Weston-super-Mare 48, 55, 98, 143, 168–69, 173

Westonzoyland 92, 97, 115

Wincanton 37, 66–68, 79, 185, 190

Winsford 55, 146, 158

Withycombe 69, 88

Wiveliscombe 142

Wookey Hole 61–64, 134, 140, 167, 189

Yatton 24, 117, 171–72

Yeovil 71, 136, 147, 174, 183, 186